Fundamentals of Motivational Interviewing

Fundamentals of Motivational Interviewing

Tips and Strategies for Addressing Common Clinical Challenges

JULIE A. SCHUMACHER

MICHAEL B. MADSON

OXFORD
UNIVERSITY PRESS

Oxford University Press is a department of the University of
Oxford. It furthers the University's objective of excellence in research,
scholarship, and education by publishing worldwide.

Oxford   New York
Auckland   Cape Town   Dar es Salaam   Hong Kong   Karachi
Kuala Lumpur   Madrid   Melbourne   Mexico City   Nairobi
New Delhi   Shanghai   Taipei   Toronto

With offices in
Argentina   Austria   Brazil   Chile   Czech Republic   France   Greece
Guatemala   Hungary   Italy   Japan   Poland   Portugal   Singapore
South Korea   Switzerland   Thailand   Turkey   Ukraine   Vietnam

Oxford is a registered trademark of Oxford University Press
in the UK and certain other countries.

Published in the United States of America by
Oxford University Press
198 Madison Avenue, New York, NY 10016

Library of Congress Cataloging-in-Publication Data
Schumacher, Julie A.
Fundamentals of motivational interviewing : tips and strategies for addressing common clinical
challenges / Julie A. Schumacher, Michael B. Madson.
    pages cm
ISBN 978-0-19-935463-4 (paperback)
1. Interviewing—Psychological aspects.   2. Motivation (Psychology)   3. Interviewing in
psychiatry.   I. Madson, Michael B.   II. Title.
BF637.I5S38 2015
158.3'9—dc23
2014022206

9 8 7 6 5 4 3 2 1
Printed in the United States of America
on acid-free paper

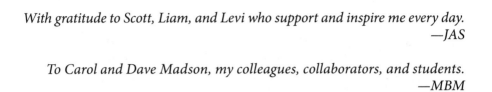

With gratitude to Scott, Liam, and Levi who support and inspire me every day.
—JAS

To Carol and Dave Madson, my colleagues, collaborators, and students.
—MBM

CONTENTS

ACKNOWLEDGMENTS

We are forever grateful to Drs. Bill Miller and Steve Rollnick for their commitment to the ongoing evolution of MI and their altruistic generosity for sharing their knowledge with others. Their dedication to MI guides us all! We are thankful to be a part of the Motivational Interviewing Network of Trainers—MINT—and value the energy and discussions about MI among its members. As researchers, we are honored to have colleagues in the international MI research community who advance our knowledge of the application of MI through their critical evaluations. It is through the work of these researchers that the understanding of MI and evidence of its effectiveness have been generated. We are grateful to these individuals. In particular, we are thankful to have great research collaborators—Drs. Scott Coffey and Claire Lane as well as numerous students and fellows we have had the privilege of mentoring over the years. Our appreciation of MI has developed through the various trainings we have provided, clients we have treated, and cases we have supervised. We are thankful to the students, community providers, and clients who helped us deepen our knowledge of how to practice and teach MI! It is through our experiences with each of these individuals and groups that our ability and inspiration to write this book developed. Finally, we want to acknowledge Margo Villarosa for her careful review of this book.

PART I

Motivational Interviewing Overview

Introduction

As described more fully in chapter 2 of this book, motivational interviewing, or MI, is a communication style that providers can use to help facilitate client change. If you are new to motivational interviewing and have just begun reading *Fundamentals of Motivational Interviewing: Tips and Strategies for Addressing Common Clinical Challenges*, you are probably asking yourself two key questions: (1) "Does MI work?"; and 2) "How do I learn MI?" Whether you are a novice or experienced provider of MI, you are probably asking yourself, "How will this book be helpful to me?" Here we provide answers to these vital questions about MI and outline the key features of this book, its intended audience, and how to use what you learn.

DOES MOTIVATIONAL INTERVIEWING WORK?

Although initially developed and written about by Dr. William R. Miller as an intervention for alcohol use disorders (1983), in the more than 30 years since the original article on MI was published, MI has been applied successfully to promote positive change in areas ranging from reducing problem drinking (Vasilaki, Hosier, & Cox, 2006), to weight loss (Armstrong et al., 2011), to reducing criminal offenses (McMurran, 2009), to utilization of life-saving clean water technologies in Zambia (Thevos, Quick, & Yanduli, 2000). To say research on MI has been burgeoning may be an understatement. Lundahl and Burke (2009) reported that entering the term "motivational interviewing" into a single research database (PsycInfo) in March 2009 resulted in the retrieval of 707 articles published during the decade from 2000 to 2009! Although the potential uses of MI are seemingly boundless, it is important that all providers who wish to use MI are aware of the current evidence supporting (and in some cases failing to support) various applications of MI.

At least four comprehensive reviews of the MI literature using a statistical approach called meta-analysis have been published in the last decade (e.g., Burke, Arkowitz, & Menchola, 2003; Hettema, Steele, & Miller, 2005; Lundahl, Kunz, Brownell, Tollefson, & Burke, 2010; Rubak, Sandbaek, Lauritzen, & Christensen, 2005). These reviews have statistically combined the findings of numerous randomized controlled trials to draw more robust conclusions about the efficacy of MI than can be gleaned from a single study. Overall, these meta-analyses suggest fairly unequivocal support for MI as an intervention for alcohol and drug problems, especially when compared to things like a wait list, reading materials, or non-specific treatment-as-usual. For these problems, MI is generally equivalent but not superior to other specific interventions, although in some cases MI may require a smaller dose of treatment to achieve comparable effects (Lundahl & Burke, 2009). These researchers also found emerging support for MI for improved general health behaviors (e.g., diet and exercise) and health indices (e.g., cholesterol, blood pressure, body mass), gambling, parenting practices, and safe water use. Support was not found for MI improving emotional/psychological well-being, eating problems, and HBA_{1c} (an indicator of diabetes control), though it is important to note that research to date on eating problems and HBA_{1c} is very limited. Mixed support was found for MI as an intervention for HIV risk behaviors and cigarette smoking in the general meta-analyses. However, recent systematic reviews and meta-analyses focused just on smoking cessation (Heckman, Egleston, & Hoffman, 2010; Hettema & Hendricks, 2011) provide stronger evidence that MI can be efficacious for smoking cessation.

Importantly, while MI research literature is burgeoning, there are several promising areas of research on MI that are still in their infancy. This is especially important to note, given ongoing anecdotal evidence we receive as MI trainers, that MI may be utilized most broadly in some of the areas for which it has the most limited support. Four such areas are corrections, group therapy, mental health, and high school counseling. Although MI is widely used in corrections, a recent review of the literature suggests research supporting this application of MI remains limited (McMurran, 2009). Likewise, although many facilities and providers prefer group treatment approaches and offer MI as a group intervention, there is far less research on MI as a group intervention, and the research that has been conducted suggests that outcomes are not as strong for group-delivered MI (Lundahl & Burke, 2009; Wagner & Ingersoll, 2013). There is also increasing discussion of how MI might be applied in mental health settings to perhaps enhance treatment engagement and augment outcomes for cognitive behavioral therapy for problems such as depression and anxiety (Arkowitz, Westra, Miller, & Rollnick, 2008; Westra, 2012). In support of those discussions, Lundahl et al. (2010) found promising evidence that MI impacts non-specific treatment factors, including increasing treatment engagement, increasing client intention to change, and reducing client distress. However, as Burke (2011) notes, there is currently insufficient research to support the definitive conclusions that integration of MI with cognitive behavioral treatments does in fact improve mental health outcomes. Finally, whereas there is compelling evidence for the efficacy of MI for adolescent substance use and health behaviors (Jensen et al., 2011; Naar-King & Suarez, 2011), there is little research that MI enhances achievement or reduces the dropout rate among high school students. Nonetheless, there is increasing discussion of the promise MI holds for enhancing school achievement and engagement (Atkinson & Woods, 2003; Frey et al., 2011). Given that findings for MI are always emerging and sometimes surprising, providers of MI are encouraged to stay apprised of the MI literature to ensure that it is applied where it is useful and avoided where it is not.

HOW DO I LEARN MI?

Given its broad applicability, it is not surprising that individuals from many professional disciplines including, but not limited to, nurses, dieticians, physicians, counselors, social workers, psychologists, addiction professionals, probation officers, clergy, battered women's advocates, and laypeople have sought to learn MI so they can be instrumental in helping others make positive changes in their lives (Madson, Loignon, & Lane, 2009; Soderlund, Madson, Rubak, & Nilsen, 2011). The good news is that although individuals from different professional backgrounds may encounter unique challenges in trying to learn MI (Schumacher, Madson, & Nilsen, 2014) there is evidence that individuals from a variety of backgrounds and professions can achieve equal outcomes when delivering MI (Barwick, Bennett, Johnson, McGowan, & Moore, 2012; Lundahl et al., 2010).

Despite its increasing popularity across disciplines, there is also a mounting body of research to indicate that MI is not "practice as usual" nor is it "easy to learn" (Miller & Rollnick, 2009). Our combined 21 years' experience learning MI, training countless others from varying backgrounds in MI, and doing research on MI training is consistent with those conclusions. Although MI sounds familiar and intuitive to many professionals and laypersons alike, for many the practice of MI seems to run directly counter to the strategies commonly relied upon when helping others discuss important life changes. In fact, what seems to come most naturally to many we train (and to us, for that matter!) are strategies that are actually inconsistent with the practices and principles of MI. For example quickly giving advice when someone mentions a problem they are having (e.g., asking, "Why don't you try…?" or "Have you tried…?") or directly confronting other's statements that do not support change we view as necessary or important for them (even when such confrontations are well-intentioned, as in the case of telling someone who says "I just can't do it"—"Yes, you can!").

The amount and type of training necessary to achieve provider proficiency in MI is both uncertain and more extensive than commonly believed. Although workshops are the most common continuing education model, research suggests that skill improvements are often not achieved or short-lived with such training (Walters, Matson, Baer, & Ziedonis, 2005) and may be particularly limited when training is urged or required by an employer (Miller & Mount, 2001) rather than independently sought by the trainee (Miller, Yahne, Moyers, Martinez, & Pirritano, 2004). Miller and colleagues (2004) found that for highly motivated providers (i.e., providers who self-selected and made expenditures for training) with high levels of baseline skill: (1) 2-day workshop training alone produces substantial but non-enduring skill increases;

(2) small doses of both feedback and coaching help maintain training gains; and (3) the combination of feedback and coaching is required to produce desired changes in client utterances during MI sessions. Close examination of the findings of Miller et al. (2004) study suggests that a combination of training, feedback, and coaching was sufficient for most, but not all, providers to achieve and maintain beginning proficiency in MI, but that few providers achieved expert competence in MI. Anyone familiar with the general literature on becoming an expert will not be surprised by that finding; becoming an expert at anything generally requires copious amounts of supervised practice (Ericsson & Charness, 1994). Importantly, Moyers et al. (2008) built on this study by examining the training model with providers who had fewer basic counseling skills and expressed less motivation to learn MI. They found that for this group only 4.3% to 10.3% of participants met all beginning proficiency criteria, many training gains eroded by 4-month follow-up, and personalized feedback and consultation did not enhance outcomes. A study examining live-supervision revealed similarly that five post-workshop supervision sessions were insufficient for many providers to achieve proficiency (Smith et al., 2007; Smith et al. 2012).

In our own work, similar findings have emerged. We have found that extended and accelerated training approaches that incorporated experiential learning activities (e.g., skill practice and real play practice sessions) have resulted in achievement of beginning MI proficiency by many participants (Madson, Schumacher, Noble, & Bonnell, 2013). However, participants rarely achieved the expert level after this training. In contrast, when we received and coded participant work samples and provided feedback and coaching, more participants approached or reached expert level (Schumacher, Madson, & Norquist, 2011; Schumacher, Williams, Burke, Epler, & Simon, 2013). Anecdotally, we observed that it was in these coaching sessions that participants developed a deeper understanding of MI, its foundational spirit, and how to apply the techniques and strategies in an MI-consistent fashion.

Thus, the research is very clear that despite the broad appeal and seeming intuitiveness of the approach, development of skill in MI rarely occurs in the absence of formal training and coaching. Moreover, development of true expertise in this approach requires a hefty dose of training and coaching for most—even those who already have substantial experience in counseling or psychotherapy (Schumacher et al., 2013). Thus, in the interest of complete transparency, we would like to state directly that we do not believe that reading this book and applying the suggested principles and skills on their own are likely to make anyone an expert at MI. MI is a very powerful communication style and therapeutic approach that involves more than simply applying a particular technique to a particular situation (Miller & Rollnick, 2009). Nevertheless, interventions that involve the selective application of principles and practices of MI may help improve outcomes, as in the case of screening and brief intervention for alcohol problems in the emergency department (D'Onofrio & Degutis, 2002).

WHAT DOES THIS BOOK OFFER?

Fundamentals of Motivational Interviewing: Tips and Strategies for Addressing Common Clinical Challenges evolved out of our years of experience: (1) conducting MI sessions with clients; (2) developing, implementing, and researching novel applications of MI (e.g., Madson, Bullock-Yowell, Speed, & Hodges, 2008; Schumacher, Coffey, et al., 2011; Zoellner et al., 2011); (3) surveying expert MI trainers and reviewing the literature about how people learn MI, which aspects of MI they find most difficult to learn or implement, and which methods facilitate learning (Madson, Lane, & Noble; 2012; Madson, Loignon, & Lane, 2009; Schumacher et al., 2012; Schumacher, Madson, & Nilsen, 2014; Soderlund et al., 2011); (4) providing training and coaching in MI to countless study therapists, undergraduate and graduate students, addictions counselors, nurses, mental health professionals, allied health professionals, medical students and physicians, probation officers, and lay volunteers (e.g., Madson, Landry, Molaison, Schumacher, & Yadrick, in press; Madson et al., 2013; Madson, Speed, Bullock-Yowell, & Nicholson, 2011; Schumacher, Madson, & Norquist, 2011; Schumacher et al., 2013); and (5) developing and evaluating methods to assess MI competency and facilitate coaching (Madson, Campbell, Barrett, Brondino, & Melchert, 2005; Madson & Campbell, 2006; Madson et al., 2013). The book was written with the highly pragmatic reader in mind; the reader who hopes to read all or even portions of this book and come away with not only knowledge about MI, but an ability to apply the principles and concepts of MI to their daily work.

The book is organized into two sections: Motivational Interviewing Overview (Chapters 1–3) and Motivational Interviewing for Clinical Challenges (Chapters 4–8).

Since the publication of the original article on MI by Miller in 1983 and the original MI text by Miller and Rollnick in 1991, MI has evolved and changed (Miller & Rollnick, 2002; Miller & Rollnick, 2013). Although the essential elements remain unchanged, definitions, emphases, and terminology have shifted over time as researchers uncover more about how and why MI helps individuals change (Miller & Rose, 2009) and how providers learn MI (Miller and Moyers, 2006). Thus, chapters 2 and 3 of this book are designed to provide the reader with a clear, concise, and current description of foundational principles, practices, and processes of MI. In addition, these chapters illustrate key concepts with vignettes and examples depicting MI-consistent, somewhat MI-consistent, and MI-inconsistent interactions from a variety of settings (e.g., healthcare, substance abuse treatment, criminal justice, and mental health).

The chapters in this book on how to apply MI to various clinical challenges (chapters 4 through 7) evolved primarily out of our years of experience as MI trainers with varied audiences. Time and time again, individuals we've trained and coached in MI have asked for guidance in applying the practices, principles, and processes we are teaching them to various specific clinical challenges. Although the specifics of the challenging situations in which those we've trained have sought to apply MI vary greatly depending on the setting within which a particular provider works, their underlying questions are very similar. Questions such as: *"How do I use MI to involve someone more actively in creating a treatment plan?"* or, *"What do you do when a client tries to get you to do all the work for them?"* or,*"How do you help someone who won't comply with treatment?"* When we address these questions with our training audiences and in chapters 4 through 7 of this book, many times the answers are simple: *"You might try agenda setting or elicit–provide–elicit to help engage the client at the beginning of the session."* Other times the answers are more complex, and may require the provider to change not only what they say and do with the client but also how they fundamentally think about the client. Our goal is to provide you with clear advice and suggestions about how concepts, principles, and skills from MI can be applied to the most difficult situations you encounter in your work.

Chapter 4 addresses how practices and principles of MI can be applied to the challenge of clients who are *Less Ready to Change*. In particular, we focus on the nearly ubiquitous problems of no-shows and non-adherence, as well as special considerations and strategies to enhance engagement of clients involved in the legal system. The last section may be of interest even to readers who do not work with legally involved clients, as many clients feel coerced to change by loved ones, employers, or others in much the same way that legally involved clients do. Chapter 5 delves into the challenges associated with *Loss of Momentum*. In this chapter we discuss how MI can be applied to clients who experience slow progress or setbacks (i.e., lapses or relapses), as well as clients with overly ambitious expectations about how quickly change will progress.

Although chapter 6 focuses on *Psychiatric Symptoms and Disorders*, specifically depressive, anxiety, trauma- and stressor-related, obsessive compulsive and related disorders, and psychotic disorders, this chapter may be of great interest to non–mental health providers—first, because psychiatric disorders are highly prevalent, and thus clients who are experiencing these symptoms and disorders are likely to present in every setting where MI might be utilized; and second, many of the challenges related to these symptoms and disorders such as poor concentration, disorganized thinking, and lack of motivation are also commonly observed in individuals who do not suffer from these symptoms or disorders. In the final chapter of the section on clinical challenges, chapter 7, we address how practices and principles of MI can be used to address challenges commonly encountered when *Working with Multiple Individuals*, specifically parents and groups.

In chapter 8 we provide a series of tips and strategies for learning MI that we have identified over our years as MI trainers. We also describe two challenges we have identified that seem to impede MI learning and implementation for many providers—namely, feelings of frustration with difficult clients and assumptions that what worked for the provider personally (when they stopped smoking, quit drinking, lost weight, went straight, etc.) is also the best solution for their client. As noted, there is no "quick fix" solution for learning MI, but we have found that following some of the tips and tactics and targeting the challenges outlined in chapter 8 may facilitate learning and implementation of MI for some providers.

FOR WHOM IS THIS BOOK INTENDED?

This book is intended as a resource for individuals interested in applying the principles and practices of MI to their work (paid or volunteer), helping to guide others in making positive changes in their lives. It is intended as a resource for those who are already expert in MI, those who are learning MI, and those who have no prior training in MI, including students. Those who are already expert in MI may find the updated review of MI practices, principles, and processes in chapters 2 and 3 to be an efficient way to get up to speed on newer concepts and terms. Experts may also identify applications of concepts and skills to common clinical challenges (chapters 4–7) that they had not previously considered in their own work. Individuals with some prior MI training may find the concise and efficient review of key concepts and practical guidance on how to apply the skills and concepts to common clinical challenges a useful complement to their other MI training materials. The MI novice will likely find this book a useful, easy-to-read introduction to what MI is and how it can be used to improve clinical practice and clinical outcomes across a variety of domains and situations. Although for those desiring to achieve expert competence in MI, this book is not intended as a substitute for formal MI training and coaching, even those without such a foundation will likely find practical and easy-to-implement strategies to common clinical challenges in (chapters 4–7). These chapters may also serve as a nice complement to the information presented in the most recent edition of *Motivational Interviewing: Helping People Change*, 3rd edition (Miller & Rollnick, 2013) or to formal workshop training in MI.

Importantly, across various professional disciplines and even within these disciplines across various settings, different terminology is used to refer to the population being served and the individuals who serve them. However, given the similarities we've noted in working with providers across disciplines and settings, we have elected to rely primarily on standardized terminology in this book. Any time we use the term "client" in this book, we are referring to the individuals who will receive a motivational interview. Any time we use the term "provider" in this book, we are referring to YOU. Whatever your specific job or role within your organization or agency (whether paid or volunteer), odds are you have a part to play in helping the individuals you serve make positive changes in their lives. Although many specific examples of applications of MI concepts and strategies will be superficially applicable to a particular setting or population, all examples were selected and written to illustrate concepts that are relevant to most or all MI providers. Readers are encouraged to read all examples, not simply those that depict interactions that might commonly occur in their work setting.

As noted by Miller and Rollnick (2013), MI is a compassionate approach that puts the needs of others above self. Thus this book is not intended for use by individuals who seek to use its principles and practices to promote their own self-interest or manipulate others. Depending on the context in which a provider works and his or her relationship to clients within that context, the provider's ability to place the best interests of the client ahead of self-interest or agency interest can be more difficult to navigate. In our discussion in chapter 4 of how MI principles and practices can be applied to clients with legal involvement, we provide further discussion and guidance on how providers can compassionately apply the principles of MI in cases where the client is being offered or required to participate in services he or she did not seek. As a final note, although many of the professionals and volunteers we have trained who are also parents or spouses have reported that using reflective listening and asking open questions (which are not unique to MI) have improved communication in their personal relationships, MI is not intended for use in personal relationships with spouses, children, or friends.

HOW TO USE THIS BOOK

Whereas MI-novice readers may choose to read this book from cover to cover, experienced MI practitioners may choose to read only a few relevant chapters. Whether you have thoroughly read none, one, a few, or all of the chapters in this book, we have designed the book to be useful as a quick reference. When you encounter a particular clinical challenge or feel stuck, we encourage you to flip to the table of contents of this book and read those chapters or sections most relevant to the challenge you face. For example, if you have a client who has started to miss appointments and you suspect it may be because he or she has anxiety about coming to see you, you might choose to read the section in chapter 4 on no-shows and the section in chapter 6 on anxiety. However you choose to use this book, we hope you will find it a helpful guide in how to apply the practices and principles of MI to help resolve a number of ubiquitous clinical challenges.

2

Foundational Concepts and Skills

WHAT IS MOTIVATIONAL INTERVIEWING?

Motivational interviewing (MI) was initially described as a counseling approach based on methods from Carl Rogers's person-centered therapy and social-psychological principles such as cognitive dissonance and self-efficacy to help increase client motivation to change problem drinking behavior (Miller, 1983). However, over the past 30 years, the definition has become broader and is applicable to a range of professional disciplines and target populations. In 2009, Miller and Rollnick redefined MI as "a collaborative, person-centered form of guiding to elicit and strengthen motivation for change" (Miller & Rollnick, 2009, p. 137). Miller and Rollnick (2013) recently expanded on this definition to provide a more comprehensive understanding of what MI is for, how it works, and why you may want to use it. Miller and Rollnick's (2013) expansion includes:

What is MI for? MI is a conversation between individuals, often a provider and a client, about change. Rather than telling clients what to do, the MI-consistent provider would collaborate with them in an attempt to strengthen their personal motivation for change.

Why should you use MI? An MI-consistent conversation focuses on clients' motivations for change and in particular feelings of ambivalence they have about changing. Although ambivalence about change is commonly experienced, failure to address such ambivalence can keep a person from changing (Wagner & Ingersoll, 2013).

How does MI work? By adopting a collaborative partnership with clients, the MI-consistent provider engages in a conversation about change. In this conversation, the provider intentionally attends to client statements about change and intentionally uses communication strategies to elicit and explore a client's own arguments for changing while minimizing arguments about remaining the same (Miller & Rose, 2009; Wagner & Ingersoll, 2013).

There is commonality across all three of these definitions. These commonalities are essential components of any MI interaction and any training or research related to MI. These common elements include:

- MI is a particular kind of intentional communication about change. This communication style can be used whether a provider is offering counseling, assessment/test feedback, supervision, or consultation.
- MI is collaborative. In using MI, the provider is focused on being a partner—NOT an expert!
- MI is evocative. To be MI-consistent, the provider's focus is on eliciting clients' motivations and ideas about change versus prescribing them.

WHAT MOTIVATIONAL INTERVIEWING IS NOT

In 2009, Miller and Rollnick attempted to clear up several misconceptions about MI. In doing so, they developed a list of the common misunderstandings people have about this approach. Corrections to these misconceptions include:

Motivational Interviewing is Not Based on the Transtheoretical Model (TTM)

TTM and the accompanying stages of readiness change represent a set of attitudes, intentions and behaviors related to change that a person may hold depending on their readiness to change (Connors, DiClemente, Velasquez, & Donovan, 2013). In particular, the stages of readiness to change (precontemplation, contemplation, preparation, action, and maintenance) provide a framework for thinking about where clients are in the change process (Prochaska & Diclemente, 1983). Clients at the first two stages of change are not committed to making change. A client who is at the precontemplation stage is not aware of a need to change whereas the client at the contemplation stage is considering the pros and cons of changing or not. The client at the preparation stage is putting plans into place to begin changing. Clients at the action and maintenance stages are actively working to modify a behavior or maintain changes already achieved.

Early writings about MI linked it to the TTM (DiClemente & Velazquez, 2002; Miller, 1983; Substance Abuse and Mental Health Services Administration, 1999). Often this led people to think that MI cannot be used without the TTM. Although MI works well with the TTM and in particular the stages of change, it is not dependent on them. In particular, MI would be valuable for use with individuals in the precontemplation, contemplation, and preparation stages more so than it would at the action and maintenance stages (Adams & Madson, 2006). The TTM provides a way of thinking about how people might approach change whereas MI provides us with an evidence-based communication approach that fits well with many theories of change (Naar-King & Suarez, 2011). Although MI can be used at certain stages of readiness to change, its use is not dependent on these stages.

Motivational Interviewing Is Not a Way of Tricking People into Doing what They Don't Want to Do

Many individuals we train have commented that MI seems like reverse psychology. The concept of reverse psychology refers to one person's advocacy for a belief or behavior that is opposite to the one they desire for another person for the express purpose of manipulating the other into do something they are against doing. Not only is this not what MI is, the idea is contradictory to: the foundation of MI, the compassion necessary to practice MI, and the ethical application of MI (Miller & Rollnick, 2013). In fact, to be MI-consistent, the provider is focused on the client's own concerns, perception of the problem, motivations and recognizing their autonomy to choose solutions that fit best for them and not the provider's own goals.

Motivational Interviewing Is Not a Technique

You can't "MI" someone! On the surface MI looks easy, but it is a complex, planned communication process that requires active and intentional listening and selection of strategies by the provider. There is also a foundational spirit that is essential to being an MI-consistent provider. By ignoring this spirit for technique a provider would only be going through the motions, not using MI. We have observed many trainees "go through the motions" in trying to implement MI which resulted in poor client outcomes.

Motivational Interviewing Is Not Simply a Decisional Balance

Decisional balance is one strategy that can be used to elicit change talk. However, there are a variety of MI-consistent strategies that can be used in MI without ever using a decisional balance (Rollnick, Miller & Butler, 2008; Rosengren, 2009). Further, people we have trained and coached have incorrectly believed they were doing MI when they used the decisional balance while completely neglecting other MI principles and strategies. Thus, a provider can use a decisional balance without necessarily being MI-consistent.

Motivational Interviewing Is Not just Client-Centered Therapy or a Form of Psychotherapy

Madson, Schumacher, and Bonnell (2010) highlighted the similarities and differences between MI and client-centered therapy (Rogers, 1959). We expand this differentiation by comparing MI to other common psychotherapies to demonstrate how it differs from these approaches (see Table 2.1). The fact that MI is a communication style, not a type of psychotherapy, lends to its broad

Table 2.1. COMPARISON OF MOTIVATIONAL INTERVIEWING AND COMMON
PSYCHOTHERAPIES

Feature	Person-Centered	MI	Cognitive	Behavioral
Level of direction	Following	Guiding	Directing	Directing
Focus in session	Feelings	Change talk	Cognitions	Behaviors
Form of psychotherapy	Psychotherapy	Communication style	Psychotherapy	Psychotherapy
Length of contact	Long-term	Brief	Brief	Brief
Essential ingredients	Core conditions	Spirit	Challenging maladaptive thoughts/ beliefs	Learning a healthy opposite to problem behavior
Focus in session	Exploration	Increasing change talk and minimizing sustain talk	Maladaptive thoughts and beliefs	Problem behaviors
Transformative element	Resolving incongruence	Change talk	Learning adaptive thoughts and beliefs	Learning healthy behaviors
Theory of personality	Developed	None	Developed	Developed
View of psychopathology	Incongruence	None	Learned patterns of thinking	Learned behaviors

applicability. This diverse applicability has contributed to the widespread proliferation of MI across different disciplines within and outside mental health and
substance abuse treatment.

Motivational Interviewing Is Not Easy

There is vast empirical support that developing competency in MI entails
practice of skill and coaching to develop basic proficiency (Madson, Loignon,

& Lane; 2009; Madson, Schumacher, Noble & Bonnell, 2013; Schumacher, Madson & Norquist, 2011; Walters, Matson, Baer, & Ziedonis, 2005). In fact, the current gold standard for MI training involves practice with observation and feedback to develop competency (Miller, Yahne, Moyers, Martinez, & Pirritano, 2004). Similarly, MI is not simply what you have already been doing. Collectively, we have spent 21 years learning, practicing, training and evaluating MI. Our evolution involved relearning skills and a mind-set that was based on but different than what we had learned previously about working with clients. We have found that that our personal MI learning experience as psychologists is consistent with the learning experience of professionals across the disciplines that utilize MI—certain communication styles and attitudes need to adjust to develop an MI-consistent practice (Schumacher, Madson & Nilsen, 2014).

Motivational Interviewing Is Not an Answer for Everything

MI is not a panacea, and there are times when MI is not appropriate. For instance, when an individual is actively changing a behavior, you would want to employ active behavior-change interventions. At times like these MI would be contra-indicated (Adams & Madson, 2006). However, it is important to recognize that behavior change waxes and wanes. Thus, MI can be integrated with other change interventions at those times (Westra, 2012). In fact, given that MI is a communication style focused on the client's change, it can be successfully integrated with traditional change approaches such as medication management (Interian, Lewis-Fernández, Gara, & Escobar, 2013), case management (Leukefeld, Carlton, Staton-Tindall, & Delaney, 2012), patient education (Gance-Cleveland, 2007), and cognitive and behavioral interventions (Naar-King, Earnshaw, & Breckon, 2013) you may currently be using. In fact, a major goal of this book is to help you learn how you can integrate MI with your current approaches to address specific challenges you may face in working with clients.

QUICK REFERENCE

Motivational Interviewing Is Not

Based on the transtheoretical model
Reverse psychology
A technique
Just using decisional balance
Person-centered therapy
A form of psychotherapy
Easy to learn or use
An answer for everything

TWO COMPONENTS OF MOTIVATIONAL INTERVIEWING

In 2009, Miller and Rose described a theory of how MI facilitates change through a combination of relational and technical components. The relational and technical components of MI are not incompatible but are suggested to be underlying processes of MI (Madson et al., 2013; Martino et al., 2008; Moyers & Martin, 2006).

Relational component: Grounded in the client-centered approach of Carl Rogers, this component includes an empathic, affirming, non-judgmental and autonomy-supportive counseling style intended to create a safe environment in which clients can explore their own wishes, fears, and concerns (Moos, 2007). In other words, the provider avoids imposing an agenda, basing acceptance on conditions, or arguing with or confronting clients, and instead actively listens to the client's spoken and unspoken messages in order to remain MI-consistent.

Technical component: Built on the relational foundation, a provider uses strategies aimed at eliciting clients' in-session change talk and decreasing their sustain talk with the overarching goal of evoking commitment to change (Amrhein, Miller, Yahne, Palmer, & Fulcher, 2003; Miller & Rose; 2009; Moos, 2007). In other words, the provider works with clients, listens intently, engages in MI-consistent behaviors, and utilizes strategies that elicit and reinforce client statements about desire, ability, reason, and need to change (Moyers & Martin, 2006).

THE FOUNDATIONAL SPIRIT OF MOTIVATIONAL INTERVIEWING

The foundation of MI, often called the "spirit," can be summarized by four characteristics that need to be present in any MI-focused provider-client relationship. These characteristics are collaboration, evocation, acceptance, and compassion (Miller & Rollnick, 2013). These characteristics are necessary for a provider to successfully use MI and are more important than any specific strategy. In fact, the spirit of MI is the foundation from which any MI interaction develops. For this reason we provide further explanation of each characteristic of the MI spirit with MI-consistent and MI-inconsistent examples.

COLLABORATION

MI depends on a relationship between the client and provider that resembles a partnership. Instead of directing the client and using the presumed power difference, providers and clients participate in a discussion regarding behavior change. As such, it is important that providers recognize that they have certain expertise or experience, and at the same time their clients also have expertise and experience about themselves and previous change efforts. This collaboration is a defining point of MI because ultimately behavior change is in the hands (or control) of the client. This relationship is conducive (i.e., facilitative or contributing) to change, not coercive.

Example: MI-Consistent/Inconsistent Collaboration

Client Statement: *"Look, I just smoke a little pot [marijuana]. I don't think it is that big of a deal, but I failed a drug screen at work and they made me come here. So, I have to quit now, even though I don't see anything wrong with it."*

MI-Inconsistent: *"Pot is illegal and against your work policy. If you want to stop, this program will get you on track."*

This response is considered MI-inconsistent because the provider assumes an expert/authoritarian role. In this role, the provider is not working as a partner but is "telling" the client how it is and how to behave. This response is more likely to increase discord (discussed later) between the client and provider, not develop a partnership.

Somewhat MI-Consistent: *"You're faced with a forced change to keep your job and that isn't too exciting for you. I've told you about our program. How will it work for you?"*

This response is somewhat but not completely MI-consistent. The provider reflects the client's concern about being forced to change and attempts to elicit solutions from the client. However, the provider still communicates that the client must figure out how to make the program work, which communicates an expert role.

MI-Consistent: *"Sounds like you are really frustrated and feel like you are being forced into changing. Since the circumstances are the way they are, I wonder if we can brainstorm and work together to come up with some ideas on how we can make the most of our time together."*

This response is an MI-consistent, collaborative response. Not only does it acknowledge the way the client is feeling about the session without correcting the client about using marijuana, but the provider adopts an egalitarian approach asking how the two can best utilize their time. The statement also communicates that the provider wants to work with the client in best utilizing their time versus imposing an agenda of what to address. Thus, the two are partners.

EVOCATION

Traditionally, many behavior change approaches tend to focus on determining what clients lack or need and on filling that gap (e.g., medication, knowledge, skills). Thus, providers often adopt a prescriptive approach determining what clients need and telling them how to change. Clients often push back to this approach, explaining why it may not work. Rather than engage in that back and forth, the MI-consistent provider focuses on drawing information out of the client (Miller & Rollnick, 2002). This may include eliciting from clients (1) their perspective of the problem; (2) why they may want or need to change; (3) how they would change; (4) personal goals and values; (5) why they may not want to change; or (6) why they may want to stay the same. While a client may lack the "desired level" of motivation, all individuals are somewhat motivated to make changes and every client has ambitions, values, and concerns. A goal in MI is to establish a personal connection between the change focus and what the client values. By identifying client's aspirations and perspectives, a provider can evoke from clients their own arguments for making changes. In MI, this is referred to as "change talk."

Example: MI-Consistent/Inconsistent Evoking

Client Statement: *"Well I'm here. My physician said I needed to see you about my diet and exercise before I had my procedure."*

MI-Inconsistent: *"It is good you are here. We need to get you on a healthy diet and exercising each day. I have a plan that has been really successful"*

This is an MI-inconsistent response because the provider does not evoke anything from the client. The provider also prematurely focuses on a change target and adopts an expert/authoritarian role. The provider is not attempting to understand any aspect of the client's view of the concern. It is highly likely that the discussion will evolve with the client explaining why the plan wouldn't work. Without understanding the client, the provider is likely to evoke more sustain talk than change talk.

Somewhat MI-Consistent: *"Thanks for coming in today at the request of your physician. What things should you change about your diet?"*

This response is somewhat but not completely MI-consistent. The provider affirms that the client followed through on the request of the physician in an MI-consistent fashion. The provider also asks an open question. However, the specific open question selected by the provider focuses the encounter on changes in diet in a non-collaborative fashion—the provider chooses what is important without seeking client input. Additionally, the choice of the word "should" communicates that the client has to do something.

MI-Consistent: *"It sounds like your physician wanted you to see me to work on your diet and exercise. What are your thoughts about seeing me?"*

This is an MI-consistent, evocative response as it not only reflects the client's understanding of the referral but it also elicits from the client his/her own ideas about the consultation. The response communicates that the client's ideas are the important ones in this conversation. This avoids the premature focus and assuming an expert role. Responding in this way also avoids the trap of taking sides. Unlike previous responses, this one does not align the provider with the physician—taking sides.

ACCEPTANCE

Although not new to counseling or to MI; acceptance has recently been explicitly identified as the third foundational component of MI (Miller & Rollnick, 2013; Wagner & Ingersoll, 2013). Acceptance involves appreciating what the client brings to the interaction. In MI, an accepting environment helps the client explore all aspects of change. This does not mean that the provider has to approve of the client's actions or give in to the status quo (Miller & Rollnick, 2013). Acceptance, as outlined by Miller and Rollnick includes four aspects.

Absolute Worth

A basic tenet of person-centered therapy is that every human is trustworthy and has potential to change and to do the best for themselves (Rogers, 1959). Recognizing the potential and worth in every client is essential to developing a solid relationship and communicating acceptance.

Accurate Empathy

To be MI-consistent, a provider has to have a genuine interest in and desire to appreciate and understand the client's situation. This does not mean feeling sympathetic towards or identifying with clients. It does mean that MI-consistent providers actively seek to understand the world of their clients and how that relates to their change or lack of change. For instance, if a client was not taking her/his medication, a provider would be MI-consistent by seeking to better understand the client's situation, values, and goals to see how they relate to change versus simply lecturing the client about the need to take the medication. Accurate empathy communicates that the provider is interested in clients' experience and wants to learn what it is like for them.

Respecting Client Autonomy

MI depends, in part, on the provider's separation from the client's final decision to make a change. This does not mean that MI-consistent providers avoid caring about their clients; instead, it implies recognizing that individuals are responsible for their decision making. This is a difficult concept for many providers to accept. However, we often remind those we train that they do not follow their clients 24 hours a day, 7 days a week. Clients must make their own decisions about what they think is best for them all the time—so why not embrace this fact? A provider can offer information, advice, and feedback, but ultimately, the decision to make a change is on the client. Acknowledging the clients' autonomy to decide often aids in the process of change as they recognize they have the freedom and ultimate responsibility for making changes how they deem appropriate.

Affirmation

As a strength-based approach to counseling, MI-consistent providers strive to recognize, comment on, and elicit client strengths and resources (Madson, Loignon, Shutze, & Necaise, 2009). Most individuals who seek help, whether by choice or coercion, have likely attempted to change in the past with variable success. Often clients focus on failures at change or thwarted efforts. In affirming clients, the goal isn't to be a cheerleader or offer positive affirmations—it is to help clients see their strengths, resources, and previous success from which this change effort may be built

Example: MI-Consistent/Inconsistent Acceptance

Client Statement: *"Look at this scar on my face. I don't know why the police arrested me, I was just defending myself. She's crazy!"*

MI-Inconsistent: *"I hear you. An important part of fixing this problem is accepting responsibility for your behavior. That will help keep you out of jail."*

This response is MI-inconsistent because the provider directly confronts the client. The response conveys that the provider has taken the side of the client's partner and the criminal justice system, is not interested in hearing the client's perspective, does not respect the client's right to make choices, and is critical rather than affirming. It is highly likely that this response would reduce the client's ability to engage with the provider and use the interaction to actively consider what types of changes he might need or want to make in his life.

Somewhat MI-Consistent: *"You do not believe that the police listened to your side of the story and are uncertain you belong in this treatment. How can we ensure you keep out of trouble?"*

This response is somewhat MI-consistent. The provider resists the righting reflex and instead reflects the client's perception of the situation. The provider also attempts to evoke potential solutions from the client. However, there is little effort to communicate the elements of acceptance.

MI-Consistent: *"You do not believe that the police listened to your side of the story and you are not certain that you belong in this treatment. Given that you feel that way, I appreciate that you kept this appointment and showed up anyway. Ultimately you will have to decide what if anything you can learn from this program."*

This response is MI-consistent because it conveys that the provider has heard and is trying to understand the client's perspective on his current situation, and thus conveys empathy. The response also affirms that the client's willingness to keep his appointment is a strength and acknowledges that the client has the autonomy to decide what he will do. Taken together, this willingness to listen to the client, support his autonomy, and recognize his strengths convey clearly that the provider values the client and recognizes his absolute worth as a person.

COMPASSION

Compassion is an authentic, emotional response when perceiving others' suffering and results in a desire to help (Seppala, 2013). In other words, compassion includes a sense of responsibility and care for human beings that intensify their motivation and drive to better their clients' lives (Fromm, 1956). Thus, in practicing in an MI-consistent fashion, it is essential to always have the best intentions for your clients and genuinely care about their welfare. However, it is important to avoid the righting reflex (discussed later) as a result of concern for the welfare of and wanting to do good for others.

Example: MI-Consistent/Inconsistent Compassion

Client Statement: *"Isn't there anything you can do to save my foot?"*

MI-Inconsistent: *"We have been working with you for years to try to get you to better manage your blood sugar. I'm sorry but at this point there is nothing we can do. Hopefully this situation will help you better manage your diet and medications in the future so you don't also lose your other foot."*

This response is considered MI-inconsistent, and might well represent a response from a provider who is experiencing burnout. Although the response contains factual information that addresses the question asked by the client, it does so in a confrontational fashion and without compassion for the client's current state of emotional distress and need for comforting and reassurance as well as information.

Somewhat MI-Consistent: *"You are very upset about losing your foot. What can you take from this situation about how to avoid future losses?"*

This response is somewhat MI-consistent. The provider reflects the client's feelings and attempts to elicit rather than confront the client. However, the client may experience the response as judgmental and non-compassionate given the focus isn't on relieving the pain but how the client can learn from this experience.

MI-Consistent: *"I can tell you are very upset about losing your foot, and I wish there was something I could recommend that would save it."*

This response is an MI-consistent, compassionate response because it conveys empathy with the client's current emotional distress as well as a desire to resolve that distress. This response may open the client up to using the provider as a source of emotional support during a difficult life transition and to working with the provider to try to better manage his or her diabetes in the future.

Foundational Motivational Interviewing Spirit Components

Entering into a collaborative working relationship
Eliciting from clients versus prescribing to them
Appreciating client worth and autonomy, affirming strengths, and empathizing with their situations
A sense of care and responsibility for the welfare of clients

---

FOUR GUIDING PRINCIPLES

Although not included in some of the most recent writings on MI (e.g., Miller & Rollnick, 2013), in our work as MI trainers, we have found that the four guiding principles of MI, as elaborated by Rollnick, Miller, and Butler (2008), help many providers improve their grasp of the foundational spirit of MI. These principles are (1) resisting the righting reflex, (2) understanding and exploring the client's motivations, (3) listening with empathy, and (4) empowering the client and encouraging hope and optimism. It can be helpful for providers to remember the acronym, RULE: Resist, Understand, Listen, and Empower in relation to remaining MI-consistent.

R: Resist the Righting Reflex

Providers tend to want to heal pain, make things right, and endorse well-being. Thus, when providers witness someone making poor choices, they have a strong urge to try to stop the individual or set them in the "right direction." This motivation is what makes the desire to correct someone's behavior an automatic reflex (i.e., righting reflex). However, providers who give into the urge to correct often experience the opposite of what they hope to achieve. Instead of choosing to change a behavior when they are told to do so, clients often resist change, particularly when they sense persuasion. This is not because clients are lazy, contrarian, or even in denial concerning their need to make a change. Instead, people are naturally inclined to push back against another's attempt to influence their behavior (Leffingwell, Neumann, Babitzke, Leedy, & Walters, 2007). This push-back is particularly powerful when someone is experiencing ambivalence (i.e., feeling two ways about the same thing) toward a behavior. For example, overeaters often are aware that their eating is problematic, and they are often aware of some of the negative consequences of their eating. At the same time, these individuals enjoy food, recognize the role food may play in socialization, and do not want to see themselves as having an "eating problem." Instead they would rather see their eating as normal. Thus, these individuals often simultaneously feel two ways about their eating behavior—both for *and* against changing it.

When clients see providers "taking sides" with the healthy part of the client's ambivalence, making a case for why they need to change, their natural response will be to make an argument against making a change (Leffingwell et al., 2007). Consequently, the provider's reflex may be to make a stronger argument, which will likely cause a client to argue more. Because people have a tendency to believe what they hear themselves say, a provider's arguing with a client may actually be solidifying the client's argument *against* making a behavior change. In MI, the client should be the one who is making a case for change, not the provider. Because many clients are ambivalent about making changes, it is the provider's job to help them work through this ambivalence and aid them in making a case for a change. To be MI-consistent, a provider needs to understand ambivalence as a natural part of change and not as pathological. This stance helps providers avoid educating or persuading clients to change—resisting the righting reflex. Therefore, MI-consistent providers use a variety of strategies to highlight and explore client ambivalence, including questioning, simple and complex reflections, affirmations, and summaries (Miller & Rollnick, 2002).

Example: Resisting the Righting Reflex

Client Statement: *"Look, I wish everybody would just leave me alone about my HIV. I get what they are saying about needing to stay on top of my treatment and sexual behavior, but I feel fine and all my friends have unprotected sex."*

MI-Inconsistent: *"You don't seem to be as worried about your HIV as everyone else. Don't you think it is important to address?"*

"What about trying to always have a condom with you in case you have sex?"

These two provider statements are MI-inconsistent and illustrate two different ways the righting reflex can manifest itself in working with ambivalent clients. The first statement directly confronts the client's ambivalence as denial in a direct attempt to get the client to reconsider his or her perspective. Likely this statement will engender discord between the client and provider. In the second statement, the provider succumbs to offering unsolicited advice and prescribes a solution. It is likely that the client will respond by discussing how the solution will not work.

Somewhat MI-Consistent: *"You recognize that change is hard and also recognize that others have concerns about your HIV and believe that you may need to change your behavior. It seems important to keep yourself and others safe in the future."*

This response is somewhat MI-consistent. The provider provides a nice double-sided reflection that highlights the client's ambivalence. However, rather than simply highlighting the ambivalence, the provider attempts to resolve it for the client by siding in favor of change. The client is likely to respond with talk about not changing.

MI-Consistent: *"You recognize that change is hard and also recognize that others have some reasonable concerns about your HIV and believe that you may need to change your behavior. Tell me where this all leaves you."*

The provider is reflecting the ambivalence the client obviously feels about making changes to his or her HIV-risk behavior. This helps convey to the client that the provider understands his or her dilemma and is not judging the client. By following up with a "Tell me" statement that invites the client to explore further why he or she might consider reducing HIV-risk behavior, the provider actively works to help client resolve ambivalence.

U: Understand the Client's Motivations

Each client has reasons for making a change, and those reasons will be more likely to persuade them to change than your reasons (Neighbors, Walker, Roffman, Mbilinyi, & Edleson, 2008; Rollnick et al., 2008). Being interested in a client's own motivations and values is an important part of eliciting from clients and increasing their motivation to change. Because consultation time with each client is limited, this may sound unreasonable and like a waste of time. However, as previously outlined, the provider voicing of reasons for change can actually be counterproductive and cause the client to voice arguments against change. Thus, from an MI perspective, your limited time is better spent asking clients why they are interested in making a change than telling clients why they should change. This principle again is focused on the client voicing the reasons for change, not the provider.

L: Listen to the Client

MI requires listening to clients with empathy in order to understand their reasons for making a change. Although providers are often viewed as the "experts" on a subject (e.g., good nutrition, medication, behavior change), typically answers to questions involving how and why change will occur for a particular client come from the client. The skill of listening is essential for gathering these answers.

E: Empower the Client

When clients take an active role in the decision-making process and feel empowered to make a change, the outcomes are typically more positive and changes are often made. While providers may be knowledgeable regarding specific aspects of changing such as how to diet, take medications, manage anxiety, and how change will improve the client's life, the client is the expert on how to fit the change into his or her daily life. Therefore, a client will likely know how to best accomplish the goal of change. In this process, it is the provider's role to offer support of the client's belief that he or she can make a change and to help the client feel comfortable sharing his or her expertise in the consultation.

BASIC MOTIVATIONAL INTERVIEWING SKILLS

Basic counseling skills are vital to interactions across several helping professions from medicine to corrections. In MI, these basic counseling skills are used intentionally and purposefully during the course of an interaction in order to facilitate client discussions about changing (change talk) and to minimize discussions about not changing (sustain talk). In other words, providers can use these basic counseling skills to elicit and selectively reinforce client discussions in favor of changing and to guide clients away from discussions related to not changing. The skills emphasized in MI are represented by the acronym OARS—Open questions, Affirmations, Reflections, and Summaries (Miller & Rollnick, 2013).

Open Questions

The appropriate use of questions is an important aspect of MI. Providers must be mindful in sessions to avoid the question and answer trap. This trap is a client/provider interaction in which the provider overuses questions (often closed questions) and the client simply answers the questions with limited responses. This trap results in a question-after-question and answer-after-answer process that prevents a deeper discussion of the topic (Miller & Rollnick, 2002). MI-consistent providers avoid trying to ask more than one question in a row to avoid this trap!

Open vs. closed question: A closed question implies or requires the client to give a one- or two-word answer (e.g., yes or no) and is used to gather specific information (Hill & O'Brien, 1999; Seligman, 2008). An open question is broad; encourages clients to talk about thoughts, feelings, behaviors, and/or experiences; and give clients flexibility in how to respond (Hill & O'Brien, 1999; Seligman, 2008). In MI, the use of open questions is preferred to closed questions as open questions are more eliciting and invite clients to provide more information than closed questions.

Example: MI-Consistent/Inconsistent Questions

Client Statement: *"I can't seem to remember to take my evening medications."*

MI-Inconsistent Closed Questions:

"Have you been following your diet?"

"Don't you think it is important to take your medications?"

These questions are MI-inconsistent, and not simply because they are closed questions. The first question is not in sync with what the client is talking about and could communicate that the provider is not listening or does not care about the client's concerns. The second question, while on topic, is a rhetorical question that could appear judgmental to the client and engender discord.

Somewhat MI-Consistent Closed Questions:

"Have you thought about setting an alarm as a way to remind yourself?"

"Do you use a pill organizer to help you keep up with your pills?"

These closed questions are not as MI-inconsistent as the prior examples, but are also not fully MI-consistent. Although the provider is not directly giving unsolicited advice about how to improve medication adherence, which would clearly be MI-inconsistent (Miller & Rollnick, 2013), the provider *is* using these closed questions as an indirect way to give such advice.

MI-Consistent Closed Questions:

"How long have you had this difficulty?"

"Do you have difficulty taking your other medications?"

While these are closed questions, they are MI-consistent as they are attempting to elicit from the client his or her thoughts about the problem and avoid prescribing a solution or placing judgment on the situation.

MI-Inconsistent Open Questions:

"How can I make you understand the importance of taking your medications?"

"How has your diet been?"

These questions, while open, are MI-inconsistent. With the first question, the provider seeks to directly confront the client about medication compliance, which is MI-inconsistent. The second question is not in sync with what the client is discussing and thus shows a lack of collaboration and empathy.

Somewhat MI-Consistent Open Questions:

"What will help you remember?"

"What are your thoughts about using a pill-minder to help you remember?"

These questions, while open and inviting the client to talk, are not fully MI-consistent. The first question immediately attempts to identify solutions and a plan for changing. It is not fully MI-consistent as it doesn't consider client motivation for changing or not. There is a potential for the discussion to quickly evolve to the point at which the provider offers solutions and the client rejects them (i.e., righting reflex). The second question is used to elicit the client's reactions; however, the question is focused on the provider's solution, rather than eliciting solutions from the client. Thus the provider is using the question as an indirect way to offer unsolicited advice.

MI-Consistent Open Questions:

"What concerns you about taking and not taking your medications?"

"What exactly happens in the evening?"

"What are some reasons you want to take your meds?"

These questions are MI-consistent because they invite the client to talk and they elicit the client's expertise about the situation thus allowing providers to gain a better understanding of the client's motivations and concerns. In fact, a question like the third question is likely to elicit change talk (discussed later)—an important aspect of MI as it relates to increasing motivation. The first two questions will help the client discuss concerns associated with medications and barriers that might need to be addressed to enhance motivation for changing.

Affirmations

When clients are attempting to change, it is common to focus on the problem or past failed attempts. Correct use of affirmations is a method through which client strengths can be emphasized. Affirmations, in MI, involve actively seeking to uncover, recognize, and discuss client strengths and positive actions (Hohman, 2012; Pirlott, Kisbu-Sakarya, DeFrancesco, Elliot, & MacKinnon, 2012). To accomplish this, a provider may comment on a strength, attribute, skill, or action; reframe an action, situation, or attribute in a positive light; or elicit affirmations from the client. Using affirmations does not mean a provider acts like an overzealous physical trainer or cheerleader, but that the provider *genuinely* elicits, recognizes, and comments on client strengths. Therefore, affirmations should focus on the client, should not be "praise," and should avoid using the word "I" as in "I approve". In the helping professions, it is common for providers to use comments like "that is good/great" or "I am so proud of you." There is no doubt in our mind that these comments are meant to be supportive; however, they are not fully MI-consistent as they violate these rules.

Example: MI-Consistent/Inconsistent Affirmations

Client Statement: *"My family says I am depressed but I am not sure. I go to work and socialize. Don't depressed people just sit at home and sulk."*

MI-Inconsistent: *"You are depressed and not sure what to do about it."*

Although this is a nice example of a simple reflection (discussed later), it focuses solely on client weaknesses and problems. Thus, there is little attempt to recognize or comment on strengths. Additionally, it has the potential to engender discord between the client and provider as the client has communicated uncertainty about being depressed.

Somewhat MI-Consistent: *"Your family thinks you're depressed but depressed people do not behave the way you are. I am happy you still came in."*

This statement is an example of a good reflection of content. However, the provider misses an important opportunity to affirm the client by commenting on strengths, successes, or positive behavior. Further, the provider by using "I" puts the focus on her or his approval versus the client's inherent strengths or abilities.

MI-Consistent:

Comment on positive action: *"You came here at the request of your family even though you are unsure if it is needed. You must care a lot about them."*

Reframe situation: *"You are feeling depressed and are coping with it pretty well. You're still able to work every day and go out with friends."*

Elicit from client: *"What sets you apart from those people who sit at home and sulk?"*

Each statement is an MI-consistent affirmation as they follow the rules outlined earlier, focus on strengths, and are likely to engage the client in further discussion versus engendering discord between the client and provider. The first statement acknowledges that the client is uncertain about having depression yet highlights the care for family members resulting in coming to the appointment. The second statement reframes the client's focus on sitting home and sulking to focus on the strength of being active. The third statement elicits from the client qualities that can be used as strengths in changing.

Reflections

As the primary basic counseling skill used in MI, reflections are important as they help bridge the meaning between what the client is communicating and what the provider hears, and allow providers to check their understanding of what was said (Passmore, 2011; Rosengren, 2009). It is important to note that when offering a reflection, the tone of voice is just as important as the words uttered. To reflect, the voice should inflect down at the end of the statement. An up-inflection at the end of the statement, which seems to come most naturally to most people we have trained in MI, communicates a question—a closed question. To be MI-consistent voice tone should also be devoid of inflections that convey sarcasm, hostility, or condescension.

Reflections are valuable as they can (1) help demonstrate that a provider is listening, (2) express provider empathy, (3) communicate an understanding and appreciation of the client, and (4) help the provider guide the client to a deeper discussion of the topic. For these reasons, it is also important to avoid tagging on a question such as "Right?" or "Is that correct?" Those types of questions can convey to the client that the provider does not really understand them and must check-in frequently in order to follow them. Reflections should also be used intentionally in MI to strategically reflect sustain talk, discord and change talk as providers seek to guide clients toward change. The goal in using reflection with discord is to join with the client rather than confront him or her about their ambivalence toward change. When intentionally reflecting discord, a provider is continuing to understand and foster an engaging working relationship (Miller & Rollnick, 2013). Change talk is a key aspect for facilitating change in MI, and as such the MI-consistent provider reflects change talk in an attempt to reinforce and strengthen it (Miller & Rollnick, 2013).

An MI reflection is categorized as simple or complex.

SIMPLE REFLECTIONS

Reflections that remain very close to what the client said, adding little additional information, are simple reflections (Moyers, 2004). Simple reflections are often used to acknowledge and validate what the client is saying (Rosengren, 2009; SAMSHA, 1999). Thus, simple reflections may include statements about basic client feelings and thoughts or session content. Sole reliance on simple reflections can slow progress of the discussion to more meaningful aspects of the client's concerns. Often when our trainees felt their sessions went around in circles with little progress, we found that they relied mainly on simple reflections and didn't deepen the discussion.

Example: MI-Consistent/Inconsistent Simple Reflections

Client Statement: *"My wife bugs me about eating healthy. I can't believe she made me come here."*

MI-Inconsistent: *"Your eating is bad."*

This reflection is MI-inconsistent because it negatively labels the client's eating and is likely to engender discord. The reflection prematurely focuses on the eating behavior and misses the client's message about being upset over being forced to come to the session. This missed opportunity to reflect the client's concern could slow engagement and the development of the working relationship. Instead, the client could become defensive about his eating behavior.

Somewhat MI-Consistent: *"Sounds like you and you wife are having some difficulties."*

This reflection is somewhat MI-consistent. It is a reflection of the session content but is likely to focus the discussion on the client's wife or marital relationship. Thus, the discussion may end up off moving away from the potential change target and may lose focus.

MI-Consistent: *"You can't believe you're here."*

This reflection is MI-consistent because it focuses on the message communicated by the client. By reflecting the content of the statement, the provider validates the client's comment and is more likely to foster trust and engagement. The reflection communicates that the provider hears where the client is coming from and that his situation is appreciated. Therefore, this reflection is less likely to engender discord.

COMPLEX REFLECTIONS

Complex reflections are an important ingredient in helping to facilitate client change within the framework of MI because they expand on the discussion. Complex reflections are provider restatements of session content, and client thoughts and/or feelings with substantial emphasis or meaning added to facilitate movement toward positive change (SAMHSA, 1999).

Types of Complex Reflection

Double-sided Reflection: The double-sided reflection is often used in MI. A double-sided complex reflection occurs when the provider restates a client statement that captures both sides of ambivalence (Miller & Rollnick, 2002). Thus, use of double-sided reflections helps to bring to awareness the ambivalence the client is experiencing without siding one way or the other.

Example: MI-Consistent/Inconsistent Double-sided Reflection

Client: *"I know people want me to completely stop smoking, but I am not going to completely quit."*

MI-Inconsistent: *"Smoking is good and you don't want to quit."*

The provider's response is a nice reflection of sustain talk. However, it is not an MI-consistent, double-sided reflection because it does not capture both sides of the client's ambivalence. The reflection only focuses on why the client wants to continue smoking. This could result in the client talking further about not quitting.

Somewhat MI-Consistent: *"You are aware that others are concerned about your smoking and at the same time are not ready to quit smoking completely."*

In this reflection the provider captures both sides of the client's ambivalence. However, it is somewhat MI-consistent as the second half of the double-sided reflection focuses on not changing. Given that clients are likely to pick up the conversation where providers leave off, this client is likely to talk more about continuing to smoke instead of changing smoking behavior. Although an expert-level MI provider might sometimes intentionally structure a double-sided reflection in this way, generally speaking this is not the most MI-consistent ordering.

MI-Consistent: *"You are not ready to quit smoking completely, and at the same time you are really aware that others are concerned about your smoking."*

In this reflection, the provider captures both sides of the client's ambivalence, recognizing the concern about smoking and the lack of readiness to quit. Thus, both sides are reflected back to the client without an emphasis on either. There are two important nuances in this reflection. First, notice the use of *and* versus *but* when using a double-sided reflection as it emphasizes feeling two ways. Next, notice that the side of ambivalence related to changing is presented last. This point highlights one of the intentional aspects of MI. People often continue to talk about the most recent thing another person states. Thus, the client is more likely to continue talking about reasons to change because the provider ended the double-sided reflection with the pro-change side of the ambivalence.

Amplified Reflection: This type of complex reflection occurs when a provider restates what the client has said, but in a stronger or even more extreme fashion than what the client communicated (Miller & Rollnick, 2002; SAMHSA, 1999). Amplified reflections are particularly helpful in responding to client sustain talk as it amplifies the client's communication about not changing beyond what the client is saying, yet does not confront or challenge it. When using amplified reflection, it is important to remain supportive and avoid a tone that could be perceived as judgmental or condescending as this could engender discord.

Example: MI-Consistent/Inconsistent Amplified Reflection

Client: *"I don't understand why my wife is so concerned about my cholesterol. My results suggest it is borderline high, not high."*

MI-Inconsistent: *"You really don't have any problems whatsoever."*

This amplified reflection is MI-inconsistent for two reasons. First, we highlight the potential tone of the word "really" as this could be perceived by the client as judgmental. Avoiding qualifiers such as this might reduce that perception. Second, using "whatsoever" could be perceived as sarcastic and confrontational and could communicate that the provider does not believe the client.

Somewhat MI-Consistent: *"Your wife shouldn't have any concerns about you."*

In this reflection the provider is amplifying the client's statement. However, the statement is a more global statement about the client's relationship with his wife versus an amplified statement about the change target. The client may respond with discord or the conversation may drift off topic and lose focus.

MI-Consistent: *"Your wife is worrying needlessly about your cholesterol."*

In this reflection the provider is amplifying the client's statement about his wife's concern by adding the word "needlessly". By adding this word the provider is taking the client's statement to an extreme that the client may actually disagree with and correct the provider.

Summaries

Summaries fall on the advanced end of reflections. In essence, summaries are provider statements that pull together and synthesize a group of client statements. To put it in the metaphorical terms of one of our non-MI passions (making

Southern barbeque): if reflections are individual spices, then summaries are the exquisite spice rub that pulls all of the individual flavors together to give your barbeque just the right taste. Summaries can be used to begin and focus a session, close a topic, conclude a session, connect session content, and/or help a client reflect on what he or she has said (Ivey & Bradford Ivey, 2003; Seligman, 2008). Summaries are valuable to discussions about change as they allow clients to hear multiple aspects of their conversation all at once. In MI, you use summaries to selectively attend to key concepts (i.e., change talk) when choosing what to include. Three different types of summaries have been discussed and are described here.

Example: Summaries

Provider Question: *"If you were to be successful in making the changes to your drinking we've talked about, what would be different in your life a year from now?"*

Client Statement: *"Well, if I make it through this DUI [arrest and conviction for driving under the influence of alcohol] and get my license back, I'd have a job again."*

Provider Response: *"So one thing is that you'd be able to get a job again. What else would be different?"*

Client Statement: *"Well, this isn't really a change from now, but it is a change from before—now that I don't go to the bars, I'm spending more time with my kids. Doing homework, eating dinner with them; you know, just normal family stuff."*

Provider Response: *"So being a more involved father is something you've been doing and you think would continue a year from now. What else might be different if you were successful in changing your drinking?"*

Client Statement: *"I'm not sure. I would hope maybe I'd be able to quit smoking. I've tried to quit before, and going to bars always makes me want to smoke. I guess if I didn't go to bars maybe I could quit smoking."*

Collecting Summaries: These are summaries that reflect information gathered over a period of time that are intended to simply continue the conversation (Rosengren, 2009). In essence, the provider is recalling several things a client recently stated. We have discussed with trainees that collecting summaries can be a great way to remain MI-consistent in intake or assessment sessions as they communicate the provider is listening and enable probing for more information about a topic without simply asking questions.

Example: MI-Consistent/Inconsistent Collecting Summaries

MI-Inconsistent: *"So you recognize the way your behavior has damaged your family both financially and emotionally and you plan to finally be a responsible father and provider."*

This summary is MI-inconsistent because it not only summarizes the client's statements, but it also labels the client's behavior in a negative way that does not convey acceptance.

Somewhat MI-Consistent: *"So you hope to have a job. You also said you'd like to quit smoking. Am I hearing you correctly?"*

This response is somewhat MI-consistent as is summarizes pieces of the discussion. The focus of the summary is on the two things the client wants to change without including the benefits of the changes discussed by the client. Thus, this summary may or may not promote positive change. The provider also uses a closed-ended question to "check" the accuracy of the summary.

MI-Consistent: **"So one thing you hope would be different a year from now is that you will have a job. You have been spending more time with your kids and want that to continue. You also said you'd like to quit smoking and you think that might be possible if you aren't drinking at bars. What steps have you already taken toward making the changes in your drinking that will make all of those things possible?"**

This summary is MI-consistent, because it pulls together what the client has said without labeling or judging what has been said, and it also focuses on the elements of what the client has said that are most likely to promote positive changes in the client's drinking.

Linking summaries: When a provider wishes to connect information expressed by a client with previous information, a linking summary can be used (Rosengren, 2009). In using linking summaries the provider is intentionally trying to bridge different things the client has stated.

Example: MI-Consistent/Inconsistent Linking Summaries

MI-Inconsistent: *"In looking through your chart, I see that this is your fourth time in treatment. I can't believe you are still getting DUIs and going to bars almost every night. You need to get your act together and take treatment seriously this time."*

This summary is MI-inconsistent because it confronts the client about his drinking behavior and also blames him for past treatment failures.

Somewhat MI-Consistent: *"So it sounds like a lot would be possible if you quit drinking, including smoking cessation. I'm glad to hear that you are considering smoking cessation now. That's a big change. I can see from your chart that you've declined smoking cessation counseling the last several times it has been offered."*

This summary is a somewhat MI-consistent linking summary. The provider uses a summary to link something the client has just said to information from the client's treatment record. However, the summary is not fully MI-consistent, because the provider shifts the established focus of the session from reducing alcohol consumption to smoking cessation.

MI-Consistent: *"So you think a lot of important goals, like getting back to work, spending time with your kids, and quitting smoking might be possible if you were to make changes to your drinking. This sounds similar to the way you turned your life around when you left the gang to join the military when you were 18."*

This summary is MI-consistent because it links what the client has just said about making changes in his drinking to comments he made about other successful behavior changes, in a way that is likely to promote the client's sense of self-efficacy about the current behavior change.

Transition summaries: The intention when using a transition summary is to shift between topics or to change topics (Rosengren, 2009). Transition summaries can be particularly useful during data-gathering interviews such as intake or diagnostic interviews as they communicate that the provider is listening and they help ease into the next aspect of the interview.

Example: MI-Consistent/Inconsistent Transition Summaries

MI-Inconsistent: *"So it sounds like this DUI was finally the wake-up call you needed. You've recognized that your drinking is destroying you and your family. Admitting you have a problem is the first step. How long have you been drinking?"*

This provider utterance is MI-inconsistent. With the summary, the provider twists the change talk the client has offered in a very negative, confrontational, and labeling way. The provider then transitions to asking structured questions without informing the client about the shift or asking permission to make the shift. Thus the provider controls the direction of the session is a very non-collaborative fashion.

Somewhat MI-Consistent: *Just to summarize, you seem clear on wanting to stop using alcohol. Now let me go ahead and ask you some questions for our intake form.*

Although this provider statement, in some sense, captures the essence of the conversation with the client up to that point, it is also not a summary. It does not bring together two or more distinct ideas expressed by the client. The provider also misses the opportunity to support client autonomy and maintain a collaborative spirit by asking permission to segue to the intake form.

MI-Consistent: *"Before I ask you the questions I mentioned earlier, let me summarize what you've told me so far, and see if I've missed anything important. You have decided to stop drinking because you have experienced your third DUI and have faced some stiff penalties. You also imagine that life will be much different, in a good way, if you are successful in making that change in your drinking."*

Although not as detailed as the collecting summary, this MI-consistent summary is a true summary in that it brings together two or more distinct ideas expressed by the client. It is MI-consistent because it does not seek to judge or label the client, but rather to emphasize those elements of what the client has said that will help promote change.

QUICK REFERENCE

Basic Motivational Interviewing Skills

Use open questions to invite discussion.

Elicit, look for, comment on, and affirm client strengths and successes.

Intentionally use simple and complex reflections to expand the change discussion.

Deliberately use collecting, linking, and transition summaries to talk about change.

CHANGE TALK AND SUSTAIN TALK

Because a major focus of MI is helping clients explore their own reasons for making a particular change, the MI-consistent provider selectively listens for and reflects client utterances that favor change—change talk. Miller and Rollnick (2013) outlined four components of motivation that are reflected in change talk: (1) wanting to change; (2) perceived ability to change; (3) identified reasons to change; and (4) importance of that change. Change talk has been classified into two categories—preparatory change talk and mobilizing change talk (Miller & Rollnick, 2013). Preparatory change talk includes statements that communicate the client is thinking about changing yet the statements by themselves do not predict client action (Amrhein et al., 2003; Carcone et al., 2013). This type of change talk is represented by the acronym DARN (*Desire, Ability, Reasons,* and *Need*).

Examples of Preparatory Change Talk

DESIRE

We often emphasize that desire statements are valuable because really wanting something to be different is important for a client to increase their willingness to act on it. In fact, wanting, wishing, or desire to change is a major component of motivation (Miller & Rollnick, 2013). Desire statements may include:

I wish my health was better.

I'd like to be calm when I drive.

I want to go out with my friends and make healthy eating choices.

I want to leave the house without having to check the lock 10 times.

ABILITY

Client expressions of what they can do or have done before are valuable statements about the client's perceived ability to change What better way is there to help clients identify solutions to a problem than hearing and reflecting their statements about what they can do or have done in the past? Thus, ability statements are important as they communicate what clients have done and what they are likely willing to do to change. Ability statements may include:

> I could probably use a designated driver more often.
> I may be able to go for a 10-minute walk each evening.
> I can get a pill box to sort my medications.
> I might be able to brush my teeth first thing in the morning.

REASONS

A common form of change talk often expressed by clients is the reasons to change. It is key to elicit and understand why it is important that a client changes because it is the client's reasons, not others', that will facilitate client change and are essential in MI. Reason statements often communicate an "if…then" message. Reason statements may include:

> If I paid attention more to my son he wouldn't get into as much trouble.
> It seems like I will have more energy if I get more sleep.
> I want to be able to enjoy things again.
> By not smoking I would save money.
> By talking more to people I might get more friends.

NEED

Clients' statements that express the importance of the change reflect how necessary and urgent it is. Miller and Rollnick (2013) highlight that need statements do not include why the change is important and if they did, the statement would reflect a reason and not a need. Need statements may include:

> I need to do something about my anxiety.
> I've got to stay out of trouble for the rest of the year.
> I must lower my blood pressure.
> I can't keep gaining weight.
> I have to get out of the house and socialize more often.

QUICK REFERENCE

Change Talk

Desire: I want to change something.
Ability: I can do this to change.
Reason: If I change then this will happen.
Need: I have to change.

Mobilizing Change Talk

Mobilizing change talk, or mobilizing statements, include client statements that communicate their commitment to and willingness to change and/or the steps they are taking already to change. This type of change talk can be thought of using the acronym CAT (Commitment, Activating, and Taking Steps) (Miller & Rollnick, 2013). Commitment statements are those that express some level of intention to make a change and are most predictive of change (Ajzen & Albarracin, 2007; Amrhein et al., 2003). Clients may express varying levels of intention to change ranging from a very low level ("I might try it.") to a very high level ("I'm definitely going to do it!"). Some clients will discuss the steps they are making to prepare for change. This has been referred to as "activating change talk" (Miller & Rollnick, 2013). Finally, some clients will discuss things they have already done to change. Statements about steps the client has already taken are called taking steps (Miller & Rollnick, 2013). Samples of mobilizing statements may include:

COMMITMENT
I guess I could try eating whole wheat toast for breakfast.
I will probably increase my walking to 5,000 steps a day.
I am not going to smoke in the car or during the middle of the night.
I am never going to drink again.

ACTIVATING
I will call the job center to see when I can have an appointment.
I plan to buy a pedometer tomorrow.
My wife and I plan to talk about how to help our son meet his probation requirements.
I got some information about different social clubs in town.

TAKING STEPS
I got rid of all of the alcohol in house.
I am now only smoking outside.
I bought some fruit at the store yesterday.
I met with the job coach yesterday.

QUICK REFERENCE

Mobilizing Talk

Commitment: I intend to do this.
Activating: I am going to do these things.
Taking steps: I did this.

Eliciting and Responding to Change Talk

The focus on eliciting and responding to change talk is arguably the aspect of MI that makes it most distinct from other counseling approaches and communication styles (Houck, Moyers, & Tesche, 2013; Westra & Aviram, 2013). When practicing MI, providers respond with interest in client change talk both non-verbally and verbally because provider behaviors have been linked with client change talk (Glynn & Moyers, 2010). Providers can use reflections, questions, affirmations and summaries to elicit and reinforce change talk.

> Questions to elicit change talk: *"What might you need to do differently about your diabetes?"*
> Asking for elaboration: *"Tell me more about that."*
> Reflecting change talk: *"It's not good, you think, for you to get as drunk as you do."*
> Summarizing change talk: *"What you seem to be saying here is that there are several reasons you need to change your eating: to feel better, have more energy, and to be a better model for your children."*
> Affirming change talk: *"It sounds like you have thought about this for some time and know you need to do something about your depression."*

SUSTAIN TALK AND DISCORD

Related to the righting reflex mentioned earlier is sustain talk and discord. Change talk is client speech in favor of change, whereas sustain talk is client speech expressing desire, reason, and need to remain the same and perceived inability to change (Miller & Rollnick, 2013). In other words, when articulating sustain talk, clients are telling you why they should not change.

Sustain Talk Example

Client Statements:

Desire: *"I want to keep eating the way I do now."*

Ability: *"I can't turn down a buffet."*

Reason: *"All of my friends eat the same way I do."*

Need: *"I don't need to change my diet."*

MI-Inconsistent: *"Well you have gained 20 pounds in the past 6 months."*

This is MI-inconsistent because it is a confrontational argument for change. Statements such are this are likely to engender discord between providers and clients. Further, the client is more likely to discuss why the provider is wrong in her response, thus becoming more entrenched in staying the way he or she is.

Somewhat MI-Consistent: *"Why might you want to change your eating now?"*

This response is somewhat MI-consistent as it is an open question that intends to elicit change talk (i.e., reasons to make a change). However, as a response to sustain talk this question is less MI-consistent as it might engender discord and increase sustain talk. More specifically, this question dismisses client sustain talk and communicates the provider has taken sides with change.

MI-Consistent:

Simple reflection: *"Your eating is not a concern for you right now."*

Amplified reflection: *"This concern about your weight is an overreaction."*

Double-sided reflection: *"Your diet is not of concern to you, and at the same time you chose to come to meet with me."*

Reframing: *"It would be difficult for you to make changes to your eating because you like food and it's an important part of your interactions with friends."*

Emphasizing autonomy: *"Ultimately, it is up to you what you decide to do or not do about your eating."*

These responses are MI-consistent because they are less likely to engender discord between providers and clients. In fact, each of them communicates that providers are joining clients where they are at in relation to the area where change is being considered. Thus, by responding to sustain talk in a MI-consistent way, providers are more likely to engage clients, reduce the discord, and open the door to explore change.

Discord

While sustain talk is client communication about a particular change, say changing a diet, discord is more about the relationship between a provider and client. In other words, discord is a signal that the provider and client are not on the same page and that there may be a rift in the working alliance (Miller & Rollnick, 2013). Thus, sustain talk and discord should be cues for providers to change their behavior and respond differently to the client. We often try to emphasize with those we train that when discord develops it is their responsibility to get "on the same page" with their clients to resolve it. To do this, a provider avoids arguing with the client, listens more carefully, changes direction, and responds to the client in a non-confrontational manner that attempts to change client energy toward discussing positive change (Miller & Rollnick, 2002).

Example: MI-Consistent/Inconsistent Responding to Discord

Client Statement: *"Well, I really don't know why I am here. I was in the wrong place at the wrong time and got an MIP [minor in possession of alcohol].*

I don't understand why they are so upset; everybody drinks on game day. I came here because the Dean told me to, but I really don't feel like I should be here, but I want to stay out of trouble. Now I have to come here and hear you lecture me about how I need to change my drinking."

MI-Inconsistent: *"If the Dean is concerned enough to ask you to come here, you must have a problem with your drinking."*

This statement is MI-inconsistent because it directly argues with the client in favor of change. This statement is likely to engender increased discord and will place the client in a position to defend him- or herself and explain why his or her drinking does not need to change. Not only is the client not talking about change based on this response, the client will be less engaged.

Somewhat MI-Consistent: *"If you'd like, I can provide you with more information about the rationale behind the alcohol policy."*

This response is somewhat MI-consistent. The provider is asking permission to provide information to address the client's statement that she does not understand why she has been referred for help. Although asking permission to give information is an MI-consistent strategy, in this case it is unlikely that the client's concern is really that she does not understand the alcohol policy. It is more likely that she is frustrated and feels singled out. Thus this response is unlikely to decrease discord.

MI-Consistent:

Apologizing: *"I'm sorry you were not given clear information about the policies."*

Simple reflection: *"It seems like you and the Dean have a different view of the situation."*

Amplified reflection: *"The University is really overacting here about your drinking given that all college students drink."*

Double-sided reflection: *"You really don't feel like you need to be here and at the same time you want to learn how to stay out of trouble."*

Affirmation: *"You have really thought through this situation."*

Shifting focus: *"You are concerned I'm going to force something upon you. I don't know enough about you yet to even start talking about what makes sense for you to do. I'd like to discuss your thoughts about what brought you here a bit."*

Emphasizing autonomy: *"You feel forced to come here and I'd like you to know that it is your choice what to do with the information we discuss in this program."*

All of these statements would be more likely to reduce discord between providers and clients as they communicate "I appreciate your situation and don't want to force you into anything." Additionally, these statements demonstrate a change in direction to avoid increasing discord. Further, the client may be more likely to respond with change talk, reduced push-back, and more willing to discuss the situation as well as more openness to provider feedback.

Responding to Sustain Talk and Discord

Reflect client's concerns about not changing.
Affirm the strengths in client's sustain talk and discord.
Validate client's concerns and shift the focus of discussion to a less contentious topic.
Explicitly comment on client's autonomy and personal choice.

CHAPTER SUMMARY

Our focus for this chapter was to introduce you to MI and provide a brief overview of the foundational components of this communication approach. In providing this overview we emphasized the importance of adhering to the MI spirit in order to develop proficiency. It is from the spirit that the MI-consistent use of basic counseling skills such as open questions, affirmations, reflections, and summaries emerge, as well as one's adherence to the principles of MI. Thus, if one embraces the spirit of MI it becomes second nature to resist the righting reflex and understand clients' motivations through listening to and empowering them. Adopting the spirit of MI as part of your philosophy can assist you in intentionally using MI skills and strategies to elicit and reinforce change talk as well as conceptualize and successfully work with sustain talk and discord. We hope that we impressed upon you the importance of adopting the spirit of MI in order to continue on your journey of developing your MI abilities.

3

The Four Processes of MI

Recent developments in the evolution of MI have moved away from the two-phase approach to MI (i.e., building motivation and consolidating commitment; Miller & Rollnick, 2002) toward four overlapping processes that make up MI-consistent interactions. The four processes are engaging, focusing, evoking, and planning. While the processes build on each other, they are not exclusive; there is not a defined beginning and end to each process (Miller & Rollnick, 2013). In other words, once a client is engaged, that does not mean providers can stop attending to client engagement. The conceptualization of the processes that unfold during a motivational interview has gotten more detailed to enhance clarity about what exactly occurs during a motivational interview. However, in our experience, the actual practice of MI has not changed. The portion of an MI session formerly termed "building motivation for change" encompassed the engaging, focusing, and evoking processes. Similarly, the portion of an MI session formerly termed "consolidating commitment to change" largely comprised what is now termed planning. In fact the MI-based interventions we have developed map on to the four phases quite well even though they were designed prior to the redefinition. The decision to redefine the two-phase approach into four processes helps to better clarify the nuances involved in a MI session (such as engaging and focusing) that were not captured by the two phases. This new approach also has promise to help providers utilize MI more effectively.

ENGAGING

The main focus in the engaging process is on developing the solid working relationship with clients that is important to most clinical encounters (Horvath, 2001). To do this, a provider must be aware of the importance that first impressions have on clients and be mindful of how provider actions influence others. In particular, providers must be cognizant of how their actions affect the perceptions and willingness of clients to enter into a working relationship with them. Helping clients feel welcome, comfortable, and safe to explore their questions and concerns about change are important goals of engaging. To be MI-consistent in engaging requires avoiding traps such as those outlined in the quick reference box (Miller & Rollnick, 2002). All of these are traps because they may lead clients to feel less welcome and safe in the relationship with a provider.

QUICK REFERENCE

Traps to Avoid

Question and answer: Asking too many closed questions.
Premature focus: Narrowing in too quickly on what to change.
Taking sides: Identifying the problem and prescribing a solution.
Expert: Communicating that you have all of the answers.

Engaging clients is vital to MI and is foundational to the other MI processes and outcomes (Boardman, Catley, Grobe, Little, & Ahluwalia, 2006; Catley et al., 2006; Moyers et al., 2005; Murphy, Linehan, Reyner, Musser, & Taft, 2012). Thus, an MI-consistent provider is always vigilant to engagement and signs of disengagement. These signs of disengagement may include the client providing short or vague responses, passively agreeing with suggestions, a closed body posture, changing the topic, interrupting the provider, or simply not saying anything.

Miller and Rollnick (2013) suggest that to appropriately engage someone in an MI interaction requires using a person-centered style that is welcoming, accepting, and genuinely focused on wanting to understand clients' concerns or problems as well as their values and goals. This requires focus on the person and listening as opposed to determining the root of the problem and the solution—remember in MI that is not the provider's job. Think of an experience you had with a helper that made it difficult for you to trust them. What was it about that experience or the person's behavior that made it hard for you to trust them? Were you open to their help or suggestions? Would you go back? These are thoughts that clients have when they first meet a provider and are things all providers should be mindful of to be MI-consistent.

QUICK REFERENCE

Motivational Interviewing Training Tip: Signs of Disengagement

Signs of disengagement may include the client providing short or vague responses, passively agreeing with your suggestions, a closed body posture, changing the topic, interrupting you, or simply not saying anything.

MI-Consistent Strategies for Engaging Clients

OARS

Use of the most basic strategies in MI, OARS (open questions, affirmations, reflections, and summaries), can be very valuable during the engaging process. These are some examples of the use of each type of OARS utterance for engaging:

MI-CONSISTENT ENGAGING OPEN QUESTIONS
"How are you?"
"What are your thoughts about being here today?"
"In your mind what does our work together look like?"
"What are your doubts/concerns about being here?"

MI-CONSISTENT ENGAGING AFFIRMATIONS
"Thank you for coming in today. A lot of clients cancel on rainy days."
"It is good to see you again. It is impressive how much you are sticking with this."
"Looks like you have been making progress."
"It couldn't have been easy to make it here today and shows your perseverance."

MI-CONSISTENT ENGAGING REFLECTIONS
Client: *[looks at watch]*/Provider: *"The wait was a bit long today."*
Client: *"Are my results in?"*/Provider: *"You're anxious to get your test results."*
Client: *"How long will this take?"*/Provider: *"You're in a hurry."*

MI-CONSISTENT ENGAGING SUMMARIES
"So you are really sticking with this and making progress. You made it in even though it was raining, you were in a hurry, and the wait was longer than usual. Let's go ahead and jump into those test results."

Exploring Goals and Values

Developing an appreciation for a client is an important aspect of an MI-consistent approach. One way to appreciate clients and their situations is to learn about their goals and values. Before a provider and client can discuss changing, it is important for the provider to understand the context that led the client to seek help and to consider personal change. Exploring goals and values is an interactive process where the provider guides the client through visualizing and articulating various objectives related to the positive changes they seek. Similarly, exploring values involves the clarification of the client's personal values, or aspects of life that the client finds particularly important. Clients are much more likely to work towards a goal that is valued. Therefore, making the connection between clients' articulated goals and values can be critical in their level of engagement and building motivation for change.

COMMON PHRASES/STATEMENTS IN THIS STRATEGY

Exploring goals and values can be introduced to the client in an open-ended interview format. Most often, a provider starts with broad, open-ended questions like, *"How would you like your life to be five years from now?"* or, *"What things are most important to you?"* These questions will begin the process of engaging and exploration and can lead the client to think about change at a high level. The order in which the client discusses their different values helps the provider better understand their relative importance to the client. As clients begin to explore goals and values, reflections of feelings and restatements can be beneficial in prompting the client to elaborate on or move forward with a train of thought (for example, *"So having financial stability for your children is very important to you,"* or, *"You seem a little uncertain about your ability to order a salad instead of something fried when eating out."*) This also serves to confirm goals and values with the client, allowing them to give the feedback to the provider concerning how well their goals and values are being understood.

MOTIVATIONAL INTERVIEWING TRAINER TIP: INDICATIONS THAT YOU ARE DOING MI-CONSISTENT ENGAGING

You spend the first few moments (or as long as it takes) getting to know the client and putting him or her at ease rather than jumping straight to "business."
The client will seem to feel comfortable talking to you!
You will feel comfortable talking to the client.
You and the client are working together.
You will be asking open, not closed questions.
You will be reflecting what you hear the client say.
You are developing an understanding of your clients and their concerns!

FOCUSING

Although a motivational interview should not proceed until a client has been engaged, MI is much more than engaging a client and creating a safe environment for the client to discuss his or her concerns. MI, like many evidence-based approaches to behavior change, is focused on helping clients make changes that solve the problems or address the concerns that led them to seek services. Providing MI involves focusing on what needs to change—the change target. Thus, the MI-consistent provider guides the client to identify what he or she wants to change and avoids prescribing or forcing a particular focus. Miller and Rollnick (2013) suggest that focusing helps to identify the client's change agenda. Table 3.1 provides several examples of MI-consistent questions that can be used to help clients focusing on change targets.

MI-Consistent Focusing Strategies

Table 3.1. MI-CONSISTENT FOCUSING QUESTIONS

Question	Why MI-Consistent
What changes might you like to make? What is worrying you most about _____?	These questions can center clients on why they are seeing you, and build rapport.
What concerns you most about changing your _____?	This question can help providers better understand the client's attitude, behavior, and where the problem lies for them.
What exactly happens when you try to _____?	Questions like this can help providers better understand the client's concerns, including potential barriers and resources.
What did you first notice about _____?	Questions like this can be helpful in guiding the client to share their expertise about their experience.

Agenda Setting

Agenda setting is a good strategy for avoiding the premature focus trap. MI-consistent agenda setting involves a brief discussion with a client during which the client assumes as much decision-making freedom as possible. This helps the provider and client determine what topics are important to discuss (Rollnick, Miller, & Butler, 2008). A client's willingness to listen to a provider's ideas increases when the provider listens and attempts to truly understand the client's view of the situation rather than focusing solely on their own concerns (Mason & Butler, 2010). However, depending on professional discipline and the practice environment, providers may have information they must deliver or topics they must to discuss. For instance, through training dieticians, we learned that they often receive orders from a physician to provide nutrition education, such as a heart-healthy diet for a patient who recently had a heart attack. These trainees would ask us "How can we allow the client to help set the agenda when we have a specific task to complete?" Our response to this question was that although these requirements may influence the nature of MI-consistent agenda setting, they do not preclude the possibility of MI-consistent agenda setting. We encouraged the dieticians to use a guiding style and look at agenda setting as a shared and collaborative process. As a good guide, it is important for the dieticians to share the doctor's concerns and recommendations and to invite the client to express his or her own concerns during the agenda-setting process. Agenda setting can be used at various times throughout a motivational interview when a provider wants to engage the client in active decision making about the direction the interview will take.

Table 3.2. Sample Feedback Form for Agenda Setting

	Healthy Range	1st Numbers	2nd Numbers	3rd Numbers	4th Numbers	5th Numbers	6th Numbers	7th Numbers
					Know Your Numbers Card			
Systolic Blood Pressure	< 120 mmHg							
Diastolic Blood Pressure	< 80 mmHg							
Waist Circumference (inches)	Men < 40 Women < 35							
Body Mass Index	18.5–24.9							
Weight	Varies							
Height	Varies							
Total Cholesterol	< 200 mg/dL							
LDL (Bad) Cholesterol	< 100 mg/dL							
HDL (Good) Cholesterol	Men > 40 mg/dL Women > 50 mg/dL							

(continued)

Table 3.2. CONTINUED

Know Your Numbers Card

	Healthy Range	1st Numbers	2nd Numbers	3rd Numbers	4th Numbers	5th Numbers	6th Numbers	7th Numbers
Blood Glucose	Pre-meal Glucose: 70–130 mg/dL Post-meal Glucose: < 180 mg/dL							
Diet: Fruits & Vegetables	4–5 cups							
Diet: Fiber	≥ 25g/day							
Diet: Sugar	~2 tsp/day (5 tbs/week)							
Diet: Calcium	1,000 mg/day							
Diet: Dairy	2 to 3 cups							
Med: Blood Pressure	Y/N and I.D.S.							
Med: Blood Sugar	Y/N and I.D.S.							
Med: Cholesterol	Y/N and I.D.S.							

Examples of Agenda Setting

"At this time, if it is okay with you, I'd like for us to take a look at the results from some of the questionnaires you completed last time we met. How does that sound? [Waits for client response]. As you can see from this form, there are several things we can discuss. What, among this information, would you be most interested in hearing first?"

"What would be most helpful for us to discuss first?"

"Given that your physician has asked me to do so, I'd like to discuss your exercise at some point today, but I also wonder what you'd most like to learn about."

You can also use an assessment feedback form to assist you in setting an agenda. An example of a feedback form called the "Know Your Numbers" card that my colleagues and I (MM) used in Hub City Steps—a healthy lifestyle intervention—is provided as an example (see Table 3.2) (Zoellner et al., 2011; 2014). This form was tailored to meet the needs of the project and focused on health indicators. A form such as this can be adapted to meet various assessment and behaviors. Providers can use the card in agenda setting similar to this:

"This is what we call your Know Your Numbers card. This card will be filled in each time you come back here. In looking at this card you will see it has information about your blood pressure....[go through sections, cholesterol, etc.] and info about where your score falls in terms of health. In reviewing these different areas, we looked at what would seem most important for you to discuss. Among these things, which do you think is most important for you to learn about...what's next..."

MOTIVATIONAL INTERVIEWING TRAINER TIP: INDICATIONS THAT YOU ARE DOING MI-CONSISTENT FOCUSING

Your clients have had a major role in developing the agenda for your conversations with them.

You have a good understanding of your clients' goals.

You recognize how consistent or different the goals are between you and your clients.

You and your clients are working together toward shared goals.

EVOKING

Traditionally, what has been described as MI can be seen in the process of evocation. After a focus for change has been identified, the MI-consistent provider elicits from clients their own reasons for wanting or needing to make the particular change—"change talk." It is this eliciting from clients that helps them identify and appreciate their own motivations for changing. In essence, the individual is talking him- or herself into changing. The expert MI provider will generally elicit multiple motivations (remember DARN [preparatory]-CAT [mobilizing] change talk from chapter 2) for change prior to proceeding with planning. Expert MI providers also generally seek to elicit change talk that focuses not only on the history of the problem, circumstance, or behavior, but also on how change (or lack thereof) might influence the present or future for a client (Moyers, Martin, Manuel, Miller, & Ernst, 2010). Conversely, the MI-inconsistent provider will lecture clients about why it is important or why clients need to change. This often counterproductive effort may actually reduce motivation and increase discord, particularly when clients are ambivalent (Miller & Rollnick, 2013).

It is important to note that the process of evoking will vary from session to session depending on the motivators for change that are most salient to a particular client. Furthermore, in keeping with the spirit of collaboration described in chapter 2, it is always essential that a provider use information and feedback from the client to guide the flow of an MI session. Nonetheless, in our work as providers and supervisors of MI, we have found a pattern that commonly emerges during a well-done evocation process. Usually, it seems most natural for providers and clients to focus first on negative consequences or problems a client has encountered as a result of the problematic behavior or life circumstance about which change is being considered. In fact, often when a provider asks: "What brings you in today?" the client will spontaneously respond with one or more negative consequences that he or she has experienced related to the change being considered. For example: "My weight has gotten over 200 pounds and none of my clothes fit any more," or "I got my third DUI [driving under the influence] and my attorney said that if I didn't come to treatment I'd probably do some jail time." After the negative consequences or problems have been explored and elaborated, a provider will often elicit anticipated outcomes of making the change or not making the change. For example, the provider might ask, "If you are successful in losing 25 pounds, how do you think your life would be better?" or "What concerns, if any, do you have about what could happen if you continue to drink and drive?"

MI-Consistent Evoking Strategies

QUESTIONS TO ELICIT DESIRE, ABILITY, REASONS, AND NEED (DARN TALK)
Desire
"What do you want (like, wish, hope) will be different?"
"Why might you want to make this change?"

Ability
"What is possible for you to do?"
"What can/could you do?"

"What are you able to do?"
"If you decided to make this change, how would you do it?"

Reason
"What would be some specific benefits?"
"What risks would you like to decrease?"
"What are the three most important benefits you see from making this change?"

Need
"How important is this change?"
"How much do you need to make this change?"

BEWARE OF MI-INCONSISTENT QUESTIONS

It is important to be intentional in the selection of evoking questions. The questions that seem to come most naturally to many of those we have trained (and presumably came most naturally to us before all of these years of MI practice and training) are questions that elicit the opposite of change talk: sustain talk. As described in chapter 2, sustain talk refers to utterances that support staying the same: Why the client does not want to change. Why the client perceives he or she can't change. Reasons the client believes he or she should stay the same. The questions that elicit these utterances from a client are things like, "Why don't you...?" or "Why can't you...?" or "Why won't you...?"

Readiness Ruler/Scaling Questions

Using a readiness ruler or rating scale can be helpful for eliciting subjective reports of motivation from clients (Lane & Rollnick, 2009). To assess readiness for change, an Importance-Confidence Scale ranging from 0 (not at all important/confident) to 10 (extremely important/confident) can assist in describing the client's developing motivation and may elicit change talk by providing a helpful perspective about the client's personal dilemma surrounding the desired change. Although verbal forms of the rating scale are commonly used, using visual forms, such as drawing a line with numbers marked 1 to 10, can also demonstrate scaling questions. (A sample readiness ruler handout is provided in chapter 7.) The choice of stem for the readiness ruler/scaling questions (e.g., "How important is it to you...?" "How confident are you...?" "How committed are you...?") will determine which dimensions of readiness for change you assess.

For instance, you can ask the client:

"How strongly do you feel about wanting to protect yourself when drinking? On a scale from 1 to 10, where 1 is 'not at all,' and 10 is 'very much,' where would you place yourself now?"

You can also assess the importance that the client places on a particular behavior:

"How important would you say it is for you to increase your safe sex practices? On a scale from 1 to 10, where 1 is 'not at all important,' and 10 is 'extremely important,' what would you say?"

This type of questioning can also be used to assess how confident or certain the client is in his or her ability to make a change.

Assessing confidence through scaling questions may be accomplished by asking:

"On a scale from 1 to 10, where 1 is 'I'm certain that I could not,' and 10 is 'I'm certain that I could,' how confident are you that you could engage in pleasurable activities?"

Particularly near the end of an encounter, this type of question can also be used to assess a client's commitment to change, as in the following example:

"On a scale from 1 to 10, where 1 is 'not at all,' and 10 is 'couldn't possibly be more,' how committed are you to your plan for walking 4 days per week?"

A key component of using the readiness rulers/scaling questions is questioning clients about why they rated themselves a particular number. When using scaling questions, one very useful follow-up is to ask what makes the number what it is and not a different number. This answer provides perspective on how and why change is important for the client. Typically, it should be asked why the client's selected score is higher than a lower number, because it elicits more reasons for changing (e.g., "What makes it an 8 and not a 5?"). A provider might also wish to ask the client what it would take to move him or her to a higher number (e.g., "What would it take to move you from a 5 to an 8?"). When it follows an importance ruler, this question creates an opportunity for the client to consider potentially undesired consequences of not making a change (e.g., "I guess if I had another heart attack I'd have to get serious about exercise."). When it follows a confidence ruler, this question often provides valuable information the provider and client can use in formulating a plan for change (e.g., "I think if I knew my family would support me, I'd feel more confident about quitting smoking."). Without these follow-up questions, a readiness ruler/scaling question may still provide valuable information about a client's level of readiness for change, but represents an important missed opportunity to evoke change talk.

BEWARE OF FOLLOW-UP QUESTIONS THAT EVOKE SUSTAIN TALK
As with the MI-consistent evoking questions described earlier, we have found that for many of those we train, the follow-up question that comes most naturally is most helpful for eliciting *sustain* talk or defensiveness. For example, if a provider asks, "On a scale from 1 to 10, how important is it for you to take your medication daily?" and the client responds "5," and the provider follows up with "Why are you at a 5 and not a 10?" it is almost impossible for the client to answer

with anything other than sustain talk (e.g., "I just can't make it a priority now because I have too many other things going on."). A client may also perceive an air of judgment in such a question (i.e., that the provider believes he or she should find it more important) and thus responds defensively. Defensive answers or answers that the client believes you want to hear also arise if rapport is poor. Therefore, good rapport and a guiding communication style more accurately assess a client's motivation for change.

Decisional Balance

The pros/cons decisional balance allows a provider and client to fully consider change by think through positives and negatives of both changing and not changing (Ingersoll et al., 2002). This strategy is typically used when clients are ambivalent about making a change in their life. This strategy helps a provider guide clients in making a decision about change. The decisional balance exercise can be introduced with provision of information about the concepts of motivation and ambivalence.

For example, a provider might say something along the lines of:

"Because most of the things we choose to do have both positive and negative aspects about them, we often experience ambivalence when we consider changing. Ambivalence means you have mixed feelings about the same matter, and those different feelings are conflicting with each other. You want to do something and at the same time you don't want to do it. When people are ambivalent, it is difficult to make decisions because it appears that nothing they do will meet all of their desires. One way to work through this is to look at both sides of the coin by examining both sides of our feelings at the time." A sample decisional balance worksheet is presented in chapter 7.

MOTIVATIONAL INTERVIEWING TRAINER TIP: INDICATIONS THAT YOU ARE DOING MI-CONSISTENT EVOKING

You have heard at least one and preferably several of your clients' motivations for changing.
You have a sense of how important change is to your clients.
You have a sense of how confident your clients are about change.
You are hearing and responding to change talk.
You are using questions and reflections to draw out change talk versus providing change reasons.
You are not the one arguing for change.

PLANNING

Developing a specific plan for change and commitment to that plan are important to guiding the client toward change. Consistent with the spirit of MI, the planning process should focus on eliciting change ideas, options, and solutions from clients versus prescribing or directing clients in how to change. This is an important point. In our experience, those we train often think that once the motivation for change is "secured" that they now have permission to be directive and "tell" clients how to change. However, to remain MI-consistent, a provider must continue to recognize that clients are experts on their own lives and as such tend to have at least some, if not all, of the solutions to their problems within themselves (Miller & Rollnick, 2013). Thus, the focus at the planning stage should be drawing these solutions out from clients and supplementing them with information the provider has about what has helped others in similar situations, what options are available to the client, or what the provider would recommend (only when necessary or when requested by the client). By doing so, the provider not only helps the client identify a solution that is the best fit for him or her, but also increases the chances that the client will commit to the solution. Think about it for a moment. Who knows you better than you know yourself? It is unlikely that we could provide a better method for you to read this book than you could develop on your own. We can make suggestions, but ultimately, you will read this book in a way that is best for you. This same principle applies to changing. As professionals, we all have education and experience with methods for changing a problem behavior. However, we do not know how these methods may or may not work for each and every client, but the client knows what will be more likely to work. We can facilitate a planning discussion through skillful use of questions, reflections, providing information and options, and summarizing.

MI-Consistent Planning Strategies

QUESTIONS
"What do you think you'll do?"
"What would be a first step for you?"
"What, if anything, do you plan to do?"
"What do you intend to do?"

Exchanging Information

Often during change planning, a client may ask or a provider may feel compelled to provide information about change options. What makes information exchange MI-consistent or MI-inconsistent is the way in which the information is presented. Traditionally, the information exchange process has been an expert–recipient approach where the "expert" shares and interprets the information. This is an MI-inconsistent approach to providing information as it neglects the client's interpretation of the information, focuses on prescribing information versus eliciting and fosters passivity in clients. An MI-consistent approach to providing information facilitates a collaborative and engaging method in which the client is asked to interpret the information.

One process to provide information in an MI-consistent way is to use the *elicit-provide-elicit* approach, which is a cyclical process of guiding clients through information exchange (Lane & Rollnick, 2009; Rollnick et al., 2008). In this process, the provider elicits from the client before providing information. For instance, in sharing information about diabetes, a provider might first ask, "What do you know about diabetes?" The client's answer to this question will help the provider better understand what information the client currently possesses, including what is accurate or inaccurate, and better focus the information offered. Following this eliciting the provider offers a small chunk of information about diabetes. After giving some information, the provider asks about the client's understanding/interpretation or reaction to the information. This information exchange process can be very valuable when providing assessment results or sharing a diagnosis.

Example of Elicit-Provide-Elicit:

Initial eliciting questions:

"You have discussed several concerns related to your alcohol use and said things have to change and you are going to do something about it. What would you like to learn most about or discuss in relation to changing?"

Client response:

"All I've heard from people is that to change you have to go to rehab and spend a lot of time away from work and family."

Provide information in manageable chunks and focus on the data and not your interpretation:

"You have heard some things about what it takes to change one's drinking behavior and are concerned about that. If I might share some information to add to your understanding, people make changes in different ways. Some people change on their own; some go to a 12-step group, while others engage in outpatient counseling services. And yes, some people do go to a facility for intensive treatment. Based on the information you gave us about your alcohol use compared to national criteria it seems like outpatient counseling may be the most appropriate place for you to address your drinking concerns."

Follow-up eliciting question:

"What do you make of this information?"

Discussing a Menu of Options

Presenting a menu of options is an approach to engaging clients in the planning process. With this approach the provider invites clients to choose the change strategies that seem best for them from a set of options the provider has prepared based on his or her expertise, best practice guidelines, etc. At the same time, when using this strategy in a fully MI-consistent fashion, the provider also encourages clients to include change ideas that may not be in the prepared set. For instance, in the following example, which might be used with college students, the menu has safe drinking behaviors that have been shown to reduce alcohol-related consequences. Note that there are open bubbles on the options sheet that would allow the client to add additional ideas they are willing to consider or are already doing. When helping the client identify a behavior change strategy the provider can open the conversation about change options using the menu (see Figure 3.1).

Sample Menu of Options

"If you'd like we can talk about some strategies you might use when drinking to reduce the risk of negative consequences. Here is a sheet that includes some behaviors that other college students from your university use to protect themselves when drinking. This area represents putting planned limits on drinking (the "know your limits" picture). This area represents mixing alcoholic and

Protective Strategy Options

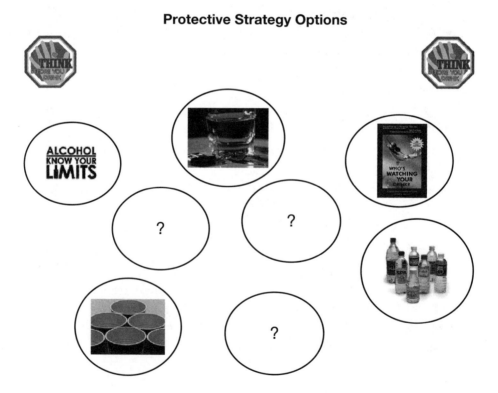

Figure 3.1 Sample Menu of Options for Safe Drinking Strategies

non-alcoholic beverages (picture of water). This area represents the manner in which you drink (the beer cups—representing beer pong). These areas represent reducing the potential for serious harm (the glass and key and the "who's watching your drink"). You will also notice some empty areas. These represent your ideas that are not represented by the other areas. Based on the drinking goals you mentioned before, which of these strategies, if any, might you use to protect yourself when drinking yet meets your goals?"

Developing a Plan for Change

The change plan is a concrete road map that the participant can follow in order to reach their change goals (Naar King & Suarez, 2011). To be effective, the change plan specifically outlines the (1) behavior to be changed, (2) reminders of the motivational factors, (3) change goals, (4) action plan, in manageable steps in order toward change, (5) potential barriers, and (6) steps to overcome those barriers. Typically the change plan is implemented when someone is ready for behavioral action. Thus, the change plan will be negotiated after enhancing motivation and commitment to make behavioral change.

Common phrases/statements that are used in this strategy:

"Now that we have discussed some aspects of your diet and exercise, what do you think you want to do about your eating and exercise?"
"Now that we have come this far, I wonder what you plan to do?"

Table 3.3. COMPONENTS OF DEVELOPING A CHANGE PLAN

Planning Goal	MI-Consistent Question	Important Points to Consider
Identify the changes the client wants to make.	"What might be some of the changes you want to make in your health?"	It is important to be specific and include goals that are positive (e.g., wanting to increase exercise, eat more fruits and veggies) and not just negative goals (e.g., stop eating fried foods).
Highlight the reasons to change.	"We discussed several reasons for changing earlier such as [summarize a few points]. For you, what are some of the most important reasons you want to change?"	Important to elicit/remind the client of the reasons the client previous provided.

(continued)

Planning Goal	MI-Consistent Question	Important Points to Consider
Eliciting why the client wants to change—the change goals.	"Tell me about your overall goals or what you hope you will achieve by making these changes."	Goals should be realistic and achievable.
Identifying what the client plans to do to change.	"There are a lot of things you can do to work toward your goals—what are some of the activities you think you will do to work toward your goals?"	Information and options—presented in an MI-consistent fashion—can help.
Eliciting reasonable first steps.	"Of those activities, what do you think you can do first?" "In making some of these changes, what are some of the first steps?" "When, where and how will these steps be taken?"	It is important to elicit specific, concrete steps.
What can interfere or derail the plan?	"Sometimes it helps to think of the things that may get in the way of your plan." "What could interfere with this plan and how can you stick to the plan?"	Remain positive and focus on identifying how to sidestep this interference.
Identify who can help the client maintain the plan.	"Who can support you in keeping to your plan?"	It is important to identify specific individuals and how they can help.
Identify how the client will know the plan is working.	"How will you know your plan is working?"	Identify specific, concrete indicators of how the plan is working or not.

Table 3.3 provides some components of change planning and examples of questions to ask clients, as well as important points to consider with each component. These components are based on the Change Plan Worksheet developed for Project Match (Miller, Zweben, DiClemente, & Rychtarik, 1992) and revised and used by us in several projects.

MOTIVATIONAL INTERVIEWING TRAINER TIP: INDICATIONS THAT YOU ARE DOING MI-CONSISTENT PLANNING

You are aware of a reasonable next step but not imposing it.

You are resisting the urge to give advice or recommendations until you have evoked solutions from the client.

You are asking permission when providing information, recommendations, or advice.

You are genuinely open to idea that the best solution for a particular client may not be the one you would recommend.

ONE ROAD MAP FOR THE FOUR PROCESSES

As providers begin to attempt to implement MI, one concern that is frequently expressed during early coaching sessions is a lack of confidence in how to navigate an MI session. In response to this concern, we have developed a "road map" for a typical MI session that many of the individuals we have trained have found helpful as they begin implementing MI (see Table 3.4). Although the skilled MI provider will rely primarily on information and feedback from a client to guide the flow of an MI session, this road map serves as an aid or crutch for early sessions during which the flow of the session is less intuitive. You will note that the primary strategies are open question, reflections, and summaries. Although they may not come as naturally as the questions, it is crucial not to skip the reflections and summaries.

THE FOUR PROCESSES OF MOTIVATIONAL INTERVIEWING: A HEALTH PROMOTION EXAMPLE

One application of MI that we have been involved with is HUB City Steps which was an MI-enhanced nutrition and exercise intervention aimed at reducing hypertension among African Americans. The project involved a three-month intervention where individuals received in person feedback about their health status and developed an individualized change plan (Zoellner et al., 2011; 2014).

Table 3.4. Sample Road Map for the Four Processes

Engaging	• Ask: *How are you doing today?* • Reflect the client's response
Focusing	• If you have an a priori target behavior, ask permission to focus on it: *If it's okay with you, I'd like to spend a few minutes talking about _____.* • If you don't have an a priori target behavior, ask: *What brings you here today?*
Evoking	• Ask: *What are the three best reasons for you to _____?* • Reflect all the reasons you have been given • Ask: *What other reasons might you _____?* • Reflect the response you are given • Ask: *How do you imagine your life would be different if you were successful in _____?* • Reflect the response you are given • Ask: *On a scale of 1 to 10, how important is it for you to _____?* • Reflect the response you are given • Ask: *Why is it a _____ and not a _____?* • Reflect the response you are given • Ask: *On a scale of 1 to 10, how confident are you that you can _____?* • Reflect the response you are given • Ask: *Why is it a _____ and not a _____?* • Summarize ALL the reasons for change you have heard (use a double-sided reflection if there is some discussion of reasons for not changing)
Planning	• Ask: *What is the next step for you?* or *What do you think you will do?* • Reflect the response you are given • Ask: *I know we've talked about this quite a bit already, but what would you say are the main reasons you want to make this change?* • Reflect the response you are given • Ask: *What are the steps you plan to take in making this change?* • Reflect the response you are given • Ask: *What are the ways other people can help you make this change?* • Reflect the response you are given

- Ask: *How will you know if your plan is working?*
- Reflect the response you are given
- Ask: *What are some things that could interfere with your plan?*
- Reflect the response you are given
- Ask: *What will you do if the plan isn't working?*
- Reflect the response you are given
- Summarize EVERYTHING you have written on your change plan
- Ask: *On a scale of 1 to 10 how committed are you to following this plan?*
- Reflect the response you are given
- Ask: *Why are you at a _____ and not a _____ (lower number)?*
- Reflect the response you are given
- Summarize the entire MI session

Trained MI coaches with nutrition or psychology backgrounds conducted the sessions (Madson, Landry, Molaison, Schumacher, & Yadrick, in press). In Table 3.5 we highlight the processes of MI using the MI feedback sessions. This example was adapted from the HUB City Steps MI counselor manual but is not a script (Madson, Bonnell, McMurtry, & Noble, unpublished manual).

THE FOUR PROCESSES OF MOTIVATIONAL INTERVIEWING: AN ALCOHOL PREVENTION EXAMPLE

For more than 20 years, the Brief Alcohol Screening and Intervention for College Students (BASICS; Dimeff, Baer, Kivlahan, & Marlatt, 1999) has been used on college campuses nationwide. The BASICS program is an alcohol prevention program focused on high-risk students with slight yet detectable evidence of alcohol abuse (e.g., evidence of heavy drinking episodes—binge drinking or drinking-related consequences). With a solid grounding in MI, the BASICS program involves a student meeting with a BASICS counselor for two sessions. Session one involves an assessment of alcohol use and related problems/risk associated with use. The second session involves personalized feedback and discussion about assessment results in a manner aimed at facilitating student motivation to better protect them when drinking. Table 3.6 provides an illustration of how the feedback session, as implemented at The University of Southern Mississippi, follows the four processes of MI.

Table 3.5. Health Promotion Example of the Four Processes

MI Process	Application to HUB City Steps
Engaging	Thank participant, engage—obtain reaction to participation in HUB Steps and set the stage for coaching session.
	"Thank you for participating in our health fair today. How was your experience with the different activities you participated in today? [Reflect client response]. My name is Mike Madson and I am a health counselor for this project. My job with HUB City Steps is to discuss with you some of the information gathered today based on what you think is important and to help you decide what, if anything, you may want to change in relation to your health and how you may go about changing. How does that sound to you?"
	[reflect]
Focusing	Agenda setting—to focus discussion on health indicators important to client by introducing Know Your Numbers card.
	"If it is okay with you, I'd like to talk about the results of your assessment today. This is what we call your Know Your Numbers card. This card will be filled in each time you come back here. In looking at this card you will see information about your results and information about where your score falls in terms of health. For example, here is information about your blood pressure and where your score falls within a healthy range. We looked at different areas that would seem the most important for you to discuss."
	[Reflect client responses].
	What is next most important for you?
	Provide feedback about health results and evoke clients' reasons, need, and ability to change.
	Using Elicit-Provide-Elicit, provide information on participant results and MI-consistent strategies to help participant increase readiness to change.
	"You indicated that you are most concerned about your blood pressure. What sort of things do you know about blood pressure? [Reflect client responses]. In looking at your blood pressure today compared to healthy levels, it appears your blood pressure is a bit high. What do you make out of that given what you know about high blood pressure?"
	[Reflect client responses].
	This process could be repeated for different concerns clients have and could be summarized after.

MI Process	Application to HUB City Steps
Evoking	Summarize and elicit.
	"You identified several factors on your Know Your Numbers card that concerned you. These included high blood pressure, higher weight than you'd like, and not having as much energy as you'd like."
	[Use MI consistent strategies to elicit]
	"How important is it for you to make some changes to your health?"
	[reflect]
	"What are some of the reasons you might want to change your health?"
	[reflect]
	"What might your life look like 5 years down the road if you changed/ didn't change your health?"
	[reflect]
	"What are some of the good things about your current behavior? What are some of the not-so-good things?"
Planning	Summarize client discussion about change.
	"If it is okay with you I would like to summarize what we discussed. You expressed concern about your health, in particular your blood pressure, weight, and limited energy. It is important to you to change some of your eating and health to be a role model for your children. You were a bit uncertain about modifying your diet because you don't want to disappoint your family by not cooking their favorite foods, and at the same time you recognize how it might be valuable to help your family eat healthier. Also, it is important for you to have more energy, and you indicated how eating healthier and increasing your physical activity would be the best ways for you to become healthier. Given all of this, what do you think you may want to do?"
	[reflect]
	Present participant with menu of change options
	"If you'd like we can talk about some changes you could make to improve your health. To help us, we have the menu of options that other individuals have used to become healthier. Here is a sheet that includes some behaviors that can be important in helping people manage similar concerns to yours. This area represents formal exercise like walking. This area represents increasing physical activity in your daily life, like taking the stairs rather than the elevator. This area represents eating healthier, which may include eating more fruit and vegetables. You will also notice some empty areas. These represent your ideas that are not represented by the other areas. What, if any, areas here would you wish to talk about, or perhaps there are other things you want to raise that are more important to you in relation to changing?"

(continued)

Table 3.5. CONTINUED

MI Process	Application to HUB City Steps
	Elicit a plan from the participant's aspects related to a specific plan.
	"What is it specifically that you may want to do?"
	[reflect]
	"What are your reasons for making this change?"
	[reflect]
	"What are your goals for making this change?"
	[reflect]
	"What might be the first step in your plan?"
	[reflect]
	"Who might help you reach your goals?"
	[reflect]
	"What sort of results do you expect from changing?"
	[reflect]
	Summarize the plan emphasizing the fit for the participant (goals, needs, intentions, and beliefs) and evoke commitment.
	"Let me see if I am following you. You want to eat more fruits and vegetables and you want to start walking each night after dinner for at least 20 minutes. For you, these two changes are important to help you manage your blood pressure, increase your energy, and to be a healthy role model for your children. The first step is to look for sales on fruits and vegetables and to get a pair of walking shoes. You indicated that your neighbor will be interested in walking with you and that you will ask her to set up a walking schedule. It is really your hope that by making these changes you will lose some weight, become less winded when walking, and feel better about yourself. Is this a plan you can commit to?"

CHAPTER SUMMARY

By learning more about and focusing on the four phases of a motivational interview, you can better appreciate how to guide clients in a discussion about changing. Many providers we have trained are tempted to jump straight to "planning" and focus an interaction immediately on identifying solutions to clients' problems. While this may sometimes be an effective strategy with clients who enter a helping relationship ready, willing, and able to change, it is not likely to be effective for clients who do not come in with that level of motivation. Understanding your clients, uncovering a shared focus for change, and evoking

Table 3.6. Alcohol Prevention Example of the Four Processes

MI Process	Application to BASICS
Engaging	Engaging in the first BASICS Session
	"Hello, my name is Mike Madson and I'm one of the BASICS counselors. Welcome to the BASICS program. Thanks for coming in today. I understand that you were asked to attend the BASICS program by your hall director. However, I would value the opportunity to understand your perspective in relation to why you are here. If you are willing, tell me a little about your perspective on what happened and what you think about having to attend BASICS." [reflect what the client has said]
	"If it is all right with you I would like to provide some information about the program and what you can expect as well as answer any questions for you. How does that sound? My job is to work with you to gather and discuss some information in relation to your alcohol use. The goal of BASICS is not to determine if you have an alcohol problem or put some label on your drinking. Instead my goal is to talk with you about the information you provide about your drinking, what that information means to you, changes you have already made, and based on what you think is important decide what, if anything, you may want to change in relation to your drinking. How does that sound to you?" [reflect]
	Engaging in the feedback BASICS session.
	"Welcome back. Thank you for coming in today. How have you been since our last meeting?" [reflect]
	"Before we begin talking about the information you provided last time we met, I wonder if you had any questions or concerns about our last meeting, or had any reactions to the meeting or the questionnaires you completed." [reflect]
	"If I might provide some information, you may remember from our last meeting that the purpose of this meeting is to discuss the information you gave about your alcohol use. It is my hope that we have a collaborative conversation, so please stop me along the way to ask questions or clarify things. Does that sound okay to you?" [reflect]

(continued)

Table 3.6. CONTINUED

MI Process	Application to BASICS
Focusing	Agenda setting to focus the discussion.
	"We have a bunch of things to discuss; are there any things that you are particularly interested in talking about?"
	[reflect]
	"One place we could begin, if you would like, is to review your self-monitoring form. How does that sound?"
	[reflect]
	Provide personal assessment feedback using elicit-provide-elicit.
	"From your perspective, in what ways, if any, has alcohol gotten in your way or resulted in unpleasant experiences? Based on the information you provided, it appears that you often do things when drinking that you later regret. What do you make of that?"
Evoking	*"People have many different reasons for drinking alcohol. What are some of the reasons you drink alcohol? How might that influence how much you drink or when you decide to stop drinking?"*
	[reflect]
	"Sometimes students decide to engage in strategies when they drink to reduce the negative consequences they experience. How might that fit or not with your goals for dinking?"
	[reflect]
	On a scale of 0 (not important) to 10 (very important), where would you place the importance of learning about new or additional ways to protect yourself from negative consequences when drinking? [Client responds saying 5]. What makes it a 5 and not a 3."
	[reflect]
	What may be some of the drawbacks to using safe drinking strategies; what may be some of the benefits?"
	[reflect]
Planning	Summarize to transition to planning
	"We started today and you were unsure whether you wanted to make any changes to your drinking. Part of you enjoys drinking the way you are now and you receive enjoyment from partying with your friends. At the same time you learned that your drinking has led to an increase in negative consequences and you have felt increasingly embarrassed by things you have done when drinking. You indicated that you would like to learn some strategies that you can use to reduce the consequences you have experienced when drinking. What, if anything, would you like to do?"

MI Process	Application to BASICS
	[reflect]
	"If you'd like we can talk about some strategies you might consider using when you drink to reduce the risk of negative consequences. What are some things that come to your mind when we talk about safe drinking?"
	[reflect] *"Here is a list that includes some behaviors that students at this university and other college students use to protect themselves when drinking. Some students use strategies to control their consumption of alcohol such as avoiding shots or chugging alcohol, or alternating an alcoholic and non-alcoholic drink. Other students use strategies to reduce serious harm associated with drinking such as using a designated driver or knowing what is in their drink. Based on the drinking goals you mentioned before, which of these strategies or others, if any, might you use to protect yourself when drinking yet meet your goals?"*
	[reflect]
	Elicit to develop a plan
	"For you, knowing what is in your drink and using a designated driver would be strategies you could use when drinking.
	What might be your reasons for using those strategies?"
	[reflect]
	"In using these strategies, what do you hope will happen?"
	[reflect]
	"Who can help you use these strategies?"
	[reflect]
	"How will you know these strategies are working?"
	[reflect]
	"Before we close today I would like to summarize your plan of action to become a safer drinker. For you, reducing the harm associated with drinking is important because you are seeing increasing problems when you drink. You expressed a willingness to become more aware of what you are drinking and making sure to use a designated driver who has not been drinking. These steps will help you to better manage your drinking and to make sure you are safe. Your hope is that these strategies will help you drink more responsibly and keep yourself out of trouble and from doing things you later regret. You identified your sorority sisters as people who can help you with this plan and that you will inform them of your plan and goals. Is this something you are willing to commit to doing?"

clients' motivations for changing are useful for helping clients develop the motivation necessary to undertake difficult changes. Many providers we train are also
tempted to focus on providing suggestions and giving advice when developing
change plans with clients. This may result in a plan that the client cannot or will
not follow. Collaboratively developing a change plan in an MI-consistent fashion
increases the likelihood that a client's plan will be successful. Our discussion of
the processes is simply an overview and readers are encouraged to read Miller
and Rollnick (2013) for more detail on the four processes.

PART II

Motivational Interviewing for Clinical Challenges

4

Less Ready to Change

Many of the strategies widely employed by helping professionals assume that clients enter the helping relationship ready to make changes. For example, immediately following an assessment of a client's smoking behavior, a smoking cessation specialist might describe the various available options for smoking cessation and ask the client to choose one. In this case, the specialist is operating under the assumption that because a client has come to a smoking cessation clinic, he or she is ready to quit smoking. The transtheoretical model (TTM; Prochaska & DiClemente, 1983) and its accompanying stages of readiness to change provide a valuable framework for understanding clients who are *less ready to change*. As mentioned in chapter 2, the TTM and MI evolved almost simultaneously and they can be used complementary to each other. Whereas MI provides a framework for understanding how provider-client interactions can influence readiness to change, the TTM helps us to conceptualize our clients' readiness to change based on attitudes, behaviors, and intentions they display according to five stages. The quick reference provides a description of the five stages.

QUICK REFERENCE

Stages of Readiness to Change

Precontemplation: Not aware a change is needed. Pros of not changing outweigh pros of changing. Avoids talking about change.
Contemplation: More aware of need to change. Recognizes the negatives of not changing. Concerned about behavior.
Preparation: Intending to change. Pros of changing outweigh pros of staying the same. More engaged and making plans to change.
Action: Taking steps to change.
Maintenance: Preventing lapses and relapse after changing.

Typically, clients who are *less ready to change* tend to be at the precontemplation or contemplation stage of readiness to change. In other words, rather than "lacking motivation," individuals who are less ready to change are often not aware of the need to change or are considering both the positives and negatives of changing and not changing. Additionally, clients may be less ready to change when they were not involved in the planning. Thus, they may be very ready to change, but less ready to implement someone else's plan. When clients are *less ready to change* they can show us in different ways, including not attending sessions, not adhering to treatment, or expressing no need to change (e.g., that they are attending simply to satisfy a mandate or referral). Fortunately, MI is helpful for working with individuals who *are less ready to change*. We provide some MI strategies for addressing challenges often associated with clients who are *less ready to change*.

CLINICAL CHALLENGE 1: NO-SHOWS

Description

A challenge encountered in almost any setting where MI might be applied to facilitate change is clients who frequently reschedule appointments (often with little notice) and clients who fail to show for scheduled appointments. There can be a number of factors that cause clients to miss scheduled appointments (with or without notice to the provider), such as problems with childcare, forgetfulness, or unexpected events. Whatever the cause, missed appointments undoubtedly reduce a provider's ability to help a client make positive changes. Missed appointments can also create systemic problems that reduce the quality of service providers can offer. For example, just like airlines and hotels, many medical clinics find it necessary to overbook schedules to compensate for anticipated canceled sessions and no-shows. Who hasn't been to the physician on a day when everybody scheduled actually shows up? Wait times are often an hour or longer, those waiting to be seen grow increasingly impatient and frustrated, and providers and office staff may feel a need to rush and thus may not offer the same level of care or service they normally would. For these reasons, no-shows are an important clinical challenge to address.

When clients are queried about the reasons for missed appointments, they will provide a range of reasons. For example, Defife, Conklin, Smith, and Pool (2010) found psychotherapy clients reported reasons for their missed appointments ranging from symptoms, to practical concerns, to motivational issues, to negative treatment effects. To providers, these reasons may range from the seemingly reasonable (e.g., "the school called to say my son had a fever and I had to pick him up") to the seemingly absurd (e.g., "my son's tarantula got out of its cage and I had to find it before I could leave the house"). Many times, particularly with clients who repeatedly miss or reschedule appointments, a provider may be left wondering whether the reasons provided are truthful, or whether the missed sessions are an indication that the client is not committed to his or her work with the provider. Possibly wondering, "Does this client also miss his appointments at the barber? Does he forget to pick his daughter up from school? Does he blow off social engagements? Or does he only do this to me?"

It is possible that provider mistrust and frustration with no-shows may be exacerbated by a difficulty understanding the perspective of the "no-shower." Speaking from personal experience, we can probably collectively count on one hand the number of times we have simply failed to show up for a scheduled appointment or canceled at the last minute. In fact, research on characteristics that have been associated with no-show suggests that individuals who serve as providers in settings where MI might be employed may often differ in important ways from their clients who no-show. For example, a study of predictors of no-shows at a community mental health center in Denmark revealed that in addition to clinical- and employment-related characteristics, age below 25 and 9 or fewer years of education were predictors of no-showing (Fenger, Mortensen, Poulsen, & Lau, 2011). Although not reported in the study, it is likely that most providers at the center were above age 25 and had 10 or more years of education. The following example illustrates a typical no-show scenario.

Example: *Mary and her primary care physician have been discussing her weight at annual check-ups for several years. Over that time, Mary has progressed from overweight but generally healthy, to obese with metabolic syndrome, to severely obese with type 2 diabetes. Mary reports that she has repeatedly attempted to lose weight, but always loses only a few pounds and quickly regains them. Mary's physician believes that successful weight loss is crucial to Mary's health, and has referred her to a dietician for nutritional counseling. Mary rescheduled her initial visit with the dietician two times, resulting in a delay of almost 3 months between the referral and her initial visit. Since the initial visit, Mary has returned for follow-up only once in the last 6 months, even though she and the dietician agreed to meet monthly to track her progress and make adjustments to her diet as necessary.*

Proposed Strategy 1: MI-Consistent Referrals

Perhaps the most difficult no-show problem to address is the client who no-shows the first appointment. Although there are a number of reasons that clients may no-show, low motivation has been identified as one reason clients might no-show for initial appointments (Peeters & Bayer, 1999). The good news is that incorporating MI into the referral process can increase initial session attendance (Seal et al., 2012). There are multiple ways to make referrals that do not actually occur within the context of a motivational interview more MI-consistent, such as asking permission (e.g., "If it's okay with you, I'd like to refer you to a dietician to provide additional support and guidance on your weight loss efforts"), emphasizing control (e.g., "I'm going to go ahead and make a referral to a dietician, but it is really up to you to decide whether that is going to be the right strategy for you"), or offering choices (e.g., "I think we have three options right now: you can continue to try to lose weight on your own using some of the ideas your friends have shared with you, I can go ahead and refer you to a dietician now so you can start working with someone on changing your diet, or I can follow up with you in 3 months and we can revisit the issue then"). Each of these strategies introduces some element of collaboration and support of autonomy, but on their own, do not make the referral fully MI-consistent.

As outlined in chapter 3, a provider and client will proceed through a series of processes during a motivational interview: engaging, focusing, evoking, and planning. Although the progression may not always be neatly stepwise and linear, each process builds upon the prior processes in important ways. For example, it would be difficult to collaboratively identify a focus for an interaction with a client who is not engaged in the interaction. As referrals occur during the planning process of a motivational interview, making a referral that is fully MI-consistent relies upon first engaging the client, collaboratively identifying a focus for the interaction, evoking the client's own motivations for making a change, and then collaboratively developing a plan for change that may include a referral.

The MI-consistent referral will be of little use to the provider who is on the receiving end of a referral that was made in an MI-inconsistent fashion and results in a client who never makes contact with the provider. Thus, we present this not as a strategy for addressing no-shows in which the client never shows up for the initial visit, but for reducing the likelihood that the clients to whom you offer referrals will end up as future no-shows.

Example: MI-Consistent/Inconsistent Referrals

The following examples will illustrate MI-consistent and MI-inconsistent referrals to a dietician for Mary, the client introduced in the earlier example.

Client Statement: *"I keep trying to lose weight, but I never lose more than a few pounds and I always gain it right back."*

MI-Inconsistent: *"You need to meet with our dietician. She can help you plan a diet you can stick to. I'll have the nurse call in the referral after this appointment."*

This is an MI-inconsistent referral because it is not collaborative. The provider tells the client what to do and makes the referral without having any understanding of whether the client is interested in working on weight loss, why she is interested, or the ways in which she prefers to approach weight loss.

Somewhat MI-Consistent: *"Many of my patients find meeting with a dietician very helpful when they get stuck. Does a referral to our dietician seem like something that would be helpful for you?"*

This referral is somewhat MI-consistent because the provider acknowledges that although a dietician has been helpful for others, it may not be helpful for this particular client. The provider also invites the client to express disagreement with the provider's views on the benefits of the referral. It is not fully MI-consistent, however, because the provider offers advice without first seeking to elicit the client's own ideas about weight loss.

MI-Consistent:

Engaging: *"That must be very frustrating [uses reflection to help engage the client]."*

Client Response: *"It is."*

Focusing: *"I do need to review a few changes in your blood sugar with you before we wrap up, but what are your thoughts about first spending a few minutes talking about the struggles you've had with your weight?" [Asks an open question that invites Mary to help focus the session].*

Client Response: *"I think that would be very helpful. I know that it is so important for my health and that maybe I could even reverse my diabetes if I lost weight. I really am trying, I just can't seem to stick to a plan."*

Evoking: *"Weight loss is hard work [offers a supportive statement to maintain engagement]. In addition to the role it might play in helping you manage and possibly even reverse your diabetes, I'm wondering what other benefits you hope you might obtain from losing weight?" [Asks an open question to evoke change talk].*

Client Response: *"I know I'd feel better about myself if I lost some weight. I've never been skinny and I don't know that I'd want to be, but I've also never been this heavy. I think my kids also worry about me now that I'm so heavy and that makes me feel really guilty."*

Planning: *"It sounds like there are a lot of reasons you'd like to lose weight. What do you think is a good first step?" [Use an open-ended question to allow the client to collaborate on the planning]*

Client Response: *"I know I eat too much, especially when I'm stressed out. Sometimes I'll order a family meal just for myself."*

Planning continued: *"It sounds like you believe making some changes to your diet is an important first step. One option you may or may not be interested in is for me to refer you to a dietician so she can help you plan a diet that would be a good fit for you. What are your thoughts about that?"*

This response is MI-consistent, because the referral is made in a collaborative fashion and only after the provider has sufficient information about the client's preferences and motivations to know that a referral to a dietician is a good fit for the client. It is also MI-consistent because the provider gives the client the opportunity to refuse the referral, which supports her autonomy.

Proposed Strategy 2: Giving Information

One of the most basic, but at times very important, strategies to address missed appointments is provision of accurate and objective information. Although giving information is not a strategy that is central to the practice of MI, when done in an objective and engaging fashion, it is MI-consistent (Lane & Rollnick, 2009). Two pieces of information that may be especially important in deterring missed appointments are: (1) the purpose of the appointment, especially as it relates to the client's goals; and (2) the provider's appointment policy (e.g., cancellation policy, penalties for missed appointments, etc.). Clients who do not understand what will happen at the appointment or who are uncertain of the benefit they are likely to receive from the appointment may be less likely to make attending the appointment a priority. This might be particularly true for clients who are referred by other providers, coerced by the legal system, or strongly encouraged by friends or family members to seek the services of a particular provider. Clients who are not made aware of the appointment policy may not understand the implications of missed appointments or the appropriate steps to take when they need to miss an appointment.

Example: MI-Consistent/Inconsistent Giving Information

The following examples will illustrate MI-consistent and MI-inconsistent strategies for giving information to clients who have missed appointments.

Provider Statement: *"I see it's been 5 months since our last appointment."*

Client Statement: *"I couldn't make it to our last appointment, because my foot was bothering me again, and then the next appointment I could get was a month later."*

MI-Inconsistent: *"Yeah. Well, it's a very full clinic, so you need to make coming in a priority. If you don't get your diet under control you run the risk of losing your foot and I know you don't want that."*

This statement gives the client some information about the appointment policy and the purpose of the appointment, but the information is not presented in an objective fashion and thus is not MI-consistent. The provider blames the client for the missed appointment (accusing her of not making it a priority), and then confronts her about her dietary control (trying to scare her into better attendance).

Somewhat MI-Consistent: *"That happens sometimes. This is a very a full clinic."*

This statement is somewhat MI-consistent. The provider offers information that is relevant to what the client has said and is objective. However, the provider does not ask permission to offer information and thus misses an opportunity to enhance collaboration and increase the client's sense of autonomy. Perhaps more importantly, the provider does not empathically address the client's seeming sense of frustration with having to wait a month for an appointment. Thus the provider's response might seem dismissive to the client.

MI-Consistent: *"If it's okay with you, I'd like to take a moment to address that concern with you. [Awaits affirmative response from client]. This is a pretty full clinic, so often the next available appointment is a few weeks or even a month after clients call. That can be a challenge because monthly appointments are considered very important for our clients who are diagnosed with type 2 diabetes: dietary management of blood sugar helps reduce risk for diabetic complications like foot problems. What are your thoughts about this?"*

This response is MI-consistent, because the provider offers the information in an objective fashion. The provider does not seek to chastise or blame the client for missing the session or scare her into coming regularly by presenting a worst-case scenario. Instead, the provider presents information that will help the client decide what level of priority she wishes to assign regular attendance of appointments. Moreover, the provider tries to express empathy with the client's underlying feelings about having difficulty getting an appointment by using words like "concern" and "challenge." Finally, the provider elicits the client's reactions to the information to enhance collaboration.

Proposed Strategy 3: Planning

Planning is another MI-consistent strategy that can be used to address missed appointments, particularly if they occur with regularity. As outlined here and in chapter 3, planning is a collaborative conversation between a provider and a client about how a client will achieve his or her goals. Planning only occurs after a client has been engaged, a focus has been identified, and a client's desire, ability, reasons, and need for change have been evoked. For clients who have expressed a commitment to attending appointments but seem to have difficulty following through on this commitment, planning that focuses specifically on appointment attendance may help them overcome practical or motivational barriers to follow-through.

Example: MI-Consistent/Inconsistent Planning

The following examples will illustrate MI-consistent and MI-inconsistent strategies for planning with clients who have missed appointments.

Provider Statement: *"I see it's been 5 months since our last appointment."*

Client Statement: *"I couldn't make it to our last appointment because my foot was bothering me again, and then the next appointment I could get was a month later."*

MI-Inconsistent: *"I think we need a plan to help you attend visits more regularly. Do you have a calendar or schedule where you could write down your appointments? If not, maybe you could post your appointment card on your bathroom mirror or refrigerator. You know, somewhere where you'll see it? I'm also wondering if the reminder calls are coming to the best phone number. Maybe you should pick a better number to make sure you don't miss the calls?"*

This provider response is MI-inconsistent because it is not a collaborative approach to planning. Instead of seeking the client's input about why attendance is difficult and what the best approach to improving attendance might be, the provider assumes the expert role and begins offering the client advice about how best to attend future appointments. This approach is likely to elicit sustain talk and discord as the client is placed in a position to defend not making her appointments or why a strategy might not work.

Somewhat MI-Consistent: *"Do you want to work together to develop some strategies to help prevent that from happening to you again?"*

This statement is somewhat MI-consistent. The provider invites the client to develop a plan to reduce no-shows in a collaborative fashion. However, the provider uses a closed question, and thus invites only a brief response. Additionally, the provider jumps to planning before reflecting or eliciting anything from the client about her desire, ability, reasons, or need to attend more follow-up visits.

MI-Consistent: *"It seems like it has been difficult for you to make it in for appointments. I wonder if before we talk about your diet, we could talk about that. [Waits for affirmative response from client]. Given that you always reschedule, I get the sense that you'd like to make it to more follow-ups. If it's okay with you, maybe we can work together to figure out how we can make that happen."*

This response is MI-consistent because the provider uses reflective listening and asks permission to introduce the change plan. It is also MI-consistent because the provider engages the client in a collaborative process of developing the change plan that begins with a reflection of the client's apparent desire to change.

Although not required, planning will often be accompanied by preparation of a written change plan (Miller and Rollnick, 2002). The sample form presented in Table 4.1 illustrates how a provider might develop a written change plan that specifically addresses "missed appointments." Although many providers prefer not to use written change plans, feedback we have received from many clients over the years is that written change plans serve as a valuable reminder of key concepts discussed with a provider.

Proposed Strategy 4: Emphasizing Autonomy

As noted in chapter 2, respecting client autonomy is part of the foundational spirit of MI. Missed appointments are an important reminder to providers that client autonomy is also a practical fact of our work as helping professionals. Providers can make referrals, schedule appointments, and even make reminder calls, but ultimately the client will decide whether he or she shows up at a recommended or required visit. Explicitly emphasizing client autonomy is an MI-consistent

Table 4.1. SAMPLE CHANGE PLAN FOR MISSED APPOINTMENTS

These are the reasons I want to attend follow-up appointments: • Regular follow-up visits keep me accountable for my diet.   • I will be more likely to lose weight if I come to follow-up visits.
My goal for follow-up appointment attendance is: • To attend all follow-up visits on the recommended schedule.
Things that have made it hard for me to attend follow-up visits are: • I feel embarrassed to tell you about things I have been eating.   • I have trouble motivating myself to leave the house and come to the appointments.
The actions I will take to overcome these barriers to attending follow-up visits: • I will remind myself that even if I don't follow my diet, going to appointments is important and something I should feel proud about—at least I'm doing something.   • I will schedule appointments on days when I have other errands, so I have to leave the house anyway.   • I will make a list of all the reasons it is important for me to come to these appointments and post it on my bathroom mirror.
You and others could help me attend more follow-up visits in these ways: • You could remind me that it is okay for me to come in even if I haven't been successful on my diet.   • My sister could help keep me accountable if I tell her I have been having trouble going and ask her to remind me.
If the plan is not working: • I will remind myself that you are not mad at me, and want to work with me to try to attend appointments.   • I will make another list of why this is so important to me and keep trying.

strategy that may help reduce missed appointments, particularly for clients who feel some level of external coercion to attend appointments.

Example: MI-Consistent/Inconsistent Emphasizing Autonomy

The following examples will illustrate MI-consistent and MI-inconsistent strategies for emphasizing autonomy with clients who have missed appointments.

Provider Statement: *"I see it's been 5 months since our last appointment."*

Client Statement: *"I couldn't make it to our last appointment because my foot was bothering me again, and then the next appointment I could get was a month later."*

MI-Inconsistent: *"You need to decide whether this is something you want to commit to or not!"*

This provider response is MI-inconsistent because the provider is giving the client a direct order. Also, the tone of voice we intended to imply by the exclamation point demonstrates a lack of empathy and unconditional positive regard, instead conveying the provider's irritation with the client.

Somewhat MI-Consistent *"You are the one who has the power to decide whether these monthly appointments are something you want to commit to or not."*

This provider response is somewhat MI-consistent. The provider emphasizes that the client has control over whether she continues working with the provider or not, which is MI-consistent. However, the provider uses the word "want," which subtly conveys that she believes the client's motivation, not foot problems or scheduling difficulties, is the root of the patient's lack of attendance. Thus the client may feel blamed or confronted by this utterance rather than empowered. The provider also fails to express empathy for the client's frustration or foot pain. This could lead the client to believe that the provider does not really care about her as a person, only whether or not she shows up for appointments.

MI-Consistent: *"I know it sometimes takes a major effort to make it here for appointments, and ultimately it is up to you to decide whether monthly appointments are something you can commit to now."*

This response is MI-consistent because the provider first supports the difficulty the client sometimes has making it to appointments, and then without sarcasm or judgment reminds the client that ultimately it is up to her to decide whether she would like to attend regular appointments or not. Using this MI-consistent strategy does not guarantee that the client will commit to coming to regular appointments—she might decide that she does not want to meet with the dietician monthly at this time. Although probably not the ideal outcome from the perspective of the dietician, this is not a bad outcome. If Mary is truly not ready to commit to monthly appointments with the dietician, it is better that she and the dietician can talk about this openly. This leaves the door open for Mary to return to the dietician when she is ready.

CLINICAL CHALLENGE 2: NON-ADHERENCE

Description

Many providers are attracted to MI as a way to help them better work with the issue of non-adherence. Consistent with the MI literature, we are choosing to use the term "adherence" versus "compliance" (Zweben & Zuckoff, 2002). You may remember from chapter 1 that MI has research support for facilitating treatment engagement and adherence (Lundhal et al., 2010). Adherence generally refers to the extent to which a client follows a provider's instructions or advice (Levensky & O'Donohue, 2006). Non-adherence is an issue often faced by providers, especially when clients are required to change in some way. Many medical treatments, including taking medications or surgery, require some form of behavior change, such as following the prescription or increased physical activity. People we train frequently express frustration with their clients' non-adherence to a treatment program because adherence is linked to positive treatment outcomes (Bisono, Manuel, & Forcehimes, 2006). With further exploration, it is often revealed that this frustration is associated with conceptualizations that non-adhering clients aren't motivated, are in denial, don't have enough knowledge or skill, or simply do not care about their health or situation. Clearly, when we conceptualize clients' non-adherence in this way, it can increase our frustration and also influence the way we respond. Many times this conceptualization of client non-adherence triggers the "righting reflex" (see chapter 2) and leads us to educate, warn, lecture, or even berate clients in an attempt to convince them of the need to adhere to our recommendations. However, those responses tend to be inconsistent with an MI approach to working with non-adherence.

Client non-adherence is expressed in several ways, and from an MI perspective it is an indicator that the provider and client are not on the same page. In fact, Levensky and O'Donohue (2006) indicated that factors such as client-provider communication, trust, and mutual conceptualization of the problem contribute to non-adherence. Some clients are considered non-adherent because they come to appointments late or simply do not attend appointments (see section on missed appointments in this chapter for further information). This form of non-adherence is common when clients come to treatment at the suggestion of someone else and not by their own choice. Thus, non-adherence may be due to the clients feeling as though they have no input into the treatment.

Example: *Shelia is a 20-year-old college student who was told to see a peer health educator by the student health services to learn to implement safer sexual practices. Immediately upon entering the room with the peer health educator, Shelia indicates that the health services worker was overreacting and that she is a normal college student and behaves the same sexually as all of her friends. Nonetheless, she agrees to attend sessions. Since that initial meeting, Shelia sporadically attends sessions and sometimes goes weeks without attending. She often arrives 10 minutes late for meetings and always has a reason for missing meetings or arriving late. When asked directly, Shelia states she is committed to attending the meetings because she was told to do so, but her behavior is inconsistent with this assertion.*

Sometimes clients do not even engage in a recommended treatment or drop out early. This form of non-adherence may be seen in allied health and behavioral health services, where clients are referred by medical providers for treatments in addition to medical interventions. However, clients may be less confident in the need for non-medical treatments or question the motives of the referral to additional treatments. As psychologists who have worked in medical settings, we often encountered clients who felt dismissed or invalidated because they had been referred to us to address medically related issues—"the doctor thinks it's all in my head." This client mindset may keep clients from engaging in treatment. Additionally, there may be financial, logistical, or other barriers that may influence clients' abilities to attend sessions.

> Example: *Karl is a veteran who was referred to a psychologist by his physician assistant to help address his chronic sleep difficulties. Before the interview begins, Karl indicates that he doesn't believe seeing a "shrink" will help his sleep and that he just needs some sleep medication. However, it becomes apparent that Karl's sleep difficulties are associated with trauma that he experienced in the military. When this feedback is shared with him and a course of treatment is suggested, he denies any problem with his military service. Karl never returns to treatment.*

Finally, clients may attend all of their scheduled sessions and be on time, but do not carry out the plans discussed for out-of-session activities, such as homework or taking medications. This form of non-adherence can be baffling for many providers who assume that when clients readily "walk in the door" that they are ready to do what is necessary to change. However, this is not often the case when it comes to behavior change, and to be MI-consistent providers need to recognize the role of ambivalence.

> Example: *Jody is a 47-year-old woman who entered psychotherapy for her social anxiety. She is also seeing a psychiatrist for medication management. She has expressed the goal of wanting to reduce her anxiety and to be able to attend more social events without worry. Jody reports that she does not take her medication regularly as she worries about developing an addiction, though her medication is not addicting. She indicates that she wants to do what it takes to become less anxious and more social; thus she agrees to treatment involving exposure and skill building. However, she has a pattern in treatment of not completing her self-monitoring, exposures, or skill practice outside of session* (for more information about specifically addressing non-adherence related to anxiety, see also chapter 6).

Regardless of how non-adherence is displayed, from an MI perspective it is an indication that the provider and client are not on the same page in relation to the change or how to go about changing (Bisono et al., 2006).

Proposed Strategy 1: Evocative Questions

Using evocative questions in relation to non-adherence can help avoid the righting reflex. Evocative questions can also help the provider adopt an approach that is grounded in genuinely trying to understand what concerns the client may have about changing or not, what their personal motivations for changing may be versus what a referral source may want, and what potential solutions seem reasonable. Remember the U from RULE in chapter 2—understanding the client's motivations. It is the client's own motivations that are more likely to predict their engagement in and adherence to treatment. Thus it is very important to elicit these from clients, especially when trying to engage them into treatment.

Example: MI-Consistent/Inconsistent Evoking

The following examples will illustrate MI-consistent and MI-inconsistent evoking for clients with non-adherence issues.

Client Statement: *"I think all I need is medicine for this problem. No offense but I don't come here as often because I don't think talking about my sleep will help."*

MI-Inconsistent: *"Do you really think that medication is the only thing that will help you sleep?"*

This question is MI-inconsistent for two reasons. This question is a closed question and unlikely to foster open discussion about the topic from the client. Additionally, the "do you really" part of the question is likely to engender discord as it can be perceived as judgmental and confrontational.

Somewhat MI-Inconsistent: *"Why don't you think therapy will be helpful?"*

This question is somewhat MI-consistent. It is an open question and thus invites the client to share. However, the "Why don't you…" phrasing of the question subtly implies that the client should think therapy will be helpful and thus may elicit discord as the client feels a need to defend his position to the provider. The phrasing of the question is also likely to evoke sustain talk (reasons not to get this particular treatment) rather than evoking the client's perspectives on what would be helpful.

MI-Consistent: *"You want to solve this sleep problem, and for you medication seems like the best option. If it is okay with you I'd like to hear your thoughts about why you think your physician referred you to me."*

This statement is MI-consistent for a few reasons. First, with the reflection, the provider communicates listening to the client and an understanding of the experience. Rather than jumping into education, the provider asks an evocative question that invites the client to comment on his/her understanding as to why the physician made the referral. This approach helps the provider avoid the righting reflex (e.g., "behavior change can help with sleep too") and fosters client engagement in the discussion.

Proposed Strategy 2: Scaling Questions

A strategy related to the use of evocative questions is to ask scaling questions, sometimes called importance and confidence rulers. In MI, these types of questions help the provider gauge whether clients' reluctance to change may be due to their perceived importance of the change or their perceived confidence in their abilities to change (Miller & Rollnick, 2013). For instance, the provider can ask *"On a scale of 0 (not at all important) to 10 (extremely important), how important is it to you to make this change?"* The use of scaling questions is not unique, but what is unique is the intentional follow-up to scaling/ruler questions. In MI, following up to ask what makes the number on the scale higher versus lower is intended to elicit reasons why change may be important or why clients may have some confidence in their ability to change.

Example: MI-Consistent/Inconsistent Scaling Questions

The following examples will illustrate MI-consistent and MI-inconsistent scaling questions for clients with non-adherence issues.

Client Statement: *"I think all I need is medicine for this problem. No offense but I don't come here as often because I don't think talking about my sleep will help."*

MI-Inconsistent: *"On a scale from 0 (not at all important) to 10 (very important) how important is it for you to attend these sessions?"*

This is definitely a scaling question but is MI-inconsistent for two reasons. First, the use of a question like this, especially in the context of missed appointments, could lead the client to become defensive and increase discord. Second, the scaling question is not really about change (i.e., improving sleep, reducing trauma symptoms); it is more about the importance of the sessions. Thus, there is a missed opportunity to explore the client's hesitancy to change or importance of change.

Somewhat MI-Consistent: *"On a scale from 0 (not at all) to 10 (very much), how important do you think this treatment is relative to the medication?"*

This scaling question is somewhat MI-consistent. The provider uses a scaling question to better understand how the client feels about psychotherapy. The use of the question also likely conveys to the client that his concerns about treatment are being taken seriously by the provider. However, the phrasing of this question is such that the discussion that follows the question is unlikely to help the client move toward the improvements he desires in sleep. Thus the utterance is empathic and collaborative, but may miss an opportunity to guide the client toward positive change.

MI-Consistent: *"You have a lot going on in your life and found the time to make it here today to address your concerns. If I might ask, on a scale from 0 (not at all important) to 10 (the most important thing for you), where does making changes to your sleep fall?"*

Client response: *"About a 4."*

MI-Consistent: *"So it is mid-range on the sale. What makes the importance a 4 and not a 2?"*

These provider utterances are MI-consistent for several reasons. First, the provider begins with an affirmation by reframing the client showing up as a positive given all of the things going on in her/his life. Next, the provider focuses on the change versus the non-adherence behaviors. By using a scaling question to focus on the importance of the behavior, the provider gets a better picture where the change fits in relation to other things in the client's life. Finally, the follow-up question is likely to guide the client to discuss why there is some importance to changing the behavior, which is more likely to build motivation.

Proposed Strategy 3: Looking Forward

Sometimes clients are less aware of how their non-adherence to treatment might have an effect on their future. As humans we tend to have narrow perspectives about our future as it relates to changing or not (Wagner & Ingersol, 2013). For instance, in a medical setting a client may "feel fine" but be pre-hypertensive. Because the client feels fine he may not see the need to address his diet or exercise to lower his blood pressure. However, unless addressed, his blood pressure is likely to get worse. Thus, one MI-consistent strategy that can facilitate adherence is helping the client connect how their current situation and non-adherence might affect their life in the future. In MI, this strategy is called looking forward.

Example: MI-Consistent/Inconsistent Looking Forward

The following examples will illustrate MI-consistent and MI-inconsistent looking forward for clients with non-adherence issues.

Client Statement: *"I think all I need is medicine for this problem. No offense but I don't come here as often because I don't think talking about my sleep will help."*

MI-Inconsistent: *"Yes, medication can help. However, if we look down the road and you don't change thoughts and behaviors related to your sleep, your sleep is likely to get worse, which will then increase your vulnerability to many other problems!"*

The provider offers accurate information about the progression of sleep difficulties and the vulnerability for other issues if the sleep doesn't change. However, the statement is MI-inconsistent as the provider is assuming the expert role and providing the information without asking permission. Additionally, rather than eliciting from the client about the future, the provider simply connects the dots for the client. This approach fosters less engagement and likely to elicit sustain talk from the client.

Somewhat MI-Consistent: *"I have a different perspective. Would it be okay if I shared it with you? [Waits for affirmative response]. I have been doing this for years, and generally people who rely on medication and don't address the other problems contributing to sleep difficulties continue to have problems with sleep."*

This response is somewhat MI-consistent. The provider asks permission before offering his professional opinion. However, the provider uses this information to try to instill motivation for treatment rather than eliciting the client's own concerns about what might happen if he does not pursue any treatment other than medication for his sleep difficulties.

MI-Consistent: *"You wonder why all of these changes are necessary when medication should help you with your sleep. I wonder if we can look 5 years down the road for a minute. Let's say you decided not to make any of these changes in relation to your sleep. What might your health look like? [client responds] How might your health be different if you decided to make some changes in your sleep behaviors?"*

This provider statement has several aspects that make it MI-consistent. The provider reflects the client's concerns about changing. The provider asks permission to look into the future and follows with two eliciting questions. This approach is more engaging and collaborative. The provider makes no assumption that the client will change and avoids the expert trap.

Proposed Strategy 4: Revising the Change Plan and Discussing Options

Often individuals are less willing to adhere to treatment when they perceive that they have few options in relation to the change; thus, they assert their independence by not adhering to the treatment plan. A concept from social psychology will help to explain this. According to Brehm and Brehm (1981), individuals have a natural tendency to react (or assert their independence) when they feel their freedom is being taken away. In other words, as humans, it is natural for us to argue against being told what to do. The ultimate way clients demonstrate this is by not adhering to the change plan. In training providers to become more MI-consistent when developing change plans, we often find that providers are far less MI-consistent in this process than they believe themselves to be. Many providers prescribe a change plan followed by a question, such as, "Does this sound okay to you?" Some providers mistakenly assume that this question makes the entire planning process MI-consistent. This strategy seems to be based on the belief that once a client indicates readiness to change it is the provider's job (as an expert) to tell him how. One way to avoid a client pushing back or not adhering to treatment is to engage the client in the planning process. For example, a provider may discuss various change options and elicit which, if any, may seem to be most appealing to the client. Given that MI-consistent planning was discussed earlier in this chapter (see missed appointments section), this discussion will focus on discussing options as part of the planning process.

Example: MI-Consistent/Inconsistent Discussing Options

The following examples will illustrate MI-consistent and MI-inconsistent discussion of options for clients with non-adherence issues.

Client Statement: *"I think all I need is medicine for this problem. No offense but I don't come here as often because I don't think talking about my sleep will help."*

MI-Inconsistent: *"For many people, medication can help but only so far. The combination of medication and cognitive behavioral therapy is generally most effective for people with your symptoms!"*

While accurate, the statement is MI-inconsistent. The statement appears to adopt an expert role commenting on the effectiveness of medication and cognitive behavioral interventions for sleep. Similarly, the provider offers information in a fashion that is not fully MI-consistent because he/she did not ask permission or announce that he/she was going to provide information. The statement is challenging to the client, prematurely focuses on a problem, and prescribes a solution. All of these aspects of the statement are likely to elicit sustain talk from the client and engender discord between the client and provider.

Somewhat MI-Consistent: *"I think we have several options here. You could continue to see me regularly and see how it goes. You could try some, but not all, of the strategies I recommend. Or you could discontinue this treatment and come back again later, if you change your mind. What sounds best to you?"*

This response is somewhat MI-consistent. The provider gives the client options and invites the client to choose which seems best. However, the provider does not ask permission before offering the options and does not leave open the possibility that the client may have different ideas about what the best solution might be. Thus although the provider seeks to be somewhat collaborative in discussing options and updating the change plan, the effort is lukewarm.

MI-Consistent: *"For you medication seems like a viable option, and you're not too sure whether also working with me to address sleep behaviors is going to give you additional benefit. At the same time, your psychiatrist has asked for you to see me which suggests she thinks working with me might be beneficial. If it is all right with you, I'd like for us to discuss some other options that I have seen clients in similar situations use to help with their sleep. I also recognize, that these options may or may not fit for you, and you may have some additional ideas."*

This provider statement has several aspects that make it MI-consistent. Beginning the statement with a reflection communicates that the provider is listening and empathizing with what the client is saying. The provider asks permission to engage in a discussion about options for change. The provider discusses options in the context of what others in a similar situation have done to help with their sleep versus prescribing options based on professional opinion or research. Finally, and discussed later, the provider emphasizes the client's personal control to choose what she/he deems best.

Proposed Strategy 5: Emphasizing Personal Control

Related to the importance of discussing options in relation to non-adherence is the need to emphasize clients' personal control to choose what they think is best for them. Miller and Rollnick (2013) highlight the fact that we really can't make clients do something they don't want to do, and clients show us by not adhering to their treatment plans. This idea also relates to reactance theory. One way to address this issue is to remind clients that ultimately the choice for change is theirs and no one else's. This is true even when they are mandated to change.

Example: MI-Consistent/Inconsistent Emphasizing Personal Control

The following examples will illustrate MI-consistent and MI-inconsistent emphasizing of personal control for clients with non-adherence issues.

Client Statement: *"I think all I need is medicine for this problem. No offense, but I don't come here as often because I don't think talking about my sleep will help."*

MI-Inconsistent: *"It is your choice what you do here, but I don't think your psychiatrist is going to be very happy with you if you don't follow his advice about adding psychological treatment."*

The provider does emphasize the client's personal control; however, the statement also includes an implied warning that the provider has to report the non-compliance with treatment back to the psychiatrist, which may lead to negative consequences for the client. In essence, by adding the warning the provider is communicating that the client does not have any control in this situation. This statement may also enhance the client's sustain talk or attempt to convince the provider that a problem doesn't exist. It also could engender discord between the client and provider as the client may feel threatened and that the provider is siding with the psychiatrist.

Somewhat MI-Consistent: *"Well it's really up to you. No one can make you come to these appointments if you don't want to."*

This statement is somewhat MI-consistent. The provider emphasizes the client's personal control, which is MI-consistent. However, the provider does so without expressing empathy or encouraging the client to further explore whether treatment termination is the best option for him, all things considered. This might leave the client with a sense that the provider really does not care whether the client's sleep improves or not, and is only interested in making sure that the treatment slot is filled with someone who comes regularly.

MI-Consistent: *"You are only here because your psychiatrist referred you here, but psychological treatments for sleep don't make a lot of sense to you. Definitely any changes you decide to make or not make, including seeing me for treatment, are up to you and I can't force you to do anything. At the same time I wonder about your thoughts as to why your psychiatrist thought that this might be beneficial for you."*

This is an MI-consistent response for several reasons. The provider avoids taking sides by empathizing with the client's frustration about being referred by the psychiatrist. Next, the provider emphasizes the client's personal control to choose to make or not make any changes. Finally, the provider invites the client to comment on what his/her ideas about why the psychiatrist may have referred him for additional treatment. A statement like this encompasses the spirit of MI, communicates acceptance and collaboration, and uses evocation. This statement is more likely to engage the client, reduce sustain talk and discord, and help the client to be more open to later suggestions.

CLINICAL CHALLENGE 3: CLIENT INVOLVED IN THE LEGAL SYSTEM

Description

Client involvement with the legal system can lead to particularly difficult client-provider interactions. Legal involvement comes in many different forms, each of which can introduce unique clinical challenges. Clients who are court-ordered, court-referred, or encouraged to seek services by an attorney prior to their court date to make a favorable impression upon the judge may enter treatment pre-contemplative about behavior change (Thombs & Osborn, 2013). That is, these clients may not perceive any reason to make changes, and may believe that the only benefit they will get from meeting with a provider is to improve their legal standing. Clients of this type are most often found in the probation/parole system, substance abuse treatment, domestic violence treatment, and similar settings.

Example: *After a substantiated allegation of child abuse, Jane was sentenced to probation and referred to an intensive parent training and anger management program. Custody of Jane's children has been temporarily granted to her ex-husband's parents and she has been informed that her children will not be returned to her custody unless she successfully completes the 12-week program and satisfies other conditions of her probation. Jane has also been informed that she may face additional legal penalties if she does not complete the 12-week program. Jane believes that stern physical discipline is an essential part of raising responsible, well-behaved children and resents her "touchy-feely, liberal" neighbor, who she is certain called in a report to the child welfare department. During her intake interview for the program, Jane is very quiet and reserved, and seems focused primarily on finding out what the program will report back to the court and probation department and what exactly the program requires to make a favorable report about her.*

Interactions with legally involved clients who present for treatment or services that are *not* required or encouraged by the legal system may still present serious clinical challenges. Clients who are involved in pending litigation or who perceive that future legal involvement is possible or likely (whether or not this is in fact true), may feel compelled to present themselves in a particular light in order to achieve legal goals, such as a favorable legal settlement, or avoid anticipated negative consequences of honest disclosure, such as a harsher sentence or loss of custody of a child.

Example: Bob is in the midst of what could best be described as a "messy divorce" and is seeking counseling to help him cope with the stress and address symptoms of anxiety and depression that have emerged since he and his wife separated. Bob would also like to use therapy as an opportunity to work on his difficulty controlling his temper, as he believes that has contributed to problems in his marriage. Bob is reluctant to disclose this problem to the therapist, however, because he is concerned that his therapy record will be subpoenaed during the divorce proceedings. Bob is afraid that admitting he has an anger problem may negatively impact him in the divorce proceedings.

Proposed Strategy 1: Giving Information

One factor that can needlessly increase discord and decrease client candor during MI sessions with clients who are involved in the legal system is uncertainty on the part of the client about whether and what types of allegiances or obligations the provider may have to the legal system. It is important to note that even clients who have no involvement with the legal system may have such concerns. For example, an individual who is being treated in the emergency room subsequent to a motor vehicle accident may be defensive or anxious when asked about her use of drugs or alcohol prior to the accident, if she believes that information will be or could be reported to police. Thus a very simple, MI-consistent strategy we have found very useful in addressing this challenge is giving information.

At the outset of an interaction with clients who have legal involvement of any sort (or who may perceive legal involvement), it is important to provide clear, unambiguous information about the provider's role, if any, in the legal system. As described further in chapter 3, to be MI-consistent, it is also important that any information given to the client is delivered in an objective manner. Although not technically required (Moyers, Martin, Manuel, & Ernst, 2010), it is more MI-consistent and generally beneficial if providers ask permission before giving information. In the case of probation, parole, or similar contexts, providers should fully disclose the dual roles they have with clients. In one role the provider represents the criminal justice system, reporting the client's progress on meeting the conditions of his or her probation or parole, including violations. In the other role, the provider acts as an advocate for the client and tries to help him or her achieve important goals (Walters, Clark, Gingerich, & Meltzer, 2007). As Walters and colleagues suggest, this dual relationship may decrease the willingness of some clients to disclose certain information for fear of sanctions. However, the willingness of the provider to proactively provide full information about the dual relationship is highly consistent with the foundational spirit of MI, which emphasizes collaboration and support of client autonomy (see chapter 2). Moreover, in our experience, provision of such information may reduce client willingness to disclose select details about their past or current behavior, but it is likely to enhance client disclosures overall by fostering the client's ability to trust the provider.

In the case of a provider outside the legal system, who is simply providing a service that may be of interest to the legal system (i.e., a community-based alcohol treatment provider working with an individual convicted of driving under the influence of alcohol or another substance [DUI] who was diverted to treatment), the client should be made aware that the provider is not part of the legal system. The provider should also make the client aware of whether the legal system is likely to require a release of information and what types of information (e.g., attendance, completion, progress, diagnoses, etc.) in order to consider the client's treatment involvement in determining the client's legal disposition. The ethical imperative for disclosure of a *lack of* relationship between the provider and the legal system is not always as clear cut as the imperative for disclosure of the presence of such relationships. However, provision of information about the absence of a connection between the provider and the legal system may help reduce discord or increase client candor in situations where the client might believe such a relationship exists.

Example: MI-Consistent/Inconsistent Giving Information

The following examples will illustrate MI-consistent and MI-inconsistent strategies for giving information to clients who have legal involvement.

Client Statement: *"I haven't smoked marijuana in over a month. I don't know how the drug screen came out positive."*

MI-Inconsistent: *"Marijuana use is a clear probation violation. You need to take this treatment seriously and stop lying to us about your marijuana use. I am going to report this to your probation officer and I hope he revokes you!"*

This statement gives the client information about the relationship between the provider and the legal system, but it is MI-inconsistent because it does so in a non-objective fashion. With this response, the provider obviously discloses this information to the client to establish his own power over the client (non-collaborative) and confront the client about what the provider believes is a lack of candor.

Somewhat MI-Consistent: *"Before we continue, I feel I must remind you that I am required to report this to your probation officer."*

This statement is somewhat MI-consistent. The provider offers the information in an objective fashion. The phrasing "I feel I must" expresses that the provider values the client's right to have full information about the probation process. Thus, in a subtle way, this phrasing supports the client's autonomy. However, the provider does not express empathy for the client's current situation or support the client's autonomy in an overt way.

MI-Consistent: *"I imagine this unexpected result is upsetting and I would like to discuss how this might have happened. Before we discuss that, I would like to review what this means and doesn't mean in terms of your legal status. Would that be okay? [Waits for affirmative response]. In addition to providing reports on your treatment attendance, your probation officer also requires that we provide reports on your progress in treatment, including outcome of urine drug screens."*

This response is MI-consistent because the provider offers the information in an objective fashion. The provider also asks permission to give the information, which supports client autonomy and enhances a sense of collaboration. The provider also reflects the client's inferred emotional reaction to a positive drug screen, which demonstrates empathy.

Proposed Strategy 2: Emphasizing Autonomy

As noted in chapter 2, a key element of the "acceptance" component of the foundational spirit of MI is respecting client autonomy. Regardless of what a provider wants or hopes a client will do, the client is ultimately the one who determines what he or she actually will do. Clients who believe change is possible and have a sense of agency are more likely to be successful in making positive changes in their lives (Bandura, 2004). Many clients who are involved with the legal system actually have lost control over one or more aspects of their lives. Nonetheless, it is very important for providers to recognize and respect that even clients who are incarcerated and have lost their physical freedom retain autonomy over other aspects of their lives (Farbing & Johnson, 2008). No matter what a client's legal status, he or she generally retains the autonomy to share or not share his/her thoughts and feelings with a provider, to discount or take seriously a provider's ideas or suggestions.

Nonetheless, loss of autonomy or concern about loss of autonomy can make it difficult for clients to actively engage in the change process. Clients may view themselves as completely powerless and assume a passive role in encounters with providers. Although this might make clients easier to manage and thus be viewed as desirable in certain settings, it may ultimately undermine efforts to promote positive changes in the clients' lives (Bandura, 2004). Clients who do not collaboratively participate in the change process may have insufficient motivation to carry out change, or may seek to make changes that are not a good fit for their unique experiences, strengths, and preferences. For example, a client who is a passive participant in discussions of employment may be assigned to employment that is of little interest to the client and does not make maximum use of his or her unique skills and experience. Loss of autonomy or concern about loss of autonomy in one area of a client's life may also give rise to unsuccessful and counterproductive efforts by the client to assert their autonomy in other areas of their life (Ryan & Deci, 2000). For example, a client who feels powerless because of his or her involvement with the legal system may react negatively to other aspects of life that are less defined or constrained.

Thus, it may be very important for providers who wish to help clients with legal involvement make positive changes in their lives to be aware of the impact of a client's loss of autonomy and make attempts to restore a client's sense of autonomy. Although emphasizing a client's personal autonomy is an MI-consistent strategy that may be applied during any MI encounter, it is perhaps most powerful with clients who have legal involvement. Using the MI-consistent strategy of emphasizing autonomy involves (as you might guess) supporting a client's autonomy by emphasizing those aspects of a client's life that are within a client's control and actively working to help the client exercise that control.

Example: MI-Consistent/Inconsistent Emphasizing Autonomy

The following examples will illustrate MI-consistent and MI-inconsistent strategies for emphasizing autonomy for clients who have legal involvement.

Client Statement: *"I miss one check-in and you are talking about revoking my probation and sending me back to prison?"*

MI-Inconsistent: *"You made a bad choice, and now you're going to have consequences."*

Although this statement seems superficially like a support of the client's autonomy because it mentions "choice," it is MI-inconsistent. The provider labels the client's choice as "bad" and actually mentions choice as a way of de-emphasizing the client's autonomy by linking it to consequences the client does not desire and cannot control at this point.

Somewhat MI-Consistent: *"If I could have made sure that you attended the check-in, I would have. But I don't have that power. You are the one who has that power."*

This statement is somewhat MI-consistent. The provider emphasizes the client's autonomy by clearly stating that the client is the one who has the power to decide whether to attend check-in meetings. The provider also expresses compassion by stating, "If I could have made sure that you attended the check-in, I would have." However, by focusing primarily on what has already happened the provider is less likely to move the client toward positive change from that point forward. Moreover, given that the client did not like the consequences of the missed check-in, this emphasis of autonomy could be interpreted by the client as an attempt to blame the client for missing the appointment.

MI-Consistent: *"The conditions of your probation are set by the court, so my hands are tied as far as what the consequences will be. I know this is disappointing for you because you'd been doing well for so long. As you know from experience, your behavior from this point forward can have a big influence on what happens next, so now it is really in your hands to decide whether it's worth it to do things that will incline the court to be lenient or not."*

This response is MI-consistent because the provider emphasizes the autonomy the client *does* have to try to do things that will impress the court and may result in leniency. The provider also offers information about consequences in an objective fashion and reflects the client's inferred emotional reaction to the possibility of being sent back to prison, which demonstrates empathy.

Proposed Strategy 3: Initiating Discord

Another useful, MI-consistent strategy for working with clients with legal involvement described by Stasiewicz, Herman, Nochajski, and Dermen (2006) is initiating discord. This strategy addresses a problem commonly encountered in clients with legal involvement: a strong sense of discord (formerly termed resistance) at the outset of an interaction with a provider (before the provider has even initiated a conversation with the client). This sense of discord may have nothing to do with the provider per se, but rather the client's sense that the provider is part of a system that has wronged or harmed the client in some way. The difficulty a provider may face in addressing this discord is that the client may not feel comfortable expressing their anger or resentment at the outset of the session. A client may in fact deny that anything is bothering him or her if asked directly by the provider. However, until the client has an opportunity to express the thoughts and feelings driving the discord in their relationship with the provider, it may be difficult, if not impossible, for the client and provider to move forward in a meaningful way.

Consistent with prior terminology used to describe discord (Miller & Rollnick, 2002), Stasiewicz and colleagues (2006) termed the strategy they developed to address this type of discord "initiating rolling with resistance." As the name implies, what this strategy entails is proactively creating an opportunity for clients to express their anger, resentment, etc. early on in their contact with the provider. This allows the client and provider to work through it and more quickly focus on whether and what changes the client would like to make. In their work with DWI (driving while intoxicated) offenders, Stasiewicz and colleagues described initiating a session by empathically offering as possible topics for discussion several of the most common discordant statements they encountered when working with DWI clients. Items on this list might include the substantial monetary costs associated with a DWI conviction (e.g., attorney fees, treatment costs, impound fees, lost wages) or a belief that the legal system is harsh on DWI offenders relative to other impaired drivers (e.g., those who text and drive). Not only does this strategy create an opportunity for clients to get their negative feelings "off their chest" early in the interaction, it is also a way to express empathy; it gives clients a sense that the provider has some understanding of the experience of receiving a DWI.

The decision to use this strategy should be based upon a provider's experience in a particular context as well as indications from the client that discord is present (e.g., a feeling of tension in the room; a hostile voice tone or sarcastic comments from the client; quiet, passive responding). Providers who work in settings where clients almost invariably express anger, frustration, resentment, or similar reactions in their early interactions with providers might find it very useful to develop a list of the most commonly voiced concerns and initiate discord at the outset of initial encounters. This may include settings where legal involvement is not the source of discord. For example, providers in clinics or agencies with long wait times, older facilities, crowded waiting rooms, inconvenient hours, or other factors likely to arouse feelings of frustration or resentment in many clients might find this as a useful strategy.

Example: MI-Consistent/Inconsistent Initiating Discord

The following examples will illustrate MI-consistent and MI-inconsistent strategies for initiating discord:

Client Statement: *"Well I'm here. What's next?"*

MI-Inconsistent: *"Listen, you and I are going to be working together for the next 12 weeks, and this is going to go a lot more smoothly if you lose the attitude."*

This statement is likely to increase discord between the client and provider in a very MI-inconsistent fashion. Rather than proactively creating an empathic, supportive opportunity for the client to discuss negative thoughts and feelings he or she might have about working with the provider, the provider seeks to proactively shut this discussion down by labeling the client's thoughts and feelings as a "bad attitude" and issuing what might be interpreted as a veiled threat about what might happen if the client expresses negative thoughts or feelings. This is an example of *not* resisting the righting reflex (see chapter 2).

Somewhat MI-Consistent: *"Well, during today's visit we are going to review the circumstances of your DWI arrest and discuss the goals of this program. Does that sound okay to you?"*

This statement is somewhat MI-consistent. This statement is somewhat collaborative in that in response to the client's question, "What's next?" the provider presents the session plan and then offers the client an opportunity to either agree or disagree with the plan. However, the provider is not emphatically attuned to the client's obvious sense of frustration and does not create an opportunity for the client to express that frustration openly. Instead the provider seeks to move ahead with the session as planned in spite of the client's obvious reluctance.

MI-Consistent: *"There a few things we need to get done today, but before we dive into that, I'd like to check in with you. A lot of times people who are referred to this treatment have a lot on their minds. Some are pretty upset about what seems like bias in the legal system against them, others feel betrayed by a friend or neighbor who called the police, others think the amount of time at work they lose and the fees they have to spend to attend this group are a little ridiculous, and still others feel very anxious about what this means and what will happen to them because they've never been in trouble before. What, if any, of these thoughts or concerns do you have?"*

This response is MI-consistent, because the provider does resist the "righting reflex" and instead empathically notes from the client's words and tone that she may not be pleased with meeting with the provider. Then, in a supportive, empathic fashion, the provider offers information (a list of potential sources of discord) and an open question that invites the client to express his feelings or concerns.

CHAPTER SUMMARY

No-shows and non-adherence are perhaps among the most ubiquitous clinical challenges faced by providers across disciplines and settings. There are a broad range of MI-consistent strategies that may help providers reduce no-shows and non-adherence by helping clients increase their readiness to change. Clients who are involved with the legal system or otherwise coerced into a helping relationship are also often less ready to change, and MI-consistent strategies can be valuable in that context as well. Effectively working with clients who are less ready to change can be facilitated by viewing readiness to change as a process of different stages (e.g., "He hasn't decided for sure whether he's ready to change") through which a client may progress, rather than a static characteristic of a particular

Table 4.2. SUMMARY OF MOTIVATIONAL INTERVIEWING STRATEGIES FOR CLINICAL
CHALLENGES WITH LESS READY CLIENTS

Clinical Challenge	Suggested MI Strategies
No-Shows: Frequently rescheduling appointments (sometimes at the last minute) or not attending regularly scheduled appointments.	MI-consistent referrals: Making referrals in a collaborative fashion and only after having sufficient information about the client's preferences and motivations to know that a referral is a good fit.
	Giving information: Providing information in an engaging and objective fashion about the nature of the referral and appointment policies.
	Planning: Engaging the client in a collaborative conversation about how client will achieve his or her goals.
	Emphasizing autonomy: Explicitly communicating that ultimately it is the client's decision whether he or she attends a recommended or required visit
Non-adherence: Arriving to appointments late, no-showing, or not following a treatment plan.	Evocative questions: Using questions aimed at genuinely understanding the client's concerns, motivations, and potential approaches to change.
	Scaling questions: Using a 0–10 scale to elicit how important and confident a client feels in relation to change.
	Looking forward: Guiding client to look forward in their life and relate change or no change to potential outcomes in the future.
	Revising the change plan: Stepping back, reviewing, and renegotiating the plan for change focusing on the discussion of multiple versus a single change option.
	Emphasizing personal control: Explicitly and genuinely highlighting client's right to choose to do what they think is best for them.
Legal involvements: Seeking services because of a court mandate, referral, or suggestion from an attorney.	Giving information: With permission, provide objective, clear, and explicit information about your role in regard to the legal system, and confidentiality and its limits.
	Emphasizing autonomy: Emphasizing the aspects of the client's if that are within his or her control when he or she perceives loss of control.
	Initiating discord: Proactively creating an opportunity for client to express anger, resentment, or other concerns about the referral.

client (e.g., "He's just stubborn"). Doing so can enhance your understanding of client change (or lack thereof) and help you tailor your interventions or the delivery of your interventions to the client's level of readiness. The important thing to recognize is that clients are less ready for a variety of reasons, and utilizing some of the MI-consistent strategies outlined in this chapter can help you meet clients where they are in their change process and help them to become more ready to change. Table 4.2 summarizes the clinical challenges and suggested MI strategies.

5

Loss of Momentum

People changing often encounter faster and slower progress toward the change goals, increases and decreases in momentum, setbacks, brief returns to problem behaviors, and even complete return to problem behavior. As outlined more fully in our discussion of Prochaska and Diclemente's (1983) stages of change in chapters 2 and 4, clients cycle through these stages of readiness to change. Thus, simply because an individual enters an action or even a maintenance stage does not ensure they will not return to a previous stage of readiness to change. Although not a specific stage in the readiness to change model, recycling and relapse often accompany any discussion of the model (Connors, DiClemente, Velasquez, & Donovan, 2013).

QUICK REFERENCE

Relapse

Relapse and recycling: A part of change in which clients may return to previous stages of change (e.g., contemplation) and also reengage in problem behaviors.

Diverse reasons exist for waxes and wanes in client progress. These reasons can range from changes in importance and confidence, to external barriers like decreases in family support, to entering the change process with unrealistic expectations. Some of these reasons are more manageable for clients and some are less controllable. Whether controllable or not, it is important to recognize shifts in momentum toward a change goal and to further recognize that although a client has been actively changing, loss of momentum is a signal that something has changed that requires parallel change from the MI-consistent provider. Generally this change will be a shift from a more directive approach to an MI-consistent guiding style. By viewing shifts in momentum as an opportunity to re-engage or recycle through the readiness to change process and adopting an MI-consistent style, a provider can help clients regain the momentum toward change. In fact, the ability to integrate an MI-consistent style when clients lose momentum during the active change process seems to be one of the important benefits of this approach.

CLINICAL CHALLENGE 1: SLOW PROGRESS

Description

Individuals we have trained frequently express concern about clients who appear to be motivated to change and yet progress slowly in their change efforts. This experience can certainly be confusing and leave providers wondering exactly why their clients are not progressing faster given their expressed desire or need and perhaps even intention to change. You may remember from chapter 2 that change talk, in particular statements about intention, has been identified as a predictor of positive change outcomes (Amrhein, Miller, Yahne, Palmer, & Fulcher, 2003). In our experience, providers (including us at times) tend to assume that after clients have expressed an intention to change, we have permission to adopt an active expert role and advise clients what they need to do to change. This is why clients come to see us, right? This assumption often leads us to develop a plan of action or intervention for the client and then present it to the client. In doing this; however, we fail to honor our clients' autonomy and elicit their expertise to help us determine the best plan of action. We then experience concern, frustration, and even disillusionment with our clients' slow progress as we place all of the responsibility for their progress, or lack thereof, on them.

An example from our experience might help illustrate this point. I (MM) regularly supervise advanced doctoral students providing psychological services. Many times I have observed students meeting with clients for two sessions to "understand" the clients' concerns and treatment goals. After the second session these students sit in the clinic work space and write a treatment plan to present to the client at the third session. Several sessions later, I've had these students approach me with frustration that the client is not making progress on the treatment plan. I tend to respond in these situations with a simple question, "How much of the plan is theirs and how much of it is yours?" The point in this story and in my questioning of my supervisees is to emphasize that, from an MI perspective, we need to be collaborative and evocative in developing a change plan.

Conceptualizing slow progress as evidence of a need to reassess motivation and reevaluate the change plan may help a provider to adopt a more MI-consistent style in these situations. Miller and Rollnick (2013) and others (e.g., Westra, 2012) remind us of the need to pay attention to shifts in motivation and even the reemergence of ambivalence as clients progress through treatment. There can be various reasons why progress is slow or slows down ranging from development of the wrong plan, to unexpected difficulties with various aspects of the change plan, to life events and barriers that may take precedence over changing.

> Example: *Joel is a 40-year-old man who is seeking career counseling due to recently being laid off from his job. He worked as an accountant for a local bank and is a certified public accountant. In meeting with his career counselor he was given a list of jobs for which the counselor deemed he was qualified and told to apply for each job and return in a week. Upon returning Joel*

informed the counselor that he applied for only one of the jobs as the others didn't seem to meet his needs or interests in a career. At this information the career counselor asked Joel if he wanted a job. Joel responded to this question with a vehement declaration, "It's my top priority!" The counselor responded by adding three more jobs to the list that she thought were appropriate and sent Joel on his way to return in 2 weeks. Upon returning Joel reported applying for one of the new jobs but no others stating that they didn't seem to meet his needs and interests. Hearing this information his counselor became visibly frustrated and again asked if Joel wanted a job.

Joel's experience is a common one when there is a schism between the plan outlined or determined by the provider and the client's goals, needs, or preferences. One way of looking at Joel's situation is that he really doesn't want a job and is just going through the motions—perhaps for some secondary gain. Or perhaps finding a job isn't as urgent for him as the provider thinks it is. We have noted this perspective when medical professionals we train share their frustrations about lack of client change. They often say something like "if they knew how important or urgent it is to their health for them to lose weight they would get on it ASAP." Although believing that change is important certainly facilitates change, it is not the only factor that should be considered when trying to understand slow progress. An MI-consistent way to think about this situation is that the change plan may not have captured the best strategies for changing or something has occurred that may have led the client to be more apprehensive about a particular change strategy. Thus, when experiencing slow progress, a more MI-consistent approach would include evoking information from the client about the factors that may be slowing down progress.

Proposed Strategy 1: Evocative Questions

A good MI-consistent way to discuss slow progress with clients is to step back from being directive (e.g., offering advice, suggestions, or solutions) and use evocative questions. The use of evocative questions in these situations helps providers elicit from clients their own evaluation of how they are progressing and what might be getting in the way. Adopting this approach can help avoid the expert trap and the righting reflex by keeping the relationship collaborative. It also communicates that the provider genuinely wants to understand the client's perspective on the situation.

Example: MI-Consistent/Inconsistent Evoking

The following examples will illustrate MI-consistent and MI-inconsistent evoking when clients are progressing slowly.

Client Statement: *"I applied for one of the five jobs you provided me last week. Getting a job is really important to me."*

MI-Inconsistent: *"Securing a job is important for you and yet you only applied for one job. Don't you think it would be important to apply for all of the jobs I gave you?"*

Even though the provider begins with a reflection the response is MI-inconsistent. The reflection has a somewhat judgmental tone, primarily because of the word *only*. By using "only" the provider is communicating that the client should have applied for more than one job. Additionally, the question is a closed question and a rhetorical question that is likely to engender discord versus facilitating discussion.

Somewhat MI-Consistent: *"I hear that finding a job is really important to you. At the same time, you applied for one of the five jobs on the list. What was wrong with the other jobs?"*

This statement is somewhat MI-consistent. The provider offers a reflection that expresses appreciation for the ambivalence the client is experiencing. However, rather than stepping back to learn more about the client, the provider remains focused on the jobs that were provided to learn why they didn't work for the client. This approach could invite discord or sustain talk versus better understanding of the client's motivations.

MI-Consistent: *"I hear that finding a job is really important to you. At the same time, you applied for one of the five jobs on the list. Perhaps I got a bit ahead of us with the list I gave you and didn't spend enough time talking to you about your goals and expectations. If it's okay with you, I'd like to learn a bit about what worked for you and what didn't with the plan we developed for you to find a job."*

This statement is MI-consistent for several reasons. The provider begins with a double-sided reflection that highlights the client's desired goal and compares that with the progress. There is no judgment in the reflection; the provider simply highlights what the client has said. The provider then admits to possibly taking an expert role and jumping ahead of the client in the plan. This allows for the provider to then transition back to eliciting from the client his perception of how well or not the plan unfolded. Through this the provider communicates collaboration and wanting to understand the client's evaluation of the implementation of the plan.

Proposed Strategy 2: Assessing Importance and Confidence

As clients progress through change plans, the importance of the change and their confidence in their ability to make the change may wax and wane as they are faced with new goals, tasks, or obstacles. For example, in treating clients with obsessive-compulsive disorder, I (MM) noted that these clients often experienced reductions in importance and confidence as treatment progressed. As further outlined in chapter 6, although they are highly efficacious, exposure-based treatments for obsessive-compulsive and related disorders require clients to complete practice exercises that can result in transient intense anxiety and other negative emotions. Thus, it is not uncommon for clients to express ambivalence about doing new exposures in their treatment even if they have already successfully completed related exposures. In part this seemed due to their anxiety and desire to avoid—thus reducing the importance (e.g., "I'd rather just live with this illness than do this treatment."). However, I also noted what seemed to be a lack of confidence in the ability to do the exposure (e.g., "I want to do this. I just don't think I can go through with it today."). The mantra at the treatment facility was "just do the exposure and it will get better"—a common behavior therapy response. Although the statement is true, this approach often can lead to slower progress and impasses in treatment. By assessing importance and confidence when progress slows, a provider can engage the client in a discussion, learn what is behind the slow progress, and even help the client resolve any importance or confidence barriers. Remember that ambivalence can return when someone is actively changing. One way it might present itself is through slow or slowed-down progress.

Example: MI-Consistent/Inconsistent Reassessing Importance and Confidence

The following examples will illustrate MI-consistent and MI-inconsistent questions for reassessing importance and confidence when clients experience slow progress.

Client Statement: *"I applied for one of the five jobs you provided me last week. Getting a job is really important to me."*

MI-Inconsistent: *"So is getting a job really important to you?"*

This provider statement is MI-inconsistent for two reasons. The provider's emphasis on "really" communicates that he does not believe the client's statement about importance. The question appears to be an accusation and does not assess how important finding a job is for the client. This statement by the provider is more likely to elicit a defensive response from the client as the provider is "calling out" the client and challenging him. The question is also a closed question. By asking the question in this way, the provider is unlikely to learn about the factors that are impeding progress.

Somewhat MI-Consistent: *"On a scale of 1 to 10, how confident you are in your ability to search for a job?"*

This response is somewhat MI-consistent. Now that the provider understands how important finding a job is to the client, he or she uses a scaling question to assess his confidence in his ability to find a job. However, the provider jumps to a scaling question on a different topic (confidence versus importance) without first reflecting what the client has said. This is a missed opportunity to express empathy. If done repeatedly, this could lead the client to believe the provider is not really interested in what he or she is saying, or to a question and answer trap in which the client passively responds to provider questions.

MI-Consistent: *"Finding a job is something that is important to you. This week you were able to apply for one of the five jobs on the list. I wonder if you can share with me, on a scale of 0 to 10, how confident you are in your ability to search for a job.* [Client response: *"About a 5."*] *So you have some confidence to search for a job. What makes your confidence a 5 and not a 3?"*

MI-Consistent: *"Finding a job is important to you and you were able to apply for one of the five jobs on the list. Perhaps you can tell me on a scale of 0 to 10 where the importance of finding a job is for you at this point?* [Client response: *"About a 7."*] *So it is important to you but not of the highest importance at this time. What would need to happen for it to be a 9 or 10 and not a 7?"*

These statements are MI-consistent for several reasons. The provider uses reflection to highlight that the client was able to apply for one job on the list while also indicating it was one of five positions. There is no judgment in these reflections and they restate what the client has said. The provider's statements focus on the client and do not introduce his own interpretations of the situation. There is no assumption of how important or confident the client is in the plan. Further, the questions are presented in a way that does not imply the client is lying or that the provider doesn't believe the client.

Proposed Strategy 3: Revise the Change Plan

Sometimes slow progress might be an indicator that the original change plan that was developed (and to which the client committed) may not have been the best possible plan. This can be the case for several reasons: perhaps the provider was not fully collaborative, or all of the possible options and barriers were not considered, or the client didn't envision what it would look like when they began the plan. Regardless of the reason, slow progress by a client may signal the need to revisit the change plan to determine what aspects of the plan, if any, need to be revised to facilitate change. Stepping back to review the change plan when progress is slow communicates to clients that the provider and client are "in this process together" and that the provider is genuinely committed to helping the client develop the best personal plan of action. This approach is more MI-consistent than asking, "Why aren't you working on this plan? You agreed to it." Remember from chapter 2 that we need to respect the expertise and autonomy of the client and we want to work with them to determine what change is best and how it is best to change for each client.

Example: MI-Consistent/Inconsistent Revising a Plan

The following examples will illustrate MI-consistent and MI-inconsistent revising of the change plan.

Client Statement: *"I applied for one of the five jobs you provided me last week. Getting a job is really important to me."*

MI-Inconsistent: *"This plan doesn't seem to be working for you. Is the plan wrong?"*

The provider acknowledges that the plan may not be working for the client. What makes this statement MI-inconsistent is the closed question. Remember to be MI-consistent providers want to use more engaging and eliciting questions. A closed question rarely accomplishes this goal. Additionally, the question has the potential to engender some defensiveness in the client.

Somewhat MI-Consistent: *"You accomplished part of your plan and struggled with other parts. What needs to change to make the plan work better for you?"*

The provider affirms that the client made some accomplishments in the plan which is MI-consistent. However, the provider also emphasizes the difficulty the client had with the plan by closing the reflection with that point. This reflection combined with the question could communicate some judgment, though subtle, about the client's efforts and invite discord.

MI-Consistent: *"You accomplished part of the plan this week. In moving forward it might be helpful to revisit the change plan to see if there are things that need to be added, removed, or revised to strengthen it for you."*

This provider statement has several aspects that make it MI-consistent. The provider reflects the client's statement about progress on the plan. Additionally, there is a strength-based emphasis (i.e., "you accomplished"). Placing emphasis on what was accomplished potentially reduces the chance of eliciting defensiveness. Further, the provider raises the idea, without any judgment, of looking at the plan to see what might need to be changed. The statement also attempts to engage the client in the process of reviewing the plan. See the "Evaluating the Current Plan" box for some questions you could use in reevaluating the change plan.

EVALUATING THE CURRENT PLAN

What have you learned from trying to implement this plan?
What aspects of the plan are working?
What parts of the plan are not working?
How is the plan helping you meet your goals?
What should we add/remove from the plan?
What should we revise in the plan?

Proposed Strategy 4: Emphasizing Personal Control

Ultimately what clients decide to do with their change plans is up to them. As we have mentioned multiple times in this book, we can't make people do what they do not want to do. This fact also applies to the speed at which someone progresses on her or his change plan. Thus, it is important for us to remember, in remaining MI-consistent, that clients are in control of their change and the pace at which they change. In other words, we need to recognize that it is the client's change timetable and not ours. Ultimately, it is up to our clients how fast or slow they change. Thus, we need to be mindful of the importance of client autonomy and personal control when client progress is slow to keep us from pressuring clients. It is also something of which clients should be reminded in the face of slow progress.

Example: MI-Consistent/Inconsistent Emphasizing Personal Control

The following examples will illustrate MI-consistent and MI-inconsistent emphasizing personal control for slow-progressing clients.

Client Statement: *"I applied for one of the five jobs you provided me last week. Getting a job is really important to me."*

MI-Inconsistent: *"It is your choice how many jobs you apply for but we need to get you a job."*

The attempt to emphasize personal control was thwarted by the end of the provider's statement—"but we need to get you a job." This minimizes the client's personal control and choice in the situation by expressing something that has to happen. Further, by adding the message "you need to get a job," the provider is increasing the chances the client will engage in conversation about why it is hard to get a job or when the jobs or strategies suggested will not work. In other words, this statement is likely to elicit sustain talk and possibly discord.

Somewhat MI-Consistent: *"Finding a job is really important to you. Only you can make this happen."*

The provider begins with a reflection highlighting the importance of getting a job to the client and emphasizes personal control. However, the provider's attempt to emphasize personal control could elicit sustain talk or discord as there is a hint of judgment in the statement.

MI-Consistent: *"You are here because you want to find a job and indicated that is really important to you. Nobody knows you and what jobs fit you better than you do. And nobody other than you can decide how many jobs you apply for."*

The provider begins the statement by reflecting the client's statement about the importance of finding a job. Further, the provider makes a statement that emphasizes that the client is the expert on himself and that he is in control of his life. This includes the provider also suggesting that the pace of finding a job is completely within the client's control and not the provider's. The provider avoids including his perspective on how many jobs the client should apply for or how fast he should seek opportunities.

CLINICAL CHALLENGE 2: LAPSES AND RELAPSES

Description

It is common for clients who are changing to experience a slip or lapse, an initial setback during which they return to a previous behavior that is counter to their change effort (Marlatt & Witkiewitz, 2005). Once they experience this setback, many clients experience a relapse or a total return to the problematic patterns they were trying to change (Connors et al., 2013). Think for a moment about New Year's resolutions. At the start of every year, countless people flock to fitness centers with the goal of increasing their physical activity and becoming healthier. For some this goal is actualized; however, for many others work toward their goals tends to wane after weeks or months only to be revisited again with the next New Year's resolution. Thus, setbacks, lapses, and relapses are common occurrences when changing. Regardless of this fact, we as providers often become discouraged when a client lapses or relapses. As a result, we often respond in a fashion that is MI-inconsistent, especially in some contexts where relapse is very common. Miller, Forcehimes, and Zweben (2011) comment how it seems strange that many treatment programs and providers respond to lapses and relapses in a punitive fashion when setbacks are so common when changing. Their point is a good one: if we conceptualize slips and relapses as part of the change process, why not respond in a supportive fashion that aims to reengage the client in the change process? We certainly do not respond in a punitive fashion when someone's cancer reoccurs.

> Example: *Elaina is a 35-year-old woman who is married and has three children. She gained 75 pounds when she was pregnant with her third child 3 years ago. Then she learned that she had hypertension and her physician recommended she lose weight and change her lifestyle. About a year ago she began to work with a dietician, a personal trainer, and a behavioral specialist to develop a healthier lifestyle. For 7 months Elaina has been successful in increasing her physical activity and modifying her diet, which led to a 25-pound weight loss. However, she recently stopped exercising and returned to old eating patterns during the holiday season. She also began to avoid her counseling sessions with her team. When she finally talked with her behavior specialist, she indicated she felt terrible about her relapse and that her team would be mad at her.*

Elaina's experience is not uncommon when people are attempting lasting change. One explanation for what might have happened is the abstinence violation effect, in which clients who have made change think they "fell off the wagon" by reengaging in a problem behavior (Gaughf & Madson, 2008). Adopting a punitive stance as a provider can reinforce the abstinence violation effect and lead a client to disengage from the provider or even from considering reengaging in change. However, remembering the stages of readiness to change and maintaining an MI-consistent focus can certainly help providers react and respond to these types of setbacks in clients and reengage them in the change process. Here are some strategies for working with clients who reengage in problem behaviors.

Proposed Strategy 1: Providing Information

Providing information about the potential for lapse and relapse can be very beneficial in helping clients appreciate the waxes and wanes associated with making lasting change. Educating clients about the high-risk situations and discussing them is a valuable aspect of relapse prevention (Marlatt & Witkiewitz, 2005). However, when clients are actively making change or have sustained a change for a period of time, there can be a tendency for providers to adopt an expert role and actively prescribe what the client should do in high-risk situations. This approach would be inconsistent with MI. In chapter 3 we discussed the cyclical process of exchanging information called elicit-provide-elicit as an MI-consistent method for providing information (Rollnick, Miller, & Butler, 2008). By using elicit-provide-elicit, a provider can discuss the potential for lapses and relapses and discuss what happened during a lapse or relapse event. This approach allows the provider to explore lapses and relapses in a collaborative way that is engaging and invites clients to be the expert commentators on their situation.

Example: MI-Consistent/Inconsistent Providing Information

The following examples will illustrate MI-consistent and MI-inconsistent providing information.

Client Statement: *"I don't know what happened—before I knew it 2 months went by and I hadn't exercised. Then I just ate all the holiday goodies ignoring my diet plan."*

MI-Inconsistent: *"The holidays are a difficult time for many people to maintain healthy lifestyles. You really need to remember your plan and how it can help you avoid those temptations."*

This statement is MI-inconsistent for several reasons. First, the tone of the provider's statement is somewhat judgmental and is likely to elicit responses from the client justifying why the setback happened. Second, the provider adopts an expert role and jumps into providing information about relapse. Here the provider is missing an opportunity to engage the client as a collaborator in identifying what happened that led her to resume her eating behaviors and not exercising. Finally, the provider prescribes what the client needs to do to avoid a relapse. However, the provider is missing an opportunity to gauge the client's interpretation or reactions to the information provided.

Somewhat MI-Consistent: *"You ran into some difficulties with your plan over the holidays that you see as a setback. You may remember from past experiences that the holidays can be a particularly difficult time—we call them high-risk situations. At these times one's health plan is particularly important. How does that information match up with your experiences?"*

This statement is somewhat MI-consistent. The provider begins with a reflection that communicates empathy and understanding of the client. The provider checks in with the client again after providing information. However, the provider does not elicit from the client prior to providing information and decides what information to provide without first checking what the client already knows from her experience with previous change efforts. There is a potential that the client may respond with sustain talk.

MI-Consistent: *"You ran into some difficulties with your plan over the holidays that you see as a setback. From your past experiences trying to make changes, what do you know about difficulties changing? [Waits for client response]. If I might share with you, the holidays can be a particularly high-risk time for folks trying to change their eating and exercise behaviors for a variety of reasons, ranging from stress to tempting foods to being very busy. How does that information match up with your experiences?"*

This statement is MI-consistent for several reasons. First, the statement begins by reflecting the client's conceptualization of the problem, which validates her experience. There is also no judgmental tone and the reflection is simply reiterating the facts as perceived by the client. Next, the provider offers some information about how the holiday season can be difficult for a lot of people and provides some potential reasons why this is the case. Finally, rather than telling the client what she needs to do, the provider elicits the client's interpretation of the information. This approach can reduce the emotionality of the situation, communicate a matter-of-fact mind-set and facilitate a focus on where to go from here.

Proposed Strategy 2: Reassess Importance and Confidence

Recognizing lapses and relapses as a natural part of the lasting change process can help a provider refocus on building motivation for reengagement in active behavior change. Thus, a provider may need to revisit the client's motivation for changing (Miller et al., 2011). One approach to begin this discussion is reexamining how important the change is to client and how confident they feel in their abilities to change after a lapse or relapse. In other words, a provider can use the importance and confidence questions to begin assessing whether something has changed for the client that may have led him or her to resume problematic patterns.

Example: MI-Consistent/Inconsistent Reassessing Importance and Confidence

The following examples will illustrate MI-consistent and MI-inconsistent scaling questions for reassessing importance and confidence clients who lapse or relapse.

Client Statement: *"I don't know what happened. Before I knew it 2 months went by and I hadn't exercised, then I just ate all the holiday goodies, ignoring my diet plan."*

MI-Inconsistent: *"So is your diet and exercise still important to you?"*

This provider statement is MI-inconsistent for two reasons. First, the use of a question like this, especially in the context of a relapse, is somewhat judgmental and is likely to engender discord as it can be perceived as an accusation versus assessing how important resuming change is to the client. Second, this is a closed question, and given the tone of the question may likely elicit a short response versus a longer response. Thus, by using this question the provider has missed an opportunity to engage the client in exploring her hesitancy to change or identify why the importance of changing has reduced.

Somewhat MI-Consistent: *"How important is changing to you right now?"*

This statement is somewhat MI-consistent. The provider offers an open question that invites the client to share her perspectives. However, by jumping straight to a question, the provider misses an opportunity to express empathy, provide support, and/or affirm a client who likely feels disappointed in herself. Additionally, while the open question used is not necessarily a "bad" question, in this particular case it may imply that the provider believes the client's lapse may be an indication that she is not serious about change. This could lead to defensiveness.

MI-Consistent: *"You had a lot of things come up in the past few months with the holidays that have gotten in the way with your change plan. I wonder, for you at this point on a scale of 0 (not at all important) to 10 (the most important thing) how important it is to you to resume your change?* [Client response: *"About an 8."*] *So it is fairly important to you to resume changing. What makes the importance an 8 and not a 6?"*

MI-Consistent: *"You had a lot of things come up in the past few months including the holidays that have gotten in the way with your change plan and left you discouraged. At this point on a scale of 0 (not at all confident) to 10 (completely confident), how confident are you in your ability to resume your change?* [Client response: *"About a 4."*] *So while it is important to you, perhaps based on your recent experience, you are not as confident in resuming change. What would need to happen for it to be a 7 and not a 4?"*

These statements are MI-consistent for several reasons. First the statements begin with a reflection that validates the client's experience with the relapse.

They are matter of fact with no judgment and simply restate what the client has experienced with an added emotion. Next, the statements focus on assessing the client's perspective of how important change is and how confident she feels in resuming change. There is no assumption that the client is ready or confident in resuming change. By using a scaling question to focus on the importance of the behavior the provider gets a better sense of where the client is at in resuming her change or not. Finally, the follow-up question is likely to guide the client to provide change talk by discussing why resuming change is important and how she can become more confident.

Proposed Strategy 3: Looking Back

Once clients relapse, they may be preoccupied with the relapse and perhaps whatever has changed that has led to the return to problem behaviors. Possibly their motivation has changed because they do not recall what things were like while they were actively changing. Therefore, as part of building motivation to reengage in change after a relapse, it may be valuable to look back to the time when the client was actively changing and compare that to their current state.

Example: MI-Consistent/Inconsistent Looking Back

The following examples will illustrate MI-consistent and MI-inconsistent looking back for clients who relapsed.

Client Statement: *"I don't know what happened—before I knew it 2 months went by and I hadn't exercised. Then I just ate all the holiday goodies, ignoring my diet plan."*

MI-Inconsistent: *"Do you remember what it was like when you were actively changing before you relapsed?"*

This statement is MI-inconsistent because the provider uses a closed question. The question also could be perceived by the client as judgmental. Additionally, the provider falls into the labeling trap by using the word "relapse". Labeling words can elicit discord from clients who feel judged.

Somewhat MI-Consistent: *"You are frustrated that after you made progress you had a return to previous behavior. Perhaps we can take a moment to look back on what led up to the setback in your plan."*

The provider offers a nice reflection to communicate empathy. Traditionally, however, the looking back strategy in MI focuses on a time when the client was not engaged in the problem behavior. Thus, the application of looking back in this way is only somewhat MI-consistent, as it might focus the client on talking about the problem versus what it was like when the client was changing so she can regain her motivation.

MI-Consistent: *"You are frustrated that after making much progress you stopped exercising and started eating the holiday goodies. I wonder if we can take a moment to look back to when you were following your exercise and eating plan to see if it gives us any clues about how you might best be able to get back on track now should you want to."*

This provider statement has several aspects that make it MI-consistent. The provider reflects the client's feelings about the relapse. In this reflection the provider uses the client's own words and avoids labeling the behavior. The provider uses looking back in an MI-consistent way by looking back to when the client was not experiencing the problem to compare it to her current state.

Proposed Strategy 4: Decisional Balance

Given that a lapse or relapse is a sign that clients likely shifted in their readiness to change, it may be valuable to explore the pros and cons of changing or continuing problematic patterns. Remember from chapter 3 that an MI-consistent approach to decisional balance involves exploring all sides of the change versus advocating for or focusing on the pro-change side of ambivalence. Pro-change advocacy by the provider will place clients in a position to advocate for the status quo. Thus, even though clients have been successfully involved in maintaining change, we need to recognize that something may have occurred to tip the scale in favor of resuming problematic patterns. For instance, Miller and colleagues (2011) suggested that a client's successful change of one problem (in their example, substance use) can lead to the realization that other problems exist. This realization could lead to falling back into problem patterns. Therefore, you may need to guide the client through reevaluating changing or not.

Example: MI-Consistent—Inconsistent Decisional Balance

The following examples will illustrate MI-consistent and MI-inconsistent decisional balance for a client who has relapsed.

Client Statement: *"I don't know what happened. Before I knew it 2 months went by and I hadn't exercised. Then I just ate all the holiday goodies, ignoring my diet plan."*

MI-Inconsistent: *"So you had a relapse and it will be important to get back to your plan so you can continue losing weight and keep your blood pressure under control. Not resuming change will only make your health worse."*

This is definitely an attempt at discussing the benefits of change and negatives of not changing; however, it is MI-inconsistent. The provider has adopted an expert role and is providing the reasons why resuming change is beneficial and why not changing is a problem. This response will likely place the client in a position to defend not changing by expressing the benefits of staying the same and the cons of changing. In other words, the provider is arguing for change, which is MI-inconsistent.

Somewhat MI-Consistent: *"You are concerned about resuming some behaviors you are trying to change. What are some of the pros and cons to resuming those behaviors?"*

This response is a somewhat MI-consistent attempt at a decisional balance. The provider begins with a reflection that expresses understanding and empathy. However, in exploring the decisional balance the provider only elicits the pros and cons of resuming problem behaviors and ignores the pros/cons of resuming change. This approach may guide the client to only discuss the problem behaviors and avoid addressing change.

MI-Consistent: *"You had a brief period of time where you resumed some of the behaviors you were changing. That concerned you. What might be some of the benefits and drawbacks of staying the way you are now? What might be some of the good things and not-so-good things about resuming your change efforts?"*

This response is MI-consistent for several reasons. The statement begins with a restatement of what the client said. The statement also added that the client was concerned about the situation, which emphasized the unspoken emotion in the client's statement. The provider then facilitates the decisional balance by first asking about the client staying the way she currently is in her change effort. Next, the provider asks the client about resuming her change efforts. At no time does the provider advocate for one side or the other (i.e., changing or staying the same), which is an important feature of a decisional balance.

Proposed Strategy 5: Eliciting and Affirming Strengths

There can be a tendency when clients experience a lapse or relapse for them to focus on the mistakes they made leading to the setback, which can result in negative affect and more avoidance (DiClemente, 2003). However, before the lapse or relapse they were actively making changes. Therefore, there likely were strengths exhibited and successes achieved. Although a provider will probably eventually need to discuss the situation that led to the lapse or relapse, it is also valuable to elicit from the clients their successes and what strengths helped them in their change efforts.

Example: MI-Consistent/Inconsistent Eliciting and Affirming Strengths

The following examples will illustrate MI-consistent and MI-inconsistent eliciting and affirming strengths for clients who relapse.

Client Statement: *"I don't know what happened. Before I knew it 2 months went by and I hadn't exercised. Then I just ate all the holiday goodies, ignoring my diet plan."*

MI-Inconsistent: *"You didn't stick with the plan. What happened?"*

This type of response is commonly used by providers in an attempt to better understand a relapse. However, the provider is not commenting on the client's success and not eliciting strengths from the client. Additionally, while the intention may be to be supportive, this type of response could leave the client feeling more discouraged. It clearly communicates a failure in progress. Further there is the potential that the provider commenting on the success could lead to a response from the client focusing on the setback. Finally, the focus on what happened can lead the client to focus more on the problem that lead to the relapse including her deficits versus eliciting strengths.

Somewhat MI-Consistent: *"You seem a bit discouraged in your behavior the past few months. It could happen to anyone. Don't be too hard on yourself. I know you can get back in there and do it again!"*

This statement is somewhat MI-consistent. The provider begins with a reflection that expresses empathy. The provider then seeks to affirm the client. However, rather than commenting on the client's strengths or past successes, the provider focuses on his or her belief that the client is capable. This sort of cheerleading is an example of the righting reflex. This response is likely to elicit the opposite of change talk from the client in an attempt to correct the provider.

MI-Consistent: *"You seem a bit discouraged in your behavior the past few months. At the same time you made the decision to come back here which suggests persistence. Perhaps you can share with me what you learned about yourself during the seven months when you were very successful with your plan?"*

This statement is MI-consistent for several reasons. First, with the statement reflects an emotion the client experienced as a result of the relapse. Next, the provider affirms the client's return. Finally, the provider seeks to elicit from the client her strengths and what she had learned about her success in making a change prior to the relapse.

Proposed Strategy 6: Reframing

A return to problem patterns can also be seen by clients, and some providers, as a failure in the change effort. This view can lead to a variety of emotional, cognitive, and behavioral responses. Emotionally clients may feel guilty, sad, and anxious. Clients may also think of themselves as failures or that they can never change their problems. Behaviorally, clients may avoid professionals who were involved with their change initiatives. Unfortunately, these emotional, cognitive, and behavioral responses are more likely to entrench clients in not changing. Reframing what a lapse or relapse is can help to facilitate different emotional, cognitive, and behavioral responses that are more conducive to changing. In fact, Miller and colleagues (2011) suggest referring to a lapse or relapse as a behavior or choice. As we mentioned earlier, conceptualizing a return to problem behaviors as a natural part of the change process can help you and clients reframe the setbacks in a way that can help you better understand the setbacks and problem solve what to do next.

Example: MI-Consistent/Inconsistent Reframing

The following examples will illustrate MI-consistent and MI-inconsistent reframing for clients who experienced a relapse.

Client Statement: *"I don't know what happened. Before I knew it 2 months went by and I hadn't exercised. Then I just ate all the holiday goodies, ignoring my diet plan."*

MI-Inconsistent: *"You had a relapse. That is a normal part of changing."*

This statement represents an attempt at reframing because the provider indicates the relapse is part of changing. However, it is MI-inconsistent because the provider uses the term "relapse," which is a label, thus falling into the labeling trap. Using a label such as relapse could evoke discord from in the client. Additionally, the provider takes on an expert role in that the provider assumes he or she has a full understanding of why the client is having problems without seeking to evoke additional information about how or why the client got off track.

Somewhat MI-Consistent: *"In my experience setbacks are a natural part of changing, and I think it is great that you came in today as it shows me how committed you are to making a lasting change. I am proud of you for that."*

This response is supportive and a reframe of the relapse and may appear MI-consistent. However, it is only somewhat MI-consistent for several reasons. First, the provider falls into an expert trap by offering information without emphasizing the client's personal control or announcing or inviting the sharing of information. Additionally, the provider violates the rules for affirmations by using "I" and communicating a message that "you have pleased me."

MI-Consistent: *"Thank you for coming today. You recently chose to step away from your change plan and became discouraged in light of 7 months of success. It seems to me that your situation provides us a good learning opportunity. What are your thoughts about that?"*

This statement is MI-consistent for several reasons. First, the statement begins with an affirmation by reframing the client showing up as a positive given the relapse. Next, the provider avoids labeling and emphasizes that the client made a choice which highlights personal control. Finally, by suggesting that the provider and client have a learning opportunity reframes the relapse as a part of the change process from which they can learn.

CLINICAL CHALLENGE 3: OVERLY AMBITIOUS EXPECTATIONS

Description

A type of challenge that can influence momentum and can be uniquely demanding is the client with overly ambitious expectations. Clients may have expectations that changing will require little effort or that there is a magic cure or technique that they can use to change. When watching television, you can see advertisements for a variety of quick-change tools ranging from clothing that "melts away fat" to energy-increasing or weight-reduction pills to exercise equipment that require minimal actual physical activity to get back "that high school body." For these reasons, as well as many others, many people are seeking change initiatives that require little effort to change. Thus it is not surprising that we are often asked, "What do I do with a client whose goals are unrealistic or unattainable in our work together?"

The client with overly ambitious expectations poses an interesting dilemma for many providers. Providers may feel a strong urge to educate that client and provide suggestions for more realistic goals based on their knowledge, experience, and understanding of the research related to changing a particular problem. For many clinical approaches this would be perfectly appropriate. We remember our clinical training and the rules for developing change goals, especially the rule for keeping goals realistic and manageable to foster success. However, adopting this expert role is inconsistent with MI. In fact, informing clients that their goals are unrealistic or less likely to be obtained and prescribing alternate goals may actually reduce client motivation rather than helping them to develop more attainable change goals. Thus, the dilemma is how to be MI-consistent and to help clients manage their expectations for change, especially when they are overly ambitious and unrealistic.

> Example: *Brandy is a married woman who initiates individual therapy with concerns about her marriage and lack of communication with her husband. She has been married for 10 years and reports that her relationship with her husband has become increasingly worse since the couple had three children. Specifically, Brandy reported that when she tries to initiate conversation with her husband he becomes nonresponsive and withdraws from her even further. She has read several relationship books and has not found the perfect solution. Therefore, she has entered therapy to learn the best way to get her husband to engage with her. She wants the therapist to provide her with the method to solve her relationship problem.*

As psychologists, we often encounter clients who have certain expectations about what we can offer to help them change. These expectations often relate to what "we [the provider] are going to do to change them." We can certainly appreciate where this expectation comes from as many medical interventions, especially those for acute illnesses, rely primarily on a health care worker doing something to fix a problem. However, this model is generally not applicable to prevention and management of chronic illness and other more complex problems. The best solution to these types of problems is rarely achieved by a provider just "doing something" to the client. Instead, the solutions requires clients to "do something" to change.

Example: *Earl is a single father whose son Craig, age 10, was diagnosed with asthma 3 years ago. They are seeking counseling at the referral of Craig's physician as he is not managing his asthma very well and has been admitted to the hospital three times in the past 6 months for asthma-related problems. Earl reports that Craig is not adhering to medical recommendations for managing his asthma and he is at a loss for what to do with Craig. Earl reports that he works 10 to 12 hours per day and that he is not available to help Craig keep track of his medications or monitor all of his behavior. Earl figured he would bring Craig for counseling as that would help "straighten him out" and get him to follow medical directions.*

Finally, based on our society's focus on the "quick fix" clients may have unrealistic expectations about outcomes associated with their change and how quickly positive change will occur. They may think that by losing weight their relationships will improve or that simply attending nutrition counseling will cure their diabetes.

Example: *Steve is diagnosed with obesity, hypertension, and diabetes. He has had difficulties managing his weight since he was a little boy and has been under the care of his physician for the past 5 years. Steve, like many other people, has dieted on and off throughout his life, losing some weight only to gain it back plus some additional weight. Steve has become increasingly concerned about his weight and the associated health effects as he recently had a mild heart attack. In fact, he has expressed his commitment to losing weight. However, his expressed goal is to lose 50 pounds in the next month as he wants to lose 150 pounds by his birthday in 3 months. He is seeking guidance from a weight loss specialist on how best to meet this goal.*

Similarly, individuals who have made some progress in changing may overestimate what their progress means and decide that they are have completed change and are cured. Expectations that small gains equal complete cure can complicate that person's change initiative.

Example: *Shelia is early in recovery from a drug addiction that she has struggled with for 7 years. She has been in a residential substance abuse treatment program and hasn't used in 3 weeks. Since entering the program, Shelia has been engaged in the treatment and is showing signs of recovering physically from her addiction. Shelia is making good gains in treatment and recognizing*

*how she is improving. In a recent conversation; she stated that she believes
she now has mastery over her addiction (often referred to as the "pink cloud
effect"). She indicates that since she is doing well she wants to spend more
time away from the treatment facility.*

Whatever the reason for clients developing overly ambitious expectations
about change, it seems to create a unique challenge to remaining MI-consistent.
This challenge involves how to remain MI-consistent and at the same time help
clients develop more realistic expectations for change initiatives. In part, this
challenge arises from the righting reflex (see chapter 2) which causes providers to have a natural tendency to want to correct clients. Thus, one important
thing a provider can do to remain MI-consistent in working with unrealistic
expectations is to resist the righting reflex. The following are some strategies that
can help a provider resist the righting reflex and remain MI-consistent when
addressing unrealistic goals.

Proposed Strategy 1: Asking Permission to Provide a Concern

When discussing an unrealistic goal in an MI-consistent fashion, it is imperative
that the provider not directly assert his or her expert status by rejecting the client's goal or by offering a new goal. Many providers may feel compelled to jump
to providing facts about change and education about the change process as a
strategy for helping clients modify their expectations. In fact, some approaches
to helping call for this education at the outset of any change initiative or goal setting. In contrast, MI encourages clients to remain empowered while negotiating
their change. Directly educating clients may foster a climate of passivity in the
client-provider interaction. However a provider can certainly share information
or even a concern and remain MI-consistent.

As discussed in chapter 3, information can be shared with clients in an
MI-consistent way. First, a provider can be MI-consistent by asking permission to
share some information or announcing that he or she has some information that
he or she would like to share. Whether the provider asks permission or announces
that he or she would like to share some information, the provider is communicating that he or she values the collaborative relationship with the client, accepts
their opinions about the process of change, and wants to be engaged with the
client as a partner in the change process. Another MI-consistent approach to providing information is to emphasize the client's personal control to decide what
to do with the information provided. In addition to communicating dedication
to collaboration, emphasizing personal control communicates that the provider
accepts the client and respects his or her autonomy to decide to do what he or she
thinks is best.

Example: MI-Consistent/Inconsistent Sharing Information or Concern

The following examples will illustrate MI-consistent and MI-inconsistent strategies for sharing information or a concern.

Client Statement: *"I believe I have really progressed in treatment and am ready to spend more time away from the facility. I have this addiction under control now."*

MI-Inconsistent: *"You have been here for three weeks and you have made progress. Physically the drug has finally been eliminated from your body and you are feeling better. There is a lot of work you need to do to more fully recover from your addiction and more time away from the facility puts you at risk for relapse."*

This statement provides the client with information about the physiological aspects of recovery and that recovery is an ongoing process that takes time. Although it is not overly confrontational, it is MI-inconsistent and likely could engender discord. In particular, the provider adopts the role of an expert who is imparting the "correct" knowledge about the situation. The likelihood that the client will push back against this statement is high.

Somewhat MI-Consistent: *"You have made some progress and are feeling good about your success in treatment. One thing that concerns me is that it is common for clients to feel mastery over their addictions early in treatment and want to take more time away from the facility. Does that seem to fit with your experience?"*

This statement is somewhat MI-consistent and reflects a comment often offered by supportive providers. However, it is not fully MI-consistent because the provider does not announce the offering of information or seek permission. Similarly, the provider attempts to elicit a client response to this information with a closed question.

MI-Consistent: *"You are noticing some improvements in how you feel and in your treatment—so much so that you feel ready to spend more time away from the facility. If it is okay with you, I would like to share some information about the recovery process for your consideration. [Waits for client response]. One thing that is common in early recovery is a sense of mastery over one's addiction when you begin feeling better physically. While it is a sign of improvement, I get concerned for my clients as this feeling can lead to decisions, like ending treatment, which can increase risk for resuming the addiction."*

This statement is MI-consistent because the provider begins by reflecting the client's statement, which communicates empathy. Next the provider asks for permission to share the information and emphasizes the client's personal control to decide versus simply providing the information as an expert. Finally, the provider provides the information in a non-judgmental way and owns the concern about the situation as his own, which also communicates compassion for the client.

Proposed Strategy 2: Use Evocative Questions

Utilizing clients' expertise and eliciting from them information that can develop more realistic expectations can be a valuable tool to remain MI-consistent. As mentioned in chapter 2, clients are the experts on their lives and better understand their past experiences. By selectively using questions, a provider can draw out from clients how their experiences may or may not relate to their current expectations. By using evocative questions a provider avoids the righting reflex, respects client autonomy, and collaborates with the client versus acting as an expert. Clients likely have attempted similar change initiatives in the past and have knowledge about what worked and did not work and how realistic or unrealistic their current expectations may be. Thus, by asking evocative questions the provider can utilize the client's experiences and expertise to help the client think more realistically about their expectations.

Example: MI-Consistent/Inconsistent Evoking

The following examples will illustrate MI-consistent and MI-inconsistent evoking for clients who have unrealistic expectations.

Client Statement: *"I believe I have really progressed in treatment and am ready to spend more time away from the facility. I have this addiction under control now."*

MI-Inconsistent: *"Do you really think your addiction is under control?"*

This question is MI-inconsistent for two reasons. First, it is a closed question. Evoking questions tend to be open ended to invite the client to respond more thoroughly and freely. Second, the question is a rhetorical question that also has a value judgment to it. Thus, the question is highly likely to engender discord.

Somewhat MI-Consistent: *"You are really committed to your recovery and recognize the gains you have made. Based on what you have learned about recovery in this program, what else do you need to do to recover?"*

This statement is somewhat MI-consistent. The provider begins by offering a reflection of how the client is feeling about their progress in treatment. Next the provider asks an open question to elicit information from the client about the recovery process in relation to goals. However, rather than exploring what the client has learned from previous experiences attempting recovery, the provider asks the question in the context of what the client has learned from the treatment facility. This approach fosters an expert role on behalf of the provider and the facility and communicates that they have the expertise and not the client.

MI-Consistent: *"You are really committed to your recovery and recognize the gains you have made. Tell me about your past attempts to at recovery and what you know about how recovery works for you. How might that information help inform your choices at this time."*

This statement is MI-consistent because the provider begins by reflecting the client's statement, which communicates empathy. Next, rather than providing information about appropriate recovery, the provider uses the client's previous experience with recovery to invite her to be the expert on her experience. Finally, the provider uses eliciting to connect the client's previous experience and knowledge about herself to current decisions.

Proposed Strategy 3: Elicit-Provide-Elicit

An MI-consistent approach that combines the first two proposed strategies is the elicit-provide-elicit strategy. As discussed in chapter 3, the elicit-provide-elicit strategy fosters client engagement in sharing information and draws out information and reactions from the client. Elicit-provide-elicit invites clients to share their knowledge and to interpret the information/concern shared. This strategy also allows a provider to better understand what facts and myths the client already believes about the change initiative, and helps the provider create a better understanding by filling in the gaps or correcting misinformation. In other words, the provider knows what they client already knows and doesn't know so the information provided can be more focused.

Example: MI-Consistent/Inconsistent Elicit-Provide-Elicit

The following examples will illustrate MI-consistent and MI-inconsistent elicit-provide-elicit for clients who have unrealistic expectations.

Client Statement: *"I really believe I have really progressed in treatment and am ready to spend more time away from the facility. I have this addiction under control now."*

MI-Inconsistent: *"What we see in the research is that it is important to help you to learn how to better manage high-risk situations and that takes time."*

This provider statement is MI-inconsistent for two reasons. First, there is no eliciting from the client, and the provider jumps into providing information. Second, the provider does not elicit the client's response or interpretation of that information. Finally, a statement such as this is highly likely to engender discord as it can be perceived as judgmental.

Somewhat MI-Consistent: *"You really want to succeed in your recovery. Tell me what you already know about successful recovery. [Waits for client to respond]. If I may add to your understanding, one thing we often see that helps is learning new strategies for assisting and monitoring high risk situations, which includes gradually exposing people to these situations over time as they recover. Does that make sense?"*

This response is a somewhat MI-consistent use of elicit-provide-elicit, but is not fully MI-consistent because the provider asked a closed question after providing the information. This type of question invites only a brief response. This type of question also may subtly communicate the message "do you agree with me" and could invite passivity and less open sharing of reactions and interpretations of the information from the client.

MI-Consistent: *"You really want to succeed in your recovery. Tell me what you already know about successful recovery. [Waits for client to respond]. If I may add to your understanding, one thing we often see that helps is learning new strategies for assisting and monitoring high-risk situations, which includes gradually exposing people to these situations over time as they recover. What are your thoughts about that?"*

This statement is MI-consistent because the provider communicates empathy and reinforces the client wanting to recover. Next, before providing information, the provider elicits the current knowledge of the client about recovery. The provider announces that she would like to share some information instead of jumping into providing it. Finally, the provider elicits the client's response to the information.

CHAPTER SUMMARY

Slow progress, slips, and relapses, and unrealistic expectations are challenges that are often encountered when clients engage in behavior change. Clients change at differing paces and there are various reasons for why client progress may slow. Conceptualizing clients' slow progress and related behaviors in an MI-consistent fashion—as a natural part of the change process, recognizing that motivation to change can vary over time—will likely reduce your frustration with these challenges. Many of the MI-consistent strategies we proposed can help you and your clients step back, evaluate, and better understand what has changed or what needs to change to help clients return to a level of motivation that facilitates change. Our goal is that reading this chapter you will identify how you can utilize some of the MI-consistent strategies discussed in this chapter to help you match clients in their change process, help them better explore the slow progress, and help them to become more ready to change. Table 5.1 summarizes the clinical challenges and suggested MI strategies.

Table 5.1. SUMMARY OF MOTIVATIONAL INTERVIEWING STRATEGIES FOR CLINICAL CHALLENGES WITH LOSS OF MOMENTUM

Clinical Challenge	Suggested MI Strategies
Slow progress: Completing treatment tasks, assignments, and goals at a pace that is inconsistent with expressed intention to change.	Evocative questions: Ask questions to assess how clients perceive their progress or to identify changes that are affecting progress.
	Assessing importance and confidence: Ask scaling questions to assess if the importance of change or confidence to change has been altered.
	Revising the change plan: Step back and review the change plan to assess if it is working. Does it relate to the client's goals?
	Emphasizing personal control: Highlight the aspects of clients' lives that are within their control when they perceive loss of control.
Lapse and relapse: Returning, either temporarily or longer term, to a problem behavior after a period of maintained change.	Provide information: Seek permission and give objective, clear and explicit information about the nature of slips and relapse and how they relate to the change process.
	Reassess importance and confidence: Elicit how the lapse/relapse has affected importance of and confidence to change.
	Looking back: Review recent change efforts to identify how the change was achieved and maintained. Discuss how clients can use this information.
	Decisional balance: Ask about the pros and cons of continuing the problem behavior or re-engaging in changing.
	Eliciting and affirming strengths: Identify positive behaviors and strengths of client before the lapse/relapse.
	Reframing: Re-conceptualize lapses or relapses as learning opportunities versus failure to change.
Overly ambitious expectations: Expecting outcomes from the change process that are highly unlikely or impossible to achieve.	Asking permission to share a concern: Express your concern, with permission, about how clients' expectations impact their change efforts.
	Evocative questions: Elicit clients' expertise on previous change attempts in comparison to their expectations.
	Elicit-provide-elicit: Elicit clients' knowledge about their expectations for change, provide objective information, and evoke client's interpretation and reaction to the information.

6

Psychiatric Symptoms and Disorders

The National Alliance for the Mentally Ill (2013) defines mental illnesses as "medical illnesses that can disrupt a person's thinking, feeling, mood, ability to relate to others, and daily functioning" (p. 3). Mental illnesses are also commonly referred to as mental disorders (American Psychiatric Association, 2013), neuropsychiatric disorders (World Health Organization, 2008), and psychiatric disorders (Kessler et al., 1994). Regardless of the terms used to refer to them, mental disorders are very common. In fact, according to the World Health Organization (2008) one third of the total years lost to disability worldwide are the result of mental disorders, such as depression, schizophrenia, and alcohol use disorders. The National Comorbidity Survey Replication, a large, nationally representative, epidemiological survey of mental disorders in the United States, found that in any given year just over one fourth of Americans ages 18 and older suffer from a diagnosable mental illness (Kessler, Chiu, Demler, & Walters, 2005). Thus, even providers who do not treat mental disorders very likely provide services to individuals who are experiencing symptoms of a mental disorder. The current chapter provides guidance on MI-consistent strategies that can be utilized to address some common clinical challenges that arise when working with clients who are experiencing symptoms of depression; certain anxiety, trauma-related, and obsessive compulsive disorders; or psychotic disorders.

The goal of the current chapter is not simply to provide guidance on how to use MI to enhance treatment for these disorders. Although mental health professionals using this book will find several of the strategies described helpful for that purpose. Instead, this chapter is written with both the mental health professional and non–mental health professional in mind. As such, each section includes non-technical, descriptive information about the disorders and symptoms of focus. The clinical challenges associated with each group of disorders are challenges that might be encountered in almost any setting where MI might be employed, from probation to health care to substance abuse treatment. Similarly, the vast majority of MI-consistent strategies recommended could be employed just as easily in helping a client with a mental disorder engage in smoking cessation or fulfillment of probation requirements as in helping the client engage in treatment for the mental disorder.

CLINICAL CHALLENGE 1: DEPRESSION

Description

Major depressive disorder and other depressive disorders are characterized by various symptoms and associated features. In our own clinical practice of MI and that of others we have supervised, we have found the following features of depression can introduce particular challenges to the practice of MI: hopelessness, feelings of worthlessness or guilt, difficulty concentrating, and lack of interest in activities. Although everyone may experience hopelessness, guilt, difficulty concentrating, or lack of interest in activities from time to time, it is important to note that these experiences are more intense and impairing in the context of a depressive disorder (American Psychiatric Association, 2013). In our work as psychologists, we sometimes talk with the families and loved ones of those who are experiencing a depressive disorder. In many cases it seems difficult for these concerned loved ones to understand how different the experience of guilt, for example, can be for an individual in the midst of a major depressive episode, than it is for someone without depression. This can make it difficult for these concerned others to understand "why she doesn't just apologize and make amends—that worked for me." Thus, in working with individuals who may be experiencing depression, we believe it is vitally important for providers to maintain an MI spirit. To seek to understand how a particular client is experiencing hopelessness, guilt, difficulty concentrating, or lack of interest, and not assume that the experience is like the provider's experience or other clients' experiences.

These features of depression will likely necessitate adaptations to MI regardless of whether you are a mental health provider or a provider of another type. For example, a client who feels hopeless about the future may have as much difficulty discussing the steps she must take to satisfy probation requirements with her probation officer as she does collaborating on a treatment plan for depression with her psychiatrist. In this section we seek to describe the signs and symptoms of depression that may impact a client's ability to respond to MI, and the MI strategies that we have found most helpful in addressing these difficulties. We try to provide this information in a manner that is relevant to mental health providers and also accessible to providers who have no background in mental health.

Hopelessness

Hopelessness generally refers to a negative perspective on the future—a lack of optimism (Beck & Steer, 1988). Individuals who feel hopeless generally feel that there is something or several things about their lives that are undesirable or untenable, and that these things are unlikely to change. It is often difficult for individuals who feel hopeless to even imagine how life might be better or different. These individuals may thus have difficulty engaging in MI-consistent tasks such as envisioning (e.g., " If you were successful in making these changes, what would your life look like in five years?") and planning (e.g., "What is the first step toward getting better control of your diet?"), which require this sort of imagining. Indications that a client you are working with may be experiencing hopelessness are presented in the quick reference.

QUICK REFERENCE

Client Utterances Expressing Hopelessness

I don't know why I even bother, nothing ever works out.
Until my wife decides she is willing to quit, it's not like I can do this anyway.

Example: *Hopelessness. Mario is a 36-year-old, divorced father of three who enters a tobacco cessation clinic at the urging of his primary care physician. When asked about his confidence in his ability to quit smoking, Mario laments that he's been a smoker for 20 years and he's not sure why his doctor thinks he can quit now. He also reports that this isn't a great time for him to try to quit, because smoking is the only thing that makes him feel good.*

Proposed Strategy 1: Hypothetical Questions

Because hopelessness can interfere with a client's ability to view change as possible, it might be difficult for a client who is feeling hopeless to respond to direct questions about how they imagine life will be after they make a change. The righting reflex (as described in chapter 2) can tempt a provider to try to convince a client that change is possible, but this can result in increased verbalizations of hopelessness (i.e., the client trying to convince the provider that change is not possible). Using MI-consistent hypothetical questions (Miller & Rollnick, 2013), a provider can help a client "work around" their hopelessness to begin imagining a life that might different and how they might achieve that change, without forcing them to relinquish their hopelessness before they feel ready or able to do so.

Example: MI-Consistent/Inconsistent Hypothetical Questions

The following examples illustrate common types of hypothetical questions:

Client Statement: *"It doesn't matter what I try, I'll never be able to stop smoking."*

MI-Inconsistent: *"I don't buy that. If you try a little harder, I'm sure you can imagine what it might be like if you quit smoking."*

This utterance is MI-inconsistent because the provider directly confronts the client about his hopelessness, accusing him of being dishonest and not putting forth enough effort in an attempt to push him to envision the future.

Somewhat MI-Consistent: *"You sound really discouraged. Would a prescription for smoking cessation aids make you feel more confident?"*

This response is somewhat MI-consistent. The provider offers an empathic reflection and then attempts to get the client to envision the possibility that he might someday be able to get smoking. However, to so, the provider uses a closed question, which invites only a brief response. The question also proposes the provider's solution rather than eliciting reasons or means for change from the client.

MI-Consistent: *"Right now it is hard to imagine that you will ever be successful in your smoking cessation efforts. If you were to imagine that somehow it was possible for you to quit, what might be different or better in your life?"*

This provider utterance is MI-consistent, because it begins with a reflection of the client's hopelessness rather than a challenge of it. The provider then gently, and with respect for the client's hopelessness, invites him to hypothetically consider what his life will be like if he is successful. This is a very basic use of the hypothetical question.

MI-Consistent: *"It's been really discouraging to try so many times and not have lasting success, and it's even hard to envision a future without smoking. Just for the sake of exploring this, imagine if you will, Mario, that I had a magic cure that would make it possible for you to stop smoking for good. How would your life be better or different?"*

This provider utterance is MI-consistent because it begins with a supportive statement and a reflection of the client's hopelessness. The provider then uses a type of hypothetical question that is sometimes referred to as a "miracle question" to invite the client to consider the possibility of change without immediately letting go of his hopelessness. The utterance is also MI-consistent, because the provider gives the client permission not to imagine the miracle cure.

MI-Consistent: *"You don't feel very confident about your ability to stop smoking. What would it take to make you more confident that it might be possible?"*

This provider utterance is MI-consistent, because it again begins with a reflection. The provider then goes on to invite the client to hypothetically consider things that might favorably alter his perspective on the possibility of change. This type of hypothetical question can be used as a follow-up to a confidence ruler ("On a scale of 0 to 10, how confident are you about your ability to quit smoking?"—see chapter 3) for client's who express limited confidence in their ability to change.

Proposed Strategy 2: Planning

As the previous examples illustrate, clients who feel hopeless may have difficulty imagining the possibility of change. There is also evidence that individuals who experience depressive disorders may have difficulty engaging in problem solving (D'Zurilla & Nezu, 2007). This difficulty in identifying and implementing solutions to important life problems may contribute to the sense of hopelessness that seems to sometimes make it difficult for individuals who are experiencing depression to fully engage in an MI session. Problem solving requires a series of steps that are not dissimilar to the planning process in a motivational interview, including setting goals, generating solutions, and making decisions (D'Zurilla & Golfriend, 1971). Thus, engaging clients in an MI-consistent planning process (see chapter 3) during which clients set goals and work collaboratively with the provider to identify a workable strategy to achieve those goals may help foster client belief that change is possible.

Example: MI-Consistent/Inconsistent Planning

The following examples illustrate how an MI provider might use planning to help a client overcome hopelessness:

Client Statement: *"It doesn't matter what I try, I'll never be able to stop smoking."*

MI-Inconsistent: *"There is a new medication that was just FDA approved for smoking cessation. I'm going to write you a prescription. Many of our clients report that smoking cessation is much easier on this medication than without it."*

Although the provider acknowledges the difficulty that the client has had with prior smoking cessation attempts and attempts to instill hope by pre-scribing a new drug, this provider utterance is MI-inconsistent because it is non-collaborative. The provider assumes the expert role and seeks to make the client a passive recipient of medical advice.

Somewhat MI-Inconsistent: *"I have a change plan worksheet we can fill out together to create a strategy for change. How does that sound?"*

This response is somewhat MI-consistent. The provider suggests that a change plan worksheet be filled out and asks the client for feedback on that idea. In another context this response might be very collaborative. However, given the client's prior expression of hopelessness, the abrupt manner in which this idea was presented conveys both a lack of collaboration and a lack of empathy (i.e., in response to the client's statement that he can't change, the provider essentially says "let's talk about how you can change").

MI-Consistent: *"Right now it is hard to imagine that you will ever be success-ful in your smoking cessation efforts. This may or may not be helpful for you, but some clients have found that talking very specifically about their goals and the different strategies they might use to achieve their goals helps them to feel a bit more hopeful about the possibility of success. I'm wondering if we could do that now."*

This provider utterance is MI-consistent, because it begins with a reflection of the client's hopelessness rather than a challenge of it. The provider then provides Mario with information about planning as a potential strategy to increase his hopefulness. In doing so, the provider supports Mario's autonomy and the collaborative nature of the interaction by explaining that Mario may or may not find it helpful (see full description of planning in chapter 3 and sample change plan worksheets found in Table 6.4 and in chapter 4).

Feelings of Worthlessness or Guilt

Feelings of worthlessness or guilt are another common feature of depression that may influence how clients experience certain MI-consistent strategies. Individuals who feel worthless or experience excessive guilt may devote great amounts of time to thinking about mistakes they have made, deficits they perceive themselves to have, ways in which they have disappointed others, and so on. Thus, when asked by a provider during an MI-consistent eliciting process, "What are the reasons you want to make this change?" they may identify numerous well-articulated, thoroughly elaborated reasons why the change is necessary. In our experience as MI supervisors, we have found that it is tempting for providers to view these utterances as evidence that the MI is going very well and that the client is very engaged. However, closer examination of the content of these utterances from clients who are experiencing depression often reveals that the provider is not helping the client identify reasons for change. Rather, the provider is inviting clients to give voice to and even expound upon a destructive, self-deprecating inner monologue that occupies much of their thinking. If you think of the depressive rumination as "beating oneself up" you could almost think of using MI eliciting to encourage the client to expound upon destructive self-evaluations as "giving the client a bigger paddle with which to beat himself." Indications that your client may be experiencing feelings of worthlessness or excessive guilt include frequent or extreme self-deprecating comments: "What is wrong with me?" "I'm not very smart," "I should know better," "I don't understand why anyone would want to be around me" and/or frequent or extreme confessions: "I shouldn't have been so nasty to her," "I screwed up again," "I'm always doing stupid stuff like that."

Example: *As Mario, the 36-year-old, divorced father of three continues his initial consultation for smoking cessation, the provider asks him why he is considering quitting smoking. Mario looks at the floor and in a very low voice tells the provider that he is a terrible example for his kids and he just really needs to get his life together or maybe they'd be better off without him. The provider, using MI-consistent strategies, says, "Tell me more about why you think smoking is a bad example for your kids." Mario responds by explaining that he never does anything right and that he is sure his kids have no respect for him at all, because not only does he smoke, but he also lost his job, destroyed his marriage, and is getting fat besides.*

Proposed Strategy 3: Envisioning

As noted, clients who feel worthless or experience excessive guilt may respond to provider questions about problems or negative consequences they have experienced with self-deprecating comments that may actually hinder rather than facilitate change efforts. Remember, it is important not only for clients to view change as necessary, but also as possible. Given that affirmations from the provider or questions from the provider that invite the client to describe past successes or strengths may enhance self-efficacy (i.e., the client's belief in his or her own ability to complete tasks and reach goals) (Bandura, 1977) it is reasonable to suspect that questions from the provider that cause the client to describe past failures or weaknesses may diminish self-efficacy. Because clients who feel worthless or experience excessive guilt may view their past as littered with mistakes, shortcomings, regrets, and few accomplishments or achievements, it may be useful for a provider to instead invite the client to focus on the future. In other words, what is possible, not what has already transpired. As noted in the preceding section of this chapter, feelings of hopelessness can make envisioning difficult and may require the use of hypotheticals.

Example: MI-Consistent/Inconsistent Envisioning

The following examples illustrate how a provider might use envisioning (Miller & Rollnick, 2013) to work around worthlessness or guilt.

Client Statement: *"I can't believe I smoked at home with my kids. I'm such a bad father. If they get asthma or something, I know it will be all my fault. No wonder my wife left me. What kind of piece of garbage father would smoke with his kids around? It was stupid and irresponsible and I can't undo it."*

MI-Inconsistent: *"You've got to let that stuff go and focus on what you can do now."*

Although the provider seems to be trying to comfort the client and is coming from a position of compassion, the statement is MI-inconsistent because the provider is in essence ordering the client to stop having those thoughts. That is not collaborative and does not support the client's autonomy.

Somewhat MI-Consistent: *"The important thing is that you're here now. Let's talk about how to approach smoking cessation this time."*

This response is somewhat MI-consistent. The provider seeks to affirm the client and shift the focus to smoking cessation. However, by failing to acknowledge in any meaningful way what the client has just said, the provider conveys that he or she is not interested in the client's perspective on anything other than how smoking cessation can be accomplished.

MI-Consistent: *"I'm hearing loud and clear that you have a lot of regrets about smoking for so long and that a big part of that relates to how important it is for you to be a good father. That's really noble. Tell me how your relationship with your kids might be different if you were successful in quitting smoking."*

This provider utterance is MI-consistent, because it begins with a reflection of the client's thoughts and feelings. The provider then goes on to affirm the client for the importance he places on being a good father. Finally the provider uses an open question to try to elicit from the client change talk that is hopeful, rather than self-deprecating.

Proposed Strategy 4: Affirming

Clients who feel worthless or experience excessive guilt may have difficulty recognizing or acknowledging their strengths and successes. This can undermine their confidence in their ability to change. In working with these clients it can be especially important for a provider to be attuned to anything the client might be saying that could hint at positive qualities, strengths, or past successes. Often affirmations with clients who feel worthless or experience excessive guilt will involve reframing something the clients has presented as a weakness or failure in a more objective and positive way.

Example: MI-Consistent/Inconsistent Affirming

The following examples illustrate how a provider might use affirmations to overcome worthlessness or guilt.

Client Statement: *"I can't believe I smoked at home with my kids. I'm such a bad father. If they get asthma or something, I know it will be all my fault. No wonder my wife left me. What kind of piece of garbage father would smoke with his kids around? It was stupid and irresponsible and I can't undo it."*

MI-Inconsistent: *"Yes. Secondhand smoke is really bad for kids. Until you get a handle on this, I think your ex-wife is doing the right thing by not letting the kids be around you."*

This statement is MI-inconsistent because the provider directly confronts the client about his smoking. This statement also demonstrates a lack of collaboration and compassion because the provider expresses more concern for the client's ex-wife and children than for the client.

Somewhat MI-Consistent: *"The important thing is that you are here now."*

This response is somewhat MI-consistent. Although the provider seeks to affirm the client, the selected phrasing might be perceived as somewhat unempathic or dismissive by the client. It is obvious from the client's utterance that the important thing to him is the impact his smoking has had on his family.

MI-Consistent: *"The way you take your role and responsibility as a father so seriously is really impressive. I know you haven't been as successful as you'd like with previous smoking cessation, but it is hard to imagine anyone taking it more seriously than you do."*

This provider utterance is MI-consistent because it affirms the positive qualities and values that likely underlie Mario's self-deprecating statements. These affirmations may help Mario view himself less as a "piece of garbage" and more as a flawed human being who is still capable of change.

MI-Consistent: *"You are really dedicated to being a good father. Tell me about some other qualities such as your dedication to your family that might help you quit smoking."*

This provider response is MI-consistent because it affirms a strength of the client. The statement also explicitly encourages the client to identify other strengths he may not be recognizing at this time.

Difficulty Concentrating

Concentration generally refers to the ability to focus one's attention or thoughts on a particular object or activity, and not attending to distractions (Lezak, 1995). Difficulty concentrating often interferes with an individual's ability to learn new information. For example, as you've been reading this book, there have probably been one or more occasions when your thoughts wandered to another topic (e.g., "I have to remember to mail that letter tomorrow.") or you noticed something new in your environment (e.g., "The sky is getting dark, a storm must be rolling in."). As you noticed your distraction and directed your thoughts back to the text, you may have realized you had no idea what you had read in the past five minutes. Difficulty concentrating can also impair an individual's ability to respond appropriately and effectively in social situations. For example, multiple times while writing this book, I (JS) received a call from my husband. Not wanting to lose my train of thought before getting it down on paper, I tried to multi-task—to talk to my husband and finish typing my ideas for this book. Needless to say, my husband noticed (and commented on it!). There were inappropriately long pauses in my speaking, I sometimes provided incoherent responses to his queries, and occasionally had to ask him to repeat what he had just said. Although not unique to depression, individuals who suffer from depressive disorders often report difficulty concentrating. Individuals who experience excessive worry (generalized anxiety disorder), posttraumatic stress disorder, attention deficit hyperactivity disorder and certain other psychiatric conditions may also experience difficulty concentrating. Indications that your client may be experiencing difficulty concentrating are presented in the quick reference box.

QUICK REFERENCE

Indicators of Concentration Difficulties in Clients

Frequent requests for repetition of information or questions
Inability to respond to queries about content previously discussed in the session
The appearance of daydreaming
Losing train of thought

Example: *When Mario, the 36-year-old, divorced father of three proceeded with his intake at the smoking cessation clinic, the provider began to ask him a question about his history of smoking. Mario began telling the provider about how he started smoking at the age of 16 by stealing his father's cigarettes and buying them from a local convenience store that didn't seem to care about selling to minors. Then Mario paused for a few moments, got a confused look on his face, and asked, "I'm sorry, what was the question?"*

Proposed Strategy 5: Summarizing

As outlined in chapter 2, the basic skills of MI are open questions, affirmations, reflections, and summaries (OARS). Rosengren (2009) outlines three different primary purposes that MI-consistent summaries can serve during a provider-client interaction, including listing important things the client has said (e.g., change talk), linking something a client has just said to something said previously, or helping to transition the conversation to a new topic or new MI process (e.g., transitioning from evoking to planning). It has been our experience that summaries can also be used as a tool to enable a client who seems to have difficulty concentrating to better participate in an interaction. For clients who have difficulty concentrating, listing summaries may not only reinforce previously discussed material, but they may enable the client to grasp content of the session that was missed due to difficulty concentrating. Linking and transition summaries may help the client draw conclusions or make connections that he or she was unable to make during the session because he or she was distracted by other thoughts.

Example: MI-Consistent/Inconsistent Summaries

The following examples illustrate how a provider might use summaries to help a client who has difficulty concentrating participate more fully in an interaction.

Client Statement: *"I'm sorry. What was the question?"*

MI-Inconsistent: *"Mario, you really need to focus on what we're doing here. I asked you to tell me about your history with smoking."*

This statement is MI-inconsistent because the provider not only repeats the question, but also attempts to shame the client about his lack of concentration. The provider talks down to the client in a paternalistic fashion, which could spring the expert trap.

MI-Inconsistent: *"Don't worry about it. Let's just go on to the next question."*

Although this provider statement indicates that the provider is sympathetic to the client's difficulty concentrating, it is not collaborative. The client requested that the question be repeated and the provider in essence overrules this request and takes full control of the direction of the session.

Somewhat MI-Consistent: *"Tell me about your history with smoking."*

This provider statement is somewhat MI-consistent. The client asked a question and the provider responded. In MI, answering a question is considered a form of giving information. However, given the circumstances, the provider's perfunctory response shows a potential lack of empathic attunement to the difficulties Mario is having with the interview.

MI-Consistent: *"I had asked you about your history of smoking and you were telling me about how you started at the age of 16 with smoking your father's cigarettes and purchasing them from a convenience store that didn't check your ID."*

This provider utterance is an MI-consistent summary. It is a collaborative response to the client's question that is intended to help the client fully engage in the interaction.

Proposed Strategy 6: Using MI-Consistent Handouts

Although written change plans, decisional balance worksheets, readiness rulers, and informational handouts are considered optional components of an MI-consistent provider-client interaction, we have found that many clients, regardless of their ability to concentrate, appreciate receiving these materials. These materials can help clients recall and refer back to key elements of their interaction with the provider. For example, several clients who receive motivational interviews from psychology interns through an MI practicum I (JS) supervise at a community residential substance abuse treatment facility report posting their change plan worksheet beside their beds. They report that they like to be reminded daily of their goals and the steps they plan to take in achieving those goals. The fact that these documents are so meaningful to these clients is very telling; the motivational interview they receive represents just one hour out of 100 or more hours of treatment they receive. Similarly, the change plan work-sheet represents just one of dozens of treatment-related papers they complete during their six-week stay at the facility. We have also found that these types of aids can be particularly helpful for clients who have difficulty concentrating and thus may be less able to recall key elements of the session than typical clients.

Example: MI-Consistent/Inconsistent Handouts

The following examples illustrate the types of MI-consistent handouts that might be provided to a client to help him or her overcome deficits in concentration.

MI-INCONSISTENT
- Any materials that judge or label a client's situation, condition, or circumstances in a way that is inconsistent with how the client labels his or her own situation, condition, or circumstances (e.g., providing a handout that describes "Signs of Alcoholism" to a client who insists that he may drink a lot but is not an alcoholic.)
- Any materials that describe a treatment plan that was created without the client's collaboration or give advice with the client's permission (e.g., handing a client a "dietary guidelines" handout and telling him or her to follow it rather than asking if he or she would like the handout, or giving the client permission to use it or not by saying, "You might find this helpful.").

SOMEWHAT MI-CONSISTENT
- Handouts that provide information in an objective, non-labeling fashion that is consistent with the client's self-perception, but are not requested by the client or offered to the client with permission to disregard them if desired.

MI-CONSISTENT
- Session/consultation/meeting agendas can be negotiated and presented in written or verbal form. After the agenda has been negotiated between a provider and client, placing a written version of the agenda between the client and provider may help a client who has difficulty concentrating stay more focused during the interaction. Samples of written agenda forms can be found in Mason and Butler (2010).
- Readiness rulers are used as both an assessment tool and a technique for eliciting change talk (Rollnick, Miller, & Butler, 2008). These rulers can be administered verbally or in written form. For clients who have

difficulty concentrating or might otherwise benefit from having a
record of this exercise, a written form that includes both their rating
and a written description of the reasons for the rating might be used
(Table 6.1).

- Decisional balance (Janis & Mann, 1977), which used to be considered
a strategy for evoking change talk in MI (Miller & Rollnick, 2002) and
is now considered a neutral strategy for assisting a client in determining
whether or not they desire to change (Miller & Rollnick, 2013), involves
having a client articulate the reasons to change and the reasons to stay
the same. Decisional balance exercises are often completed in written
form and provide the client with a useful summary of all the factors he
or she considered in deciding to change (or not change). A sample form
for completing a decisional balance is included in Table 6.2. Note that
if you decide to use this technique no form is needed—we often prefer
to draw a large "+" in the middle of a blank sheet of paper and place
appropriate headings in each quadrant.

- During an MI-consistent planning process, the client and provider will
often collaboratively complete a change plan worksheet that is intended
to remind the client of key aspects of his or her change plan. Elements
you may wish to include on a change plan worksheet are the change the
client wants to make, the reasons he or she wants to make the change,
the steps he or she will take or the strategies he or she will use to
change, what supports he or she will need to change (people, treatment
programs, books, etc.), and how he or she will evaluate the plan and
make changes if it is not helping the client achieve desired results (Miller
& Rollnick, 2002). Samples of change plan worksheets are presented in
chapters 4 and 7 and Table 6.4.

Lack of Interest in Activities

Lack of interest in activities is another feature of depression that can present
unique clinical challenges. Of particular import in depressive disorders is a lack
of interest in activities that used to be enjoyed or an inability to take pleasure in
activities that were previously enjoyed. Whereas many individuals who are confronted with difficult behavioral changes such as initiating an exercise program,
starting a diet, quitting smoking, or searching for a job may find it difficult to be
interested in or intrinsically motivated to engage in activities that are not immediately rewarding or pleasurable (but do promote progress toward the goal),
most individuals will have no difficulty engaging in activities that are immediately rewarding or pleasurable. For example, I (JS) sometimes found it difficult to
get myself interested in sitting down to work on this book, even though completing the book was a goal of mine and was highly valued. In contrast, I rarely if
ever find it difficult to get myself interested in eating fries from my favorite fast
food restaurant, reading a trashy novel, or getting a massage or pedicure. These

Table 6.1. SAMPLE READINESS RULER HANDOUT

My Goal Is: _____

On a scale of 0 to 10, with 0 being not at all important and 10 being very important, I rate the importance of achieving this goal as (circle one):

0   1   2   3   4   5   6   7   8   9   10

My rating is a _____ and not a lower number for the following reasons (list reasons):

1.

2.

3.

4.

5.

On a scale of 0 to 10, with 0 being not at all confident and 10 being very confident, I rate my confidence in my ability to achieve this goal as (circle one):

0   1   2   3   4   5   6   7   8   9   10

My rating is a _____ and not a lower number for the following reasons (list reasons):

1.

2.

3.

4.

5.

Table 6.2. SAMPLE DECISIONAL BALANCE HANDOUT

Reasons to Quit Smoking	Reasons to Continue Smoking
This quadrant generally includes negative consequences the individual has experienced as a result of the target behavior (i.e., smoking) • "My doctor is concerned about my health." • "My kids hate the smell." • "My workplace is going smoke free." • "Cigarettes are expensive."	*This quadrant generally includes positive consequences the individual has experienced as a result of the target behavior (i.e., smoking)* • "Smoking helps me relax." • "I enjoy smoking."
Reasons not to Quit Smoking	**Reasons not to Continue Smoking**
This quadrant generally includes negative consequences the individual anticipates experiencing as a result of changing the target behavior (i.e., smoking) • "Now is not a good time—I'm under a lot of stress."	*This quadrant generally includes negative consequences the individual anticipates experiencing as a result of changing the target behavior (i.e., smoking)* • "I want to live to see my children get married." • "I've wanted to quit for over 10 years." • "With all the money I'd save every year, I could take my kids to Disney World."

behaviors are not particularly consistent with any important long-term life goals, but I enjoy them. In contrast, individuals who are experiencing a depressive episode may experience difficulty getting interested in or taking pleasure from activities that normally bring pleasure. For example, an individual who is experiencing a depressive episode may have no interest in accompanying me to a fast food restaurant for fries and a milkshake, even though he or she normally loves fries even more than I do. Instead he or she might decide, "I just don't feel like it." Indications that your client may be experiencing lack of interest in activities may include reports of decreased engagement in activities, an inability to generate ideas or options when asked what they would like to do, or direct statements such as "I just don't seem to get excited about anything anymore."

Example: *As Mario, the 36-year-old, divorced father of three works collaboratively with his provider to develop a plan for tobacco cessation, the provider suggests that Mario identify ways to reward himself for meeting his daily smoking goals. After a lengthy pause, the provider explains that many individuals find that giving themselves a treat such as 30 minutes playing video games or using a social networking site, eating a special food treat such as a miniature candy bar or serving of chips, or getting praise from a loved one for their successful efforts each day can help them stay on track. Mario hesitates and ponders the provider's suggestions and then explains that he cannot think of anything that he really enjoys right now or would find rewarding.*

Although the provider is attempting to be supportive and find activities that may reinforce the client's successes with smoking cessation, the discussion is likely to be circular. The more the provider succumbs to the righting reflex and suggests rewards, the more insistent Mario may become in his arguments that he simply cannot think of anything. For someone who has depression, you may have to focus on times when the client was not experiencing depression to identify rewarding activities, things clients like, or strengths.

Proposed Strategy 7: Looking Back

Although clients experiencing depression may not currently be able to identify activities they find pleasurable, attempting to elicit what things were like and what activities they enjoyed when they were not feeling depressed can help. Thus, the MI-consistent strategy of looking back may help (Miller & Rollnick, 2013).

Example: MI-Consistent/Inconsistent Looking Back

The following examples illustrate how a provider might use looking back as a strategy to address a client's current lack of interest.

Client Statement: *"I cannot think of anything that I enjoy right now."*

MI-Inconsistent: *"Mario, we all have something that we like to do. What is it for you?"*

This response is MI-inconsistent because the provider actually invalidates the client's statement and minimizes the struggle he is having. The provider falls victim to the expert trap and the response is likely to elicit sustain talk versus generating any potential solutions.

Somewhat MI-Consistent: *"What did you enjoy before you got divorced?"*

This response is somewhat MI-consistent. The provider asks an open question to help the client identify things that he used to enjoy. However, the provider asks the question without first reflecting the client's statement. Thus there is a missed opportunity to express empathy. This failure to acknowledge the client's difficulty before asking the question may also cause the client to experience this continued questioning as non-collaborative.

MI-Consistent: *"Mario, I certainly can see that it is a struggle for you to find things you currently enjoy and that it is frustrating for you. I wonder if it would be helpful for us to look back to a time before your divorce, when you were feeling much better and doing more things. What were some of the enjoyable things for you at that time?"*

This provider utterance is MI-consistent. The provider begins by validating the client's situation and feelings about not enjoying things. Next, the provider acknowledges that there was a prior time when the client was not depressed and asked the client to look back at that time for ideas.

CLINICAL CHALLENGE 2: ANXIETY, TRAUMA-RELATED, AND OBSESSIVE COMPULSIVE DISORDERS

Description

According to the *Diagnostic and Statistical Manual of Mental Disorders*, Fifth Edition (DSM-5), "Anxiety disorders include disorders that share features of excessive fear and anxiety and related behavioral disturbances" (pp. 189, American Psychiatric Association, 2013). A common behavioral disturbance shared by many anxiety disorders is avoidance. This feature is also shared by some disorders that were previously classified as anxiety disorders in the DSM including obsessive-compulsive disorder and posttraumatic stress disorder (American Psychiatric Association, 2000, 2013). Avoidance refers to efforts by an individual to avoid people, situations, stimuli, thoughts, or feelings because they arouse unpleasant emotions, particularly fear or anxiety. For example an individual who is experiencing a specific phobia of snakes may avoid looking at pictures of snakes; going to zoos, natural science museums, or pet stores where snakes might be encountered; and going outside at night or without wearing boots during the day in case snakes might be encountered.

Avoidance is of concern to those who treat anxiety disorders, because there is evidence that although avoidance may reduce anxiety in the short term, it actually serves to maintain and even increase anxiety over time (e.g., Clark, 1999). For example, an individual with a snake phobia who runs back into the house and locks the door when a neighbor calls to tell him or her that she found a harmless garden snake in her yard that morning might immediately experience a decrease in anxiety upon doing so. However, over time he or she might come to fear and avoid the back patio and backyard entirely, and may eventually refuse to leave the house unless wearing protective leather boots.

Avoidance presents clinical challenges, because many of the most effective psychotherapies for disorders such as specific phobia, obsessive-compulsive disorder, and posttraumatic stress disorder include exposure-based interventions (Doyle & Pollack, 2003). Exposure-based interventions involve having an individual who is avoiding situations, people, stimuli, thoughts, or feelings because they elicit a strong anxiety or fear reaction to intentionally come into contact with those situations, people, stimuli, thoughts, or feelings and tolerate the intense anxiety or fear (Hofmann & Smits, 2008) Whether you have worked with individuals who have anxiety, trauma-related, or obsessive-compulsive disorders; watched reality television programs that depict exposure based treatment; had friends or family members who suffered from such disorders; experienced an anxiety or related disorder yourself; or have no direct experience with anxiety or related disorders; you can probably imagine that finding the motivation to complete exposure-based treatment is a challenge. We admire the courage of the many individuals we have treated with exposure-based treatments over the years and have found the use of many MI strategies helpful in assisting these individuals to find the motivation and courage to reclaim their lives through completion of exposure-based treatment.

> Example. *Jamal is a 32-year-old man who has been diagnosed with posttraumatic stress disorder subsequent to a single car motor vehicle accident during which he was seriously injured and the driver of the vehicle was killed. Since the accident, Jamal has been unable to drive on the freeway, after dark, or in unfamiliar neighborhoods. He also becomes incredibly upset when he sees a black sedan (the car involved in the accident was a black sedan) or hears jazz music (he and the driver were listening to jazz on the radio at the time of the accident). During their second visit, a social worker provides Jamal with information about his diagnosis and exposure-based treatment. Jamal expresses that the symptoms of PTSD have ruined his life and he is willing to do whatever it takes to get past this. However, shortly after the exposure-based interventions begin, Jamal states that he is not certain he wants to continue with treatment and tries to convince the social worker that having PTSD is really not that bad.*

As illustrated in this example, avoidance can interfere with a client's ability to complete exposure-based treatment, even if he or she does not express any initial hesitation or concern about the treatment. In our own work, we find that not all clients express doubt about their ability to tolerate exposure-based treatment. In fact a significant minority express unrealistic optimism about their ability to tolerate exposure-based treatment without any difficulty. With the help of a caring, compassionate, and competent professional, there are only a handful of situations that would be considered contraindicated for exposure-based interventions (e.g., vanMinnen, Harned, Zoellner, & Mills, 2012). Nonetheless, the very nature of anxiety, trauma-related, and obsessive-compulsive disorders, as well as exposure-based treatment almost ensures that an expectation of no distress or avoidance is unrealistic for most clients. Thus we also outline MI-consistent strategies to help clients set realistic expectations for exposure-based treatment (see also chapter 5).

Avoidance related to anxiety can interfere with effective provision of interventions and services of all types, not simply those that involve exposure-based treatments (Westra, 2012). Individuals with social anxiety have intense fear or anxiety about one or more social situations that expose the individual to possible evaluation by others. This fear and anxiety stem from a belief they will act in some way that will be negatively evaluated by others in the feared social situations. As a result these situations are avoided or endured with intense fear and anxiety (American Psychiatric Association, 2013). For example, individuals with social anxiety may avoid making phone calls, coming to appointments, speaking up in groups, or engaging actively in one-on-one meetings. This fear, anxiety, and avoidance may interfere with an individual's ability to participate fully in almost any situation or setting in which MI might be utilized, from a meeting with a probation officer, to an appointment with a family care provider, to a substance abuse treatment group. In our own clinical practice of MI and supervision of others' MI practices, we have identified MI strategies that may be useful in working with individuals who avoid treatment because of social anxiety.

> Example. *Sanjay is an 18-year-old male who suffers from social anxiety. He has been referred to the counselor at his school to discuss decreasing attendance and performance. Sanjay's teachers report that he often looks at his desk or fiddles with his pen, never raises his hand to participate in class discussions, and often seems unprepared when called upon to answer a question or present information to the class. As the counselor talks to Sanjay about his problems at school she discovers that several of his classes require presentations this year and that his political science instructor, a former law professor, often calls on students randomly and expects them to know the answer. Sanjay explains that his heart races whenever he thinks about the presentations and political science class and he just knows he's going to "mess up" in front of the class and all of the kids will think he's stupid.*

Proposed Strategy 1: Empathic Listening

We know from our work with community providers who do not specialize in mental health (and even sometimes those who do) that lack of engagement due to social anxiety is often misattributed to lack of motivation or weakness. As you read these descriptions, you might have been thinking, "Who hasn't felt their heart race when they stand up to speak before a crowd of people?" or "Who hasn't shuddered a bit when they saw a particularly fearsome looking snake or spider?" As with depression, it is important to note that although everyone experiences fear or anxiety from time to time, the experiences are more intense and impairing in the context of an anxiety disorder (APA, 2013). Thus, it is very important to listen empathically and attempt to understand the clients' experience of anxiety rather than assuming that your personal experience with anxiety makes you an expert on the client's experience. This is true even if you have suffered from the same disorder the client is experiencing (see chapter 8 for additional information about the unique challenges that arise when working with clients who are similar to you).

Example: MI-Consistent/Inconsistent Empathic Listening

The following examples illustrate how to use empathic listening to understand the role anxiety may play in a client's lack of participation in an intervention:

Client Statement: *"I'm going to say something stupid and the other kids are going to laugh at me."*

MI-Inconsistent: *"Everyone gets nervous sometimes Sanjay. You just need to have faith in yourself and speak out confidently."*

Although the provider seems to be trying to express warmth and compassion to the client, this provider utterance is nonetheless MI-inconsistent. Instead of demonstrating empathy by reflecting Sanjay's concerns, the provider instead provides information as an attempt to dismiss Sanjay's concerns. The provider then goes on to tell Sanjay what to do, which is not collaborative and does not support Sanjay's autonomy.

Somewhat MI-Consistent: *"What do you think might make you feel less nervous about speaking up in class?"*

This response is somewhat MI-consistent. The provider asks an open question that invites Sanjay to share his perspectives. However, this question is asked before the provider has elicited enough information from Sanjay to really understand what his experience of anxiety is like, and what his motivations to implement strategies to reduce anxiety might be.

MI-Consistent: *"You are really worried that the other kids might think poorly of you if you speak up in class."*

This provider utterance is MI-consistent because the provider empathically reflects the client's feelings and concerns without trying to minimize them or force him to adopt a new perspective.

MI-Consistent: *"So if you felt more confident that the other kids wouldn't laugh at you, you'd be more willing to participate in class."*

This provider utterance is also MI-consistent and is also an empathic reflection. This reflection is more complex than the previous example as the provider reframes the client's concerns as a possible intervention target. A provider might choose this type of reflection to help the client begin to consider that change is possible.

Proposed Strategy 2: Assessment Feedback

In our work with individuals with anxiety disorders, obsessive-compulsive disorders, and trauma-related disorders, we have found that many clients benefit from provision of MI-consistent feedback from their diagnostic assessment (e.g., Miller, Zweben, DiClemente, & Rychtarik, 1992). An example comes from a recent clinical trial that included an MI-based intervention as a preparatory intervention for individuals who enrolled in a clinical trial for treatment of co-occurring alcohol use disorders and posttraumatic stress disorder (Coffey et al., 2013). In this study, we found that the first participants who enrolled in the study had difficulty articulating the potential benefits of receiving treatment for posttraumatic stress disorder because they did not realize that the constellation of distressing and life-interfering symptoms they were experiencing could all be traced to their diagnosis of posttraumatic stress disorder. However, once provided with objective information about the diagnosis, including feedback from their diagnostic evaluation, participants could readily articulate: (1) the ways in which the symptoms, distress, and impairment associated with posttraumatic stress disorder had negatively impacted their lives, and (2) the way their lives would be better, richer, and fuller if they were successful in treatment and no longer experienced the symptoms, distress, and impairment associated with the diagnosis.

Example: MI-Consistent/Inconsistent Assessment Feedback

The following examples with Jamal, the man described earlier who developed posttraumatic stress disorder as a result of a motor vehicle accident, illustrate how a provider might use assessment feedback to help a client with an anxiety, trauma-related, or obsessive compulsive disorder develop sufficient motivation to participate in treatment and reduce their symptoms.

Client Statement: *"My life has been ruined ever since the car accident."*

MI-Inconsistent: *"If you want to regain your life, I recommend you participate in a treatment called exposure therapy."*

This response is MI-inconsistent because the provider gives advice without permission, which reduces collaboration and may also diminish the client's sense of autonomy. The provider also fails to demonstrate empathy with Jamal's obvious angst.

Somewhat MI-Consistent: *"You have a disorder called PTSD and that is why you've been struggling so much since the accident. You can do a treatment called exposure therapy that will help you get past it."*

This response is somewhat MI-consistent. The provider offers Jamal objective information about his condition. However, the provider does not ask permission before giving the information or elicit the client's response to the information. The provider also jumps to planning (offering a treatment approach) without eliciting Jamal's motivation for treatment.

MI-Consistent: *"Jamal, would it be okay with you if I shared some feedback from your assessment that might help you better understand why things have been so difficult for you since the car accident?"*

This provider utterance is MI-consistent, because the provider asks permission to give information, which supports the client's autonomy, and also demonstrates both sympathy and empathy for the difficulty the client has experienced as a result of the car accident that took the life of his friend.

Table 6.3. EXAMPLE OF OBJECTIVE WRITTEN FEEDBACK FROM A PTSD ASSESSMENT

Posttraumatic Stress Disorder Assessment Results

TRAUMATIC EVENTS IN YOUR LIFE

_____   _____   _____

_____   _____   _____

_____   _____   _____

YOUR TRAUMA SYMPTOMS

Posttraumatic Stress Disorder (PTSD) Diagnosis   yes _____   no _____

Avoidance symptoms

_____

Re-experiencing symptom _____

Hyperarousal symptoms _____

Overall trauma symptom severity: mild   moderate   severe   very severe

---

Table 6.3 provides an example of what MI-consistent written feedback from a PTSD assessment might look like. This feedback is most helpful when presented in the context of verbal or written interpretive information that will help clients make the most of the information (e.g., Miller et al., 1992).

Proposed Strategy 3: Evocation

For clients who present with anxiety, trauma-related, or obsessive-compulsive disorders for which an exposure-based treatment is recommended, using MI-consistent evocative questions to help them articulate their own reasons for change may be essential to helping them foster the motivation and strength to overcome their avoidance and pursue treatment (Westra, 2012). Evocative questions can most easily be accomplished after clients have been provided with assessment feedback or other information that gives them a clear understanding of how the symptoms they have been experiencing are linked to their diagnosis.

Example: MI-Consistent/Inconsistent Evocation

The following examples illustrate how a provider might use evocation to help a client develop sufficient motivation to overcome avoidance and engage in treatment:

Client Statement: *"My life has been ruined ever since the car accident."*

MI-Inconsistent: *"Well, I have good news Jamal. I can offer you a treatment that is very effective for helping people move past traumatic events like car accidents."*

This provider utterance is MI-inconsistent, because the provider does not evoke the client's desire, ability, reasons, need, or commitment for change. Instead the provider assumes that because the client reports that his life is ruined that his motivation is sufficient and jumps directly to planning. The planning is MI-inconsistent because it is non-collaborative; the provider is prescribing a treatment rather than inviting the client to participate in determining what treatment will be best for him.

Somewhat MI-Consistent: *"Would you like to talk about treatment options that might help you regain your life?"*

This provider utterance is somewhat MI-consistent. The provider asks the client permission to discuss treatment options. By asking permission and using the word "options," the provider enhances the sense of collaboration and client autonomy. However, the provider does not seek to elicit the client's desire, ability, reasons, need, or commitment for change before moving to treatment planning. The provider also uses a closed question, which invites only a brief response from the client.

MI-Consistent: *"So this has been really hard on you. Tell me a little about what has been different or bad about your life since the car accident."*

This provider utterance is MI-consistent, because it begins with an empathic reflection of the client's comment about his life being ruined. The provider then invites the client to explain in more detail exactly how the car accident has negatively impacted him. The more change talk statements the provider elicits, the more likely the client will decide he is ready to commit to treatment (Amrhein, Miller, Yahne, Palmer, & Fulcher, 2003).

Proposed Strategy 4: Offering Choices

As outlined in chapter 2, a component of the foundational spirit of MI is acceptance, which includes "autonomy support"—that is, provider support of the client's right to choose the best course of action for him- or herself (see also Miller & Rollnick, 2013). Thus in discussing treatment, an MI-consistent provider should strive to offer objective information about options available to the client, including the potential pros and cons of each option. The provider should then collaborate with the client in deciding which course of action is best, keeping in mind that the client is the final arbiter of what he or she will or will not do. As I (JS) advise the medical students each year during a brief lecture on practices and principles of MI, no matter what the treatment outcome literature and practice guidelines say, a treatment that the client will not adhere to is probably not the best treatment for that client.

In the case of anxiety, trauma-related, and obsessive-compulsive disorders, clients have many treatment options ranging from no treatment, to medications, to cognitive or behavioral psychotherapies, to supportive psychotherapy. Providers should be knowledgeable about treatment outcome data and practice guidelines to offer clients accurate and objective information about the implications of selecting a particular intervention, completing between-session assignments, and/or dropping out of treatment before it is completed. Keep in mind that while it is MI-consistent for the provider to share his or her professional opinion about the best intervention option for a client (e.g., "Although what you decide is ultimately up to you, my professional opinion is that cognitive behavioral therapy would be a much better option for you than medication."), it is MI-inconsistent for the provider to impose it on the client (e.g., "Cognitive behavioral therapy is really the only option for you.").

Example: MI-Consistent/Inconsistent Offering Choices

The following examples with Sanjay, the 18-year old with social anxiety, illustrate how a provider might offer choices to a client in an MI-consistent fashion.

Client Statement: *"I don't see why I have to graduate high school. My father didn't graduate and he makes a lot of money in construction."*

MI-Inconsistent: *"Things are different now, Sanjay. It is a lot harder to make a decent living without a diploma than it used to be."*

This statement is MI-inconsistent because instead of empathically acknowledging the client's perspective, and perhaps inviting another perspective, the provider seeks to directly counter the client's perspective and impose the provider's perspective.

Somewhat MI-Consistent: *"Dropping out of high school is certainly an option."*

This statement is somewhat MI-consistent. The provider supports Sanjay's autonomy by acknowledging that dropping out of high school is an option. However, the provider does not present other options that might help Sanjay move in his preferred direction. Although Sanjay is expressing a desire to drop out, the desire seems to be driven largely if not entirely by a belief that dropping out is the only way to reduce his anxiety. As Miller and Rollnick (2013) note, there may be occasions when a provider uses MI to help a client consider goals in the client's best interest, even when a client doesn't initially endorse those goals.

MI-Consistent: *"This has obviously become unbearable for you, Sanjay, and you feel like you need to do something. You have a lot of options in how to deal with this, and dropping out of school is certainly one of them. As a school counselor, my job is to help you select the solution that is best for you all things considered. I have some ideas of things that you may or may not think will be helpful to you, such as working with a counselor like me either alone or with your parents to learn skills and strategies to attend class without feeling anxious, talking to your doctor about medications that might help you manage your anxiety, scheduling meetings to talk to your teachers about the problems you've been having and asking for their help, talking to other students who used to have the same feelings you have about how they got past it. I will tell you my thoughts about the pros and cons of each of these options, but first I'd like to hear your thoughts about these ideas and whether you maybe have some others we should put on the list for consideration."*

This provider utterance is MI-consistent, because it begins with an empathic reflection and then supports the client's autonomy to choose his own solution for the problem. It is further MI-consistent because rather than immediately telling the client what she thinks is best solution is, the provider first lists available options and seeks his perspective on them.

Proposed Strategy 5: Emphasizing Control

Many providers who treat anxiety, trauma-related, and obsessive compulsive disorders recognize that avoidance is a symptom of the client's disorder and thus feel compelled to push clients to work through and overcome it, doing so in a non-collaborative fashion that does not support client autonomy is MI-inconsistent. Although it is counterintuitive for many providers, we have found that emphasizing control when clients are having the most difficulty engaging in treatment is a very useful strategy for helping clients overcome avoidance. In our experience, clients who are particularly uncertain about their ability to tolerate treatment may begin almost every in-session exposure practice with a statement of uncertainty and reluctance about continuing with treatment. This is followed, of course, by a statement from the provider supporting the client's autonomy and right to choose what they do or do not do in a particular session.

Example: MI-Consistent/Inconsistent Emphasizing Control

The following example illustrates how a provider might use emphasizing control to address the clinical challenge of avoidance with Jamal, the man who is suffering from motor vehicle accident–related PTSD.

Client Statement: *"I'm not sure I can handle the exposure today."*

MI-Inconsistent: *"It is important for you to go on, Jamal."*

This statement is MI-inconsistent because the provider does not acknowledge the client's concerns or support his autonomy, and instead directly confronts his reluctance to participate in treatment.

Somewhat MI-Consistent: *"Why can't you handle it, Jamal?"*

This question is somewhat MI-consistent. It is an open question and thus elicits the client's perspective. However, it is a question that elicits sustain talk, and thus will encourage the client to talk about why he can't move toward his own treatment goals, rather than why he can. Additionally, the specific wording of the question ("Why can't you... ") may be perceived as confrontational by the client. It implies that the provider thinks the client should be able to handle it.

MI-Consistent: *"Jamal, you are in control here. It is entirely up to you whether you do the exposure today. As we've discussed before, you know that my recommendation is that you do it, because the more you confront what you fear, the less you will fear it. But ultimately it is up to you whether to do the practice today."*

This provider utterance is MI-consistent because although the provider reminds the client of previously discussed information about the importance of completing exposure practices, the provider also repeatedly supports the client's autonomy and right to decide not to do the practice.

Proposed Strategy 6: Planning

As outlined further in the discussion of "Proposed Strategy 7: Envisioning," many clients may underestimate the extent to which avoidance might interfere with their ability to successfully complete treatment for an anxiety, trauma-related, or obsessive compulsive disorder. Helping a client prepare for the possibility that avoidance might interfere with his or her ability to participate in a desired treatment is another MI-consistent strategy for addressing this clinical challenge. As described in chapter 3, during MI-consistent planning the provider works collaboratively with the client to devise strategies to address avoidance when and if it occurs. The provider should also revisit and update this plan as needed to ensure that the client is successful in achieving his or her goal of overcoming avoidance in order to successfully complete treatment.

Example: MI-Consistent/Inconsistent Planning

The following examples illustrate how a provider might use planning to help a client, such as Jamal, prepare to successfully overcome treatment avoidance.

Client Statement: *"I'm willing to give this treatment a try, but I'm not really sure about it."*

MI-Inconsistent: *"Jamal, your reluctance is probably based on avoidance, which is a symptom of posttraumatic stress disorder. You need to come to sessions regularly even if you don't feel like it. Will you do that?"*

Although the provider begins with information provision about avoidance, which is not MI-inconsistent, the provider goes on to tell the client what to do about the avoidance, which is MI-inconsistent. Telling the client what to do is not collaborative, and may diminish the client's sense of autonomy.

Somewhat MI-Consistent: *"Jamal, I would recommend that you use breathing exercises and positive self-statements whenever you feel uncertain about treatment. But that may or may not be the best strategy for you."*

The provider offers advice with permission to disregard, which is MI-consistent and promotes some sense of autonomy and collaboration. However, the response overall is only somewhat MI-consistent because the provider offers this advice without first eliciting Jamal's thoughts about what might help him participate in treatment. Thus the collaboration is lukewarm.

MI-Consistent: *"Jamal, if I may provide some information, your reluctance is probably based on avoidance, which is a symptom of posttraumatic stress disorder. Many clients who really want to overcome posttraumatic stress disorder, but are uncertain about treatment find it beneficial to discuss ahead of time what they will do if they begin finding it difficult to continue to treatment. Would it be okay if we did that now? [Provider waits for affirmative response]. Let's start off by discussing what types of things might make you decide that treatment is too difficult or you don't want to continue."*

This provider utterance is MI-consistent, because it begins with information provision and then segues into an invitation to the client to participate collaboratively in devising a strategy to address avoidance.

One way we have framed these plans in our own work is "Making a Plan for Successful Treatment." Change plan worksheets, such as the one in Table 6.4, are commonly used in MI (e.g., Miller & Rollnick, 2002).

Proposed Strategy 7: Envisioning

We have found that helping clients realistically envision what treatment might be like is often a useful strategy for clients who have unrealistic expectations (see also chapter 5). Given that the reality of treatment for most clients is that it is beneficial and manageable, but requires emotionally intense and perhaps time-consuming hard work, this strategy will often result in clients voicing a small amount of sustain talk. An example of the type of utterance that might result from use of envisioning with a client who has unrealistic expectations of treatment might be, "I guess maybe the exposure practices might be hard, but if I think about how much it will help me, it will keep me going." Although eliciting sustain talk is in most

Table 6.4. SAMPLE PLAN FOR SUCCESSFUL TREATMENT

Making a Plan for Successful Treatment-Example

The most important reasons why I want to successfully complete treatment are:

1. So I can get my life back.

2. So I can drive without fear.

3. So I stop thinking about the accident all the time.

4. So I don't teach my kids to be afraid of driving.

To successfully complete treatment I must:*

1. Attend treatment regularly.

2. Complete in-session practices to the best of my ability.

3. Complete all homework assignments to the best of my ability.

Some things that could interfere with successful completion of treatment are:

1. My temper—sometimes when I get scared, I get angry and just say "forget about it".

2. My priorities—I may decide that I need to work or do other things besides completing treatment.

3. Something will happen with my family that makes me feel like I need to stop treatment.

4. I may talk myself out of it.

The ways other people can help me are:

1. My family can encourage me to keep going.

2. My therapist can encourage me and remind me that the end is in sight.

3. My therapist can call me if I miss an appointment and encourage me to reschedule.

What I will do if I am not "sticking with" treatment the way I had hoped or am considering dropping out:

1. Be honest with myself, and not blame other people for my part in this difficulty.

2. Remind myself of how bad things were and how many times I've tricked myself into avoiding things because I'm anxious.

3. Remind myself that I am strong and I can do this!

4. Pray for strength, courage, patience, wisdom—whatever I need to make it through the difficult time.

5. Ask family, friends, and others for support and a pep talk.

6. Remember all the success I have had in treatment.

* Many ideas for what to list in this section may be offered by the provider as the provider will be more knowledgeable about the components of the treatment the client has selected.

cases an MI-inconsistent strategy, eliciting a small amount of sustain talk is sometimes helpful in preparing clients who do not have a realistic perspective on the potential difficulties of exposure-based treatment. Nonetheless, it is a strategy we recommend be used sparingly and only when clinical judgment suggests it is warranted. We personally use this strategy only when a client expresses a strong belief that an exposure-based treatment for anxiety will be easy and he cannot imagine encountering any difficulties when completing it. For example, if a provider says, "This exposure-based treatment for anxiety will involve repeatedly coming into contact with those things that make you most anxious and staying in the situation for a predetermined amount of time, such as 30 minutes, or until your anxiety diminished by 50%. What questions or concerns do you have?" If the client says, "I don't have any concerns, it sounds straightforward. Let's get started," the provider may wish to help the client better envision what treatment will really be like and gain a more realistic perspective on the treatment. This will help ensure that the client is not disappointed, or does not feel like a failure if he or she does experience difficulty with treatment at some later point.

Example: MI-Consistent/Inconsistent Envisioning

The following examples illustrate this likely controversial, but potentially very useful strategy as a provider and client discuss treatment for posttraumatic stress disorder.

Client Statement: *"I don't have any concerns. PTSD has ruined my life and I'll do anything it takes to get past it."*

MI-Inconsistent: *"It doesn't sound like you are being very honest with yourself."*

This provider utterance is MI-inconsistent because the provider directly confronts the client's optimism, which is not collaborative and does not support the client's autonomy.

Somewhat MI-Consistent: *"Tell me one concern that you might have about PTSD treatment."*

This provider utterance is somewhat MI-consistent. It is an open question ("tell me" statements are considered open questions in MI) and thus invites a lengthy answer from the client. However, given the context (the client has just stated "I don't have any concerns"), it is likely to elicit discord. The client may feel that the provider is not listening—or worse yet, may feel confronted by the provider.

MI-Consistent: *"So you are very confident and ready to go. Many people who go through this treatment find that it is more difficult or more intense than they expected. What do you think might happen in treatment that might make you feel less certain about wanting to continue with it?"*

Although the provider is likely to elicit a small amount of sustain talk by asking the client to envision what might be difficult in treatment, which as stated is not strictly MI-consistent, the provider does so in an MI-consistent fashion. The provider first empathically reflects the client's optimism and then objectively provides information that does not directly counter what the client has said, but perhaps gives him food for thought. Finally, the provider asks an open question seeking to elicit the client's perspective on what might happen that might be difficult in treatment. This then allows the provider to work with the client to plan for and successfully overcome these barriers as discussed in Proposed Strategy 6.

CLINICAL CHALLENGE 3: PSYCHOTIC SYMPTOMS

Description

Psychosis refers to a loss of contact with reality that usually includes false beliefs about what is taking place or who one is (delusions) or seeing, hearing, smelling, tasting, or feeling things that aren't there (hallucinations). In addition to hallucinations and delusions, other symptoms of psychosis include disorganized thoughts, speech, and behavior. Psychosis can be caused by a number of medical problems, such as alcohol and drug use or withdrawal, and diseases or tumors that affect the brain, as well as psychiatric disorders such as schizophrenia, bipolar disorder, severe depression, and some personality disorders. Although treatment depends on the cause of the psychosis, it typically includes an antipsychotic medication (Cohen, 2010). MI shows promise for helping individuals with psychotic disorders, particularly schizophrenia, better adhere to necessary medications (Drymalski & Campbell, 2009) and make other positive changes in their lives, such as decreased problematic alcohol consumption (Graeber, Moyers, Griffith, Guajardo, & Tonigan, 2003) and increased contact with smoking cessation professionals (Steinberg, Ziedonis, Krejci, & Brandon, 2004). Nonetheless, psychotic symptoms and disorders present unique challenges to the implementation of MI (e.g., Rusch & Corrigan, 2002). More than once community providers have tried to "stump" us by role playing a client with psychotic symptoms during a training event.

Example: *Roger is a 63-year-old man who has been diagnosed with schizophrenia and is being cared for in a board and care home. Roger's adherence to his antipsychotic medications has varied over the past 40 years. During periods of lower adherence, he often spends months or years living on the street until his family tracks him down and he is admitted to an inpatient psychiatric facility for stabilization. Recently, Roger's physical health has worsened, and the staff at the board and care home believe Roger will need to be cared for in a skilled nursing facility. For example, due to his medical condition Roger often falls. Because of his large stature, Regina, the weekend house manager at the board and care facility (a petite woman), has difficulty assisting Roger when this occurs. This difficulty is compounded by the fact that Roger is often shouting incoherently after a fall and has difficulty responding to Regina's instructions. Roger seems to have little insight into his physical health concerns, and has dismissed staff attempts to initiate discussions with him about their concerns. Almost as soon as these discussions are initiated, Roger insists that he is in peak physical condition because the CIA has injected him with experimental drugs to enhance his performance.*

How would you respond to Roger? Would you argue with Roger about the unreality of his beliefs? Would you recommend that the psychiatrist increase his medications so he is too sedated to leave his bed? Would you go to the court to have Roger committed to a nursing home for his own safety? Would you quit your job at the board and care home and find a less stressful position? The text will outline several MI-consistent strategies that may be useful when working with clients who have delusions, hallucinations, or disorganized thoughts and behaviors. However, it is important to note that adaptations to commonly used MI strategies are often necessary when working with individuals who suffer from psychotic symptoms or disorders. Carey, Leontieva, Dimmock, Maisto, and Batki (2007) have recommended adapting motivational enhancement protocols for individuals with schizophrenia to include more frequent, briefer sessions. Carey and colleagues describe the potential benefits of this adaptation for clients with schizophrenia as: (1) decreased demands on attention; (2) increased opportunities for clients to learn how to respond to an MI-style intervention; (3) greater repetition of and elaboration of content; (4) better integration of real-life events into discussions; and (5) attenuated impact of a "bad day" (e.g., a day on which symptoms or stressors are much worse) on overall treatment outcome. Martino, Carroll, Kostas, Perkins, and Rounsaville (2002) recommend several adaptations of MI for individuals with psychotic disorders to accommodate disordered thinking and cognitive impairments, such as simplifying open-ended questions (e.g., avoiding compound questions), emphasizing the provider role in guiding the conversation to promote logical organization and reality testing, reducing reflections focused on disturbing life experiences, and increasing emphasis on affirmations of the client. It is important to note that many of these strategies as well as those presented here, are less appropriate or less effective for clients who are highly disorganized or agitated.

Proposed Strategy 1: Giving Information

It has been our experience that some clients who have been involved in the medical, substance abuse treatment, or criminal justice systems for a long period of time experience initial surprise or uncertainty when working with a provider who is using an MI-consistent approach. For example, they may provide very short answers in response to open questions or sit in silence after a provider offers a reflective listening statement. Client uncertainty is not surprising given how dissimilar MI is from many of the directive approaches most commonly employed in those settings and from interpersonal interactions in general (Amrhein et al.,

2003). Despite this initial uncertainty, we have found that most of these clients readily adapt to MI spirit and techniques, and very actively and fully participate in the interaction within a few minutes. As Martino and colleagues (2002) note, individuals with disordered or disorganized thinking may have more difficulty adapting readily to an MI style. Thus, they recommend providing the client with an informative overview prior to an MI-style interaction. During this overview the client is informed not only of the purpose of the interaction, but also the roles that the client and provider will have during the interaction.

Example: MI-Consistent/Inconsistent Giving Information

The following examples illustrate how giving information can be used to orient clients with cognitive impairments to an MI-style interaction.

Client Statement: *"How long is this going to take? I haven't had a cigarette in hours."*

MI-Inconsistent: *"Roger, you can have a cigarette after we're done. The staff has decided that we can no longer care for you here. We are going to recommend to your case worker that you be placed in a skilled nursing facility. Do you have any questions?"*

This provider utterance is MI-inconsistent because the provider does not attempt to collaborate with Roger. Instead the provider dismisses Roger's request for information about the length of the appointment and his obvious desire for a smoke break. Then the provider assumes the expert role and tells Roger that a decision has been made about his care. The final question is almost MI-consistent, in that the provider seeks to get Roger's perspective on what he has just been told, but it is phrased as a closed question, which invites Roger to provide only a brief answer (e.g., "yes" or "no") rather than a more lengthy response.

Somewhat MI-Consistent: *"This will take about 15 minutes Roger."*

This provider response is somewhat MI-consistent in that the provider answers the client's question in an objective fashion. However, the provider does not ask the client's permission to continue the interaction or provide any information about the purpose of the interaction and thus does not support the client's autonomy or set the stage for the client to collaborate in the interaction.

MI-Consistent: *"I know you really want a cigarette right now, and at the same time I'd really like about 15 minutes of your time to discuss something important. Would that be okay? [Waits for client response]. Roger, I'd like to talk to you a little bit about the good experiences and not-so-good experiences you've had with us over the last few months and what the best options for housing might be for you. I'm really interested in learning about what you think and feel about your housing, so although I may ask you a few questions here and there, I'm really just interested in hearing what you have to say. Tell me what you like about living in this house, Roger."*

This provider utterance is MI-consistent because it begins with a reflection of Roger's desire for a cigarette and an answer to his question. This demonstrates empathy and also establishes a collaborative atmosphere. The provider asks Roger's permission to continue the interaction, which supports Roger's autonomy and further promotes a collaborative atmosphere. The provider then offers Roger information to help orient Roger to an MI-style interaction during which the pros and cons of his current living arrangement will be reviewed. This should prepare Roger to collaborate more actively in the discussion. It is important to note that using an MI style does not guarantee that Roger will agree with the staff's determination that they are no longer able to provide adequate, safe care for him and that it is time for him to move to another type of facility. Thus the staff at the board and care home may ultimately have to go against Roger's wishes to stay at their facility. Nonetheless, engaging Roger in a discussion that invites his perspective and allows him to control those aspects of the situation that are under his control (e.g., the location of the facility to which he transfers) support and emphasize the autonomy that Roger does have.

Proposed Strategy 2: Asking Permission

Asking permission before giving information or advice is an MI-consistent strategy to increase the sense of collaboration and support of client autonomy during an interaction (Moyers, Martin, Manuel, Miller, & Ernst, 2010). Asking permission can also help add additional structure to an interaction when clients have difficulty keeping their own thoughts or speech organized. This approach is not uncommon in standard implementation of MI and MI hybrid interventions such as motivational enhancement (Miller et al., 1992) or motivational interviewing assessment (Martino et al., 2006). For example, in an MI session, the transition from eliciting to planning might be marked by a provider utterance such as "If it is okay with you, I'd like to shift gears and begin developing a plan for helping your reach your goals." However, more frequent use of such utterances than would be typical may be beneficial for clients who have difficulty sustaining as structured, focused dialogue on a particular topic.

Example: MI-Consistent/Inconsistent Asking Permission

The following examples illustrate how a provider might use giving information to help a client maintain focus throughout the session:

Client Statement: *"I've been taking my medications every day. There's no problem with that."*

MI-Inconsistent: *"I know you are taking them right now, Roger, but it is important for us to talk about the times you haven't been taking them. Every time you stop taking them you decompensate."*

Although the provider acknowledges the client's recent success with medication adherence, which is MI-consistent, the provider quickly dismisses this success and shifts the focus in a non-collaborative fashion to times the client has been less successful, which is MI-inconsistent. The provider then offers information about medication adherence not to inform the client, but to confront him about the problems his past behavior has caused.

Somewhat MI-Consistent: *"If it's okay with you, I'd like for us to talk about the times when you haven't been taking your medication."*

This statement is somewhat MI-consistent because the provider seeks the client's permission to discuss medication adherence. However, given that the client has just stated that he has been compliant with his medication, the specific wording of this utterance is likely to be perceived by the client as non-collaborative. The provider also misses an excellent opportunity to affirm a client who is obviously seeking positive feedback from the provider.

MI-Consistent: *"You've been quite successful with your medications for the last several months, Roger. That's really impressive. If it's okay with you I'd like to spend at least a few minutes talking about what has sometimes made it hard to be successful in the past. Many clients find their symptoms worsen and they lose a lot of progress when they stop taking their medications."*

This provider utterance is MI-consistent because it begins with an affirmation of the client's success. The provider then asks permission to change the topic to possible reasons for past adherence, but is careful to do so in a way that does not diminish the prior affirmation of the client's success. The provider also offers information about the importance of discussing medication adherence, but does so in the third person, which makes it less likely to arouse defensiveness (Rollnick et al., 2008).

Proposed Strategy 3: Summarizing

As noted in chapter 2, summaries are an opportunity for the provider to pull together and synthesize several of statements the client has made. When used in MI, summaries are often selective. That is, the provider may choose to include key points the client has made, such as "change talk" statements, while omitting other things the client has said that are less relevant to the focus of the interaction. Martino et al. (2002) suggest that summaries can be used to provide logical organization to client statements. Thus, with clients who may have disorganized or tangential thinking, a careful summary can be used to organize a client's thoughts for him or her. Not surprisingly, reflecting or summarizing is much more challenging for providers who work with clients suffering from psychotic disorders (Martino et al., 2002), and thus may be difficult for those who are new to MI to implement effectively.

Example: MI-Consistent/Inconsistent Summarizing

The following examples illustrate how a provider might use summarizing to help a client organize his or her thoughts in a meaningful way.

Client Statement: *"I've been taking my medications every day. There's no problem with that. My case worker just wants me to go to the nursing home because she works for 'them.' I think she's been poisoning me. That's probably why I'm falling. The drugs the CIA gives me have been helping. I think they must be an antidote. Can I have a smoke break? I get really nervous when I can't smoke. I think the CIA agent is coming back tomorrow. Can you call my case worker? I want to see my sister."*

MI-Inconsistent: *"Roger, you know the CIA isn't giving you any medications."*

This statement is not a summary and is MI-inconsistent because the provider directly confronts the client's delusional thinking. Although the provider is accurate, the manner in which he addresses the client's delusional thinking is not collaborative and diminishes his sense of autonomy.

Somewhat MI-consistent: *"So you think she's been poisoning you and that she works for them."*

This statement is somewhat MI-consistent because the provider summarizes a portion of what the client has said. However, the material summarized is unlikely to move the client toward positive change. Instead, the summary is likely to get the client to expound upon his delusional beliefs.

MI-Consistent: *"You've been quite successful with your medications for the last several months, Roger. It seems like it is important to you to take care of yourself. I'm hearing that the falls are concerning to you, but you are less convinced that the nursing home is the solution. It sounds like the case worker has talked to you a bit about why the staff has recommended that for you. Would it be okay if I shared a little bit more about the types of benefits we thought a nursing home might have for you?"*

This provider utterance is MI-consistent because the provider selectively reflects statements the client made that support positive, healthy changes. The provider reflects on the client's medication adherence and guesses that this might reflect an underlying desire he has to take care of his health. The provider also reflects the client's brief mention about the falls as a potential concern. Finally, the provider asks the client's permission to share additional information about the staff's recommendation. This supports client autonomy and sets the tone for a collaborative discussion about the nursing home.

Proposed Strategy 4: Reflective Listening

In our work training providers who work with individuals who have delusional thinking, one issue that appears particularly challenging is how to stay

MI-consistent without colluding with the delusions—that is, without providing additional evidence to support the delusional belief (Nelson, 2005). During training role plays, when the "client" makes a delusional statement such as: "The house manager stole my sweater!" we find that providers generally respond in one of two ways: (1) they calmly, but directly confront the client statement: "No, she didn't. No one is stealing from you." in an effort to help bring the client back into contact with reality; or (2) they reflect the delusional content as though it were reality-based: "The house manager stole your sweater." The first statement avoids supporting a delusional belief, but is likely to increase discord in the provider-client interaction. Although more MI-consistent, the second statement may serve to reinforce the client's inaccurate paranoid beliefs about the house manager and encourage the client to continue talking about them. Instead of direct confrontation or collusion, we recommend that providers strategically reflect whatever aspect of the client statement or interaction *is* reality based. In some cases, the emotion that seems to underlie the client's statements (e.g., fear, anger) or the process unfolding between the client and provider (e.g., frustration, misunderstanding) may be the only reality-based material available. An example would be: "You sometimes feel unsure of who you can trust."

Example: MI-Consistent/Inconsistent Reflective Listening

The following examples illustrate how a provider might use reflecting to emphasize reality-based statements by a client who has disorganized or delusional thinking.

Client Statement: *"My case worker just wants me to go to the nursing home because she works for "them." I think she's been poisoning me."*

MI-Inconsistent: *"Roger, you know the case worker is not poisoning you."*

This statement is not a reflection and is MI-inconsistent. Although the provider is accurate, her direct confrontation of the client's delusional thinking is not collaborative and diminishes his sense of autonomy.

Somewhat MI-Consistent: *"Roger that must be very frightening to have the case worker out to get you."*

This statement is a reflection and technically is MI-consistent. However, because it is a reflection of a delusional belief, it does not help move the client in a direction of positive change. Instead, it may serve to more deeply entrench the client's delusional beliefs, as a person of authority has agreed with them (Nelson, 2005).

MI-Consistent: *"You're not convinced that a nursing home is the right placement for you, so you question the staff's motives for recommending one."*

This provider utterance is MI-consistent because the provider reflects the client's disagreement about the appropriateness of a nursing home and his difficulty accepting the staff's recommendation given that he doesn't agree with their appraisal of his physical condition. The statement does not directly confront the delusional belief, nor does it in any way support the client's erroneous belief that he is being poisoned or that the case worker is aligned with some nefarious organization. The utterance also helps guide the client toward a meaningful discussion of a key issue that staff needs to discuss with him—the recommendation for placement in a nursing home.

Proposed Strategy 5: Shifting Focus

Sometimes a client with psychotic symptoms is so caught up in a pattern of delusional or disorganized thinking that the best strategy may be helping the client shift attention away from the disorganized or delusional pattern of thinking. An MI strategy termed "shifting focus" can be very helpful in this regard. As Miller and Rollnick (2002) highlight, this strategy amounts to going around the barrier to productive discussion rather than trying to climb over it. It is important to note that when this strategy is applied in an MI-consistent fashion, it typically involves first acknowledging the client's concern and then guiding the client to a discussion of a workable issue. Without acknowledgement of the client's concern (be it reality-based or not), this strategy has the potential to cast the provider in the expert role and the client in a passive role.

Example: MI-Consistent/Inconsistent Shifting Focus

The following examples illustrate how a provider might use shifting focus in an MI-consistent fashion to help a client who is stuck in a pattern of delusional or disorganized thinking.

Client Statement: *"My case worker just wants me to go to the nursing home because she works for 'them.' I think she's been poisoning me."*

MI-Inconsistent: *"That's not really why I called you here today. I called you here today because we need to talk to you about your medical issues."*

This provider utterance is MI-inconsistent because the provider actively dismisses the client's concerns and shifts to the topic of medical concerns in a very non-collaborative fashion. This approach is likely to promote discord between client and the provider or cause the client to assume a passive role in the interaction.

Somewhat MI-Consistent: *"So you're still worried about your case worker. What do you think we should do about that?"*

In this response the provider first reflects what the client has said and then asks a question to gather more information. Thus, the response is somewhat MI-consistent. However, what the provider chooses to reflect and the question the provider chooses to ask focus the discussion on a topic that is not likely to lead to positive change. Since the case worker is not really poisoning the client, developing solutions to that problem is likely to have little benefit for the client and may increase the intensity of his delusional beliefs.

MI-Consistent: *"You don't feel like a nursing home is going to be the best fit for you, and you're questioning the case worker's motive for recommending it. What are the important things you are looking for in a place to live?"*

This provider utterance is MI-consistent because the provider acknowledges the client's concerns using reflective listening. Note that the provider empathically reflected the client's concerns without agreeing either implicitly or explicitly that he is being poisoned or that his case worker works for "them." The provider then uses an open question to help shift focus to a workable, but related issue: what characteristics the client looks for in a place to live.

Proposed Strategy 6: Stacked Questions

Martino et al. (2002) recommend simplifying open questions for clients with schizophrenia. Specifically, they recommend avoiding complex open questions such as, "What do you think your family would think about the nursing home and how does that impact your willingness to consider it?" A complex open question such as that can be difficult even for very high functioning individual with no cognitive impairments. I (JS) remember a time when a grand rounds speaker in our department was asked a compound open question, and as one might expect, she responded to the first part of the question and then had to ask the questioner to repeat the second part of the question because she had forgotten it. For clients who have problems with organizing their thinking, these types of questions can be very confusing and overwhelming. Simple phrasing of open questions, such as: "What do you think your family would think about the nursing home?" [Waits for client response]. "How does that impact your willingness to consider a nursing home?" are likely to be much more effective.

It has been our experience that even when phrased simply, clients with cognitive impairments such as disorganized thinking may have some difficulty responding to open questions. Sometimes, even with a simple open question, the client may feel unsure of what is being asked. The use of stacked questions can help clients who have difficulty responding to simple open questions. Asking the client an open question followed by a series of closed questions intended to give the client a sense of what types of answers would address the open question can be useful in this situation. This has been referred to as stacked questions (Moyers et al. 2010) and is useful because it gives a client the confidence and certainty to respond to an open question without narrowing the focus in the way a closed question does.

Example: MI-Consistent/Inconsistent Stacked Questions

The following examples illustrate how a provider might use stacked questions to help a client who is having difficulty responding to open questions.

Client Statement: *"My case worker just wants me to go to the nursing home because she works for 'them.' I think she's been poisoning me."*

MI-Inconsistent: *"Poisoning you? Are you sure? There isn't any evidence for that is there, Roger?"*

This provider utterance includes stacked questions, but is not MI-consistent. All of the questions are a direct confrontation of the client's statement. This diminishes the client's sense of autonomy as well as the sense of collaboration in the interview. Additionally, the questions keep the focus on the delusional content, instead of trying to guide the client toward a more productive discussion of the pressing issue at hand—how the client would like to handle his need for greater medical care than the board and care home can provide.

Somewhat MI-Consistent: *"What do you want to do? Do you want to go to the nursing home? Or do you want to see if your sister will let you move in with her?"*

This response is somewhat MI-consistent. The provider starts off with an open question that invites the client to share his preferences. By asking what the client wants, the provider also offers some support for client autonomy by expressing that what the client wants matters. However, instead of providing the client with a menu of possible ways to answer the open question, the closed questions that follow the initial question serve to narrow the range of possible answers to the question.

MI-Consistent: *"What benefits might there be to moving somewhere like a nursing home? For example, wouldn't it be nice to have people available 24-7 when you aren't feeling well? Would it be good to be somewhere closer to your family? Would you feel less anxious if you had your own room rather than having to share? ... "*

This provider utterance is MI-consistent because the provider asks an open question to gain the client's perspective. Even though the open question is followed by closed questions, the intent of these questions is to provide the client with clarity about the spirit of the provider's question as well as the sense that there are a range of "right" answers to the question that has been posed. This may enhance the client's ability and confidence to provide a meaningful answer to the question and thus collaborate actively with the provider in exploring the pros and cons of an alternative housing situation, such as a nursing home.

Table 6.5. SUMMARY OF MOTIVATIONAL INTERVIEWING STRATEGIES FOR CLINICAL CHALLENGES RELATED TO PSYCHIATRIC SYMPTOMS

Clinical Challenge	Suggested MI Strategies
Depression: Clients suffering from depression experience hopelessness, feelings of worthlessness or guilt, difficulty concentrating, and lack of interest in activities that may make it difficult for them to fully engage with a provider or change process.	Hypothetical Questions: Hypothetical questions invite a client to consider the possibility of change without committing to it. These questions can help clients who are feeling hopeless consider potential solutions or benefits of change, even if they are currently feeling pessimistic about the possibility of change.
	Planning: Planning involves helping a client think through the concrete details of how desired change will be accomplished. A concrete plan may help clients who are feeling pessimistic become more hopeful about the possibility of change.
	Envisioning: Envisioning involves asking a client to imagine what the future would be like if they were to make a change. This strategy may be helpful for clients who respond to questions about past negative consequences of their behavior in an overly self-deprecating fashion because they are experiencing excessive guilt or feelings of worthlessness.
	Affirming: Affirmations, which involve commenting on a client's strengths or abilities in any area, can help clients experiencing feelings of worthlessness or guilt to view themselves as capable of change. Summarizing: Frequent summaries of key points in the conversation may enhance engagement for clients who have difficulty concentrating. Handouts: Providing clients who have difficulty concentrating with MI-consistent handouts, such as a decisional balance or change plan, may help them better remember key points covered during a conversation about change. Looking Back: Asking a client to think about what things were like before their depression emerged can help clients who currently lack interest in activities to identify activities they might enjoy or find rewarding.

(continued)

Table 6.5. CONTINUED

Clinical Challenge	Suggested MI Strategies
Anxiety: Clients diagnosed with anxiety or related disorders may avoid essential aspects of treatment, including appointments with their provider, because participating fully in treatment causes anxiety or distress.	Empathic Listening: Listening carefully to a client in an attempt to really understand his or her perspective may help a provider to fully appreciate that the distress associated with anxiety and related disorders is more than the nervousness we all experience in certain situations.
	Assessment Feedback: Providing clients with objective feedback on an anxiety assessment may help clients better recognize the ways in which anxiety and related disorders are impacting their lives.
	Evocation: Using evocative questions to help a client articulate his or her reasons for change may help a client who has not been fully participating in an intervention due to anxiety develop sufficient motivation to endure the intervention despite their anxiety.
	Offering Choices: Offering the client choices about intervention options available to him or her enables the client to choose the intervention option that is best for him or her all things (including anxiety) considered.
	Emphasizing Control: Emphasizing that the client is the one who ultimately has to choose what he or she will or will not do may help empower a client who is avoiding treatment due to anxiety or related disorders to actively engage in treatment despite their distress.
	Planning: Clients who may avoid treatment due to symptoms of anxiety or related disorders may benefit from making a plan for what they will do if they find themselves considering avoiding an appointment or other treatment activity.
	Envisioning: Helping a client envision what treatment can be like may be helpful to clients who suffer from anxiety or related disorders and underestimate how difficult treatment might be given their symptoms.
Psychotic Symptoms: Clients who experience symptoms of psychotic disorders including disorganized	Giving Information: Before attempting to utilize MI-consistent strategies with an individual suffering from psychotic symptoms, it can be helpful to give information about the type of conversation you are hoping to have with the individual. Many MI-consistent strategies are so unlike typical communication strategies that they might lead to confusion or uncertainty without this preface.

Clinical Challenge	Suggested MI Strategies
thoughts, speech, and behavior, as well as delusions, may have difficulty actively participating in many types of interventions.	Asking Permission: Asking permission to discuss a particular topic may a useful strategy for guiding disorganized clients back to the topic of discussion each time the discussion veers off topic.
	Summarizing: Using summaries may be helpful when working with clients who have disorganized thinking. With a summary the provider may help the client organize his or her thoughts in a meaningful way.
	Reflective Listening: Providers may use reflections to selectively emphasize reality-based content embedded within a delusional client utterance.
	Shifting Focus: A provider may use an open question to shift the focus from a tangential or delusion topic to a topic that is more likely to guide the client in the direction of positive change.
	Stacked Questions: Some clients with thought disorders may be uncertain how to respond to open questions. Following an open question with a series of closed questions that seek to clarify the intent of the question for a client may be helpful for clients who feel uncertain of how they should respond to the open question.

CHAPTER SUMMARY

In our own work, we have found that the principles and practices of MI can be very fruitfully applied to some of the unique challenges encountered when working with clients who are experiencing psychiatric symptoms or disorders. These challenges include things such as hopelessness, lack of interest in activities, difficulty concentrating, avoidance, and disorganized or delusional thinking. Given that psychiatric illnesses are very common, mental health professionals are not the only ones likely to encounter these unique challenges. Thus we attempted to provide practical, non-technical descriptions of these symptoms and disorders so that non–mental health providers can more readily identify clients who may benefit from referral to mental health treatment and who may also benefit from MI-consistent strategies to help them overcome barriers to change introduced by their psychiatric illness. A summary of these strategies can be found in Table 6.5.

7

Working with Multiple Individuals

Up to this point we have discussed clinical challenges related to working with one individual. However, many providers work with multiple individuals simultaneously. This work may take the form of seeing a couple about marital issues or parenting, providing education to a group of clients, or facilitating disorder-specific treatment groups. Working with more than one person in an MI-consistent way requires simultaneously attending to a variety of concerns and client factors. Thus, the MI-consistent provider needs to attend to things like ambivalence, change talk, sustain talk, and discord as they uniquely apply to each individual. It is likely that these variables are different for each person. In other words, a provider cannot assume that there is a "shared" level of ambivalence among all clients involved in an interaction. Moreover, even if all clients are experiencing an equal level of ambivalence, this will be experienced differently by each individual. However, the MI-consistent provider must avoid simply doing "individual MI" for each person. Thus the question becomes, how does the provider consider each individual's goals, ambivalence, and needs in the context of working with multiple individuals? Furthermore, how does the provider balance these various goals and needs to keep the interaction moving forward?

As a means of helping you consider how to address this challenge, we present two unique clinical challenges related to working with multiple individuals—working with parents and working with groups. We want to emphasize that our focus in this chapter is on how to address challenges that arise when working with parents and groups in an MI-consistent way. We are not, however, providing guidance on developing MI-based interventions for parents or groups.

CLINICAL CHALLENGE 1: PARENTS

Description

We have many colleagues who work with children and offer behavioral parent training as part of their clinical services. These colleagues frequently tell us about their struggles to engage parents in parent training, especially when they expect that their child will be the only one meeting with the provider and making changes. Although it is important to consider parent preferences in selecting an intervention strategy for child behavior problems, our colleagues often express that working with only the child will result in sub-optimal outcomes. In fact, multiple approaches to addressing child behavior problems, including parent training, tend to be the best approach (Curtis, Ronan, & Borduin, 2004). For example, parent training programs are among the most robust, empirically supported interventions available for preventing, and even reversing, development of antisocial behavior in youth (Kazdin, 2005; Maughan, Christiansen, Jenson, Olympia, & Clark, 2005). A wide range of positive outcomes have been associated with parent training programs including reduced behavior problems, increased social competence, and improved academic performance among children. Positive effects for participating parents also have been demonstrated, including improved parent-child relationships, reduced parenting stress, and reduced use of corporal punishment (e.g., Nicholson Fox, & Johnson, 2005). Thus, from a provider perspective, parent training programs would in many cases be considered an optimal first-line approach to addressing child behavior problems.

While parent training programs are promising, engaging parents in parent training programs and reducing attrition rates is difficult (Sterrett, Jones, Zalot, & Shook, 2010). Parents participating in parent training classes or interventions are most often seeking services because of a perceived (and often, actual) child behavior problem such as noncompliance or aggression. In parent training classes, the focus is on the parent as the agent through whom change in the child is facilitated, which may be difficult for parents, who are focused on the child, to accept. This creates a discrepancy between the parents and the provider as to what the problem is and how to address the problem. As discussed in chapter 2 discrepancies between clients and providers are likely to produce discord and increase client sustain talk. Complicating the situation, discrepancies between parents about the degree to which they need to learn different parenting skills may exist. One parent may see the need to change her parenting skills whereas her partner may see no need to learn new skills. Thus, the couple is not on the same page in relation to what needs to be changed, and this may hinder engagement and retention in parent training. In these two situations it might be helpful to consider that one or both members of the couple are pre-contemplative about their need to change their parenting practices. Adopting an MI-consistent approach to discussing the option of parent training may help to address the common pitfalls in parent training.

Example: *Margo and Phil have an 11-year-old son, Benjamin. Benjamin has been referred to a behavior specialist by his endocrinologist to better manage his diabetes. Benjamin was diagnosed with type 1 diabetes 2 years ago and it has worsened in the past 6 months. Upon meeting Benjamin and his parents, the behavior specialist learns that Margo and Phil disagree on how much they need to monitor and manage Benjamin's adherence to his medical treatment plan, including his diet. Margo will often monitor Benjamin's diet and ensure he is taking his medications. On the other hand, Phil believes that Benjamin is old enough to monitor these behaviors. Phil also believes that 'Ben should be able to be a normal kid' and often allows Benjamin to eat whatever he wants. Thus, Benjamin often abides what his father says and rarely manages his behavior in relation to his health. This behavior has led to a worsening of Benjamin's diabetes to the point their physician has become concerned."*

This example is not uncommon when parents bring their children for assistance with behavioral concerns. Parents may not have made the association between their behavior and their child's behavior. Using some of the following MI strategies may help parents make this link without becoming defensive and ultimately help their child develop healthier behaviors.

Proposed Strategy 1: Providing Feedback and Information

Often parents are less aware of how their behavior or parenting practices may have contributed to the development and maintenance of their child's behavioral problems. One approach to addressing this lack of awareness is to provide parents with information about how multiple factors, including parenting practices, influence a child's behavior and the problems displayed. For instance, the Family Check-up is an MI-based approach that includes feedback and has empirical support (Brennan, Shelleby, Shaw, Gardner, Dishion, & Wilson, 2013; Smith, Dishion, Shaw, & Wilson 2013). Giving information is a valuable strategy in MI, and it is how the information is provided that makes the strategy more or less MI-consistent. In particular, it is important that the information-giving process is engaging and objective. Additionally, information would generally only be offered after asking permission or being invited to share the information. In relation to parenting, it seems important to offer information to clients in a fashion that attempts to minimize any defensiveness or perception of being blamed for the child's problems.

Example: MI-Consistent/Inconsistent Giving Information

The following examples will illustrate MI-consistent and MI-inconsistent strategies for giving information to clients who are ambivalent about engaging in parent training.

Client Statement: *"Margo tends to micromanage everything Benjamin does. It seems like he needs more space to be himself and be a normal kid."*

MI-Inconsistent: *"Well, Benjamin certainly is at an age where he needs to learn to better care for himself. Kids typically learn self-management behaviors from their parents and your doctor is concerned that you and Margo are not helping Benjamin to better manage his diabetes. Often when problems like these happen, parents need to change some of their parenting strategies to help their child."*

This statement gives the client some information about the connection between child and parent behavior. The provider even supports the client's perspective a bit. However, the way in which the information is provided is MI-inconsistent. The provider simply offers the information without asking permission, announcing or emphasizing personal control in providing the information. There is a potential for the information to be received as blaming by the clients, which could increase discord. Finally, the provider does not elicit the clients' responses to this information.

Somewhat MI-Consistent: *"You two are concerned about Benjamin and his health and have different opinions about how to help him manage his behavior. If it's okay with you, I'd like share some information we know about children and managing health behavior. [Waits for client response]. One thing we know is that it is important for mom and dad to have a shared perspective of how to manage their child's behavior. Sometimes when parents modify their behavior a bit, it has a remarkable effect on the child's behavior. I've got a list of strategies that will help you get on the same page."*

This provider statement is somewhat MI-consistent because it empathizes and affirms the parents and elicits a response to the information from both parents. The provider also asks permission and presents the information in a non-expert role. However, after presenting the information about the importance of a shared perspective, the provider does not elicit the reactions from each parent to the information before presenting the list of strategies. As a result, the information-sharing process is less engaging and may result in discord.

MI-Consistent: *"You two are concerned about Benjamin and his health. You have different opinions about how to help him manage his behavior. If it's okay with you, I'd like share some information we know about children and managing health behavior. [Waits for client response]. One thing we know from a professional perspective is that when mom and dad don't have a shared vision of how to manage the behavior that the child's behavior can become more problematic. Sometimes when parents modify their behavior a bit it has a remarkable effect on the child's behavior. What do you two think about this information?"*

The provider offers this information in a MI-consistent way. The provider begins by affirming the parents' dedication and concern for their child. Next, the provider reflects the discrepancy between the parent's view of the problem [and possibly solution]. This is done in a way that doesn't side with either parent. Before offering information, the provider announces that he would like to share information. The provider gives the information in the third person, in the context of what is known in the professional world versus specifically focusing on the parents, which can decrease perceptions of blame or defensiveness. Finally, the provider elicits the reaction from the parents to this information.

Proposed Strategy 2: Exploring Goals/Values

Sometimes parents are less aware of how their parenting practices might have an effect on their goals for their children. Provider-client discussions that invite clients to share their goals for their children and how their behavior facilitates or hinders achievement of these goals might help clients make key connections on their own. Such discussions can also help parents begin to consider what may need to happen to support the achievement of their goals for their child. A related approach is to explore the parents' values in relation to caring for their children and compare how current behaviors are in line or not with those parenting values. In MI these strategies are called exploring goals/values.

Example: MI-Consistent/Inconsistent Exploring Goals

The following examples will illustrate MI-consistent and MI-inconsistent exploring of goals or values.

Client Statement: *"Margo tends to micromanage everything Benjamin does. It seems like he needs more space to be himself and be a normal kid."*

MI-Inconsistent: *"Yes, there seems to be a discrepancy between your perspective and Margo's perspective on how to parent Benjamin. Your goals for Benjamin are for him to be a healthy, independent boy, yet your differences of opinion on how to achieve that are keeping him from achieving those goals!"*

These provider utterances are MI-inconsistent. Both utterances begin with MI-consistent reflections of the difference of opinion between the parents. However, the provider then assumes the expert role and draws connections between these differences of opinion and the clients' goals and values rather than eliciting from the clients how their disagreements might be related to their goals and values. The provider also blames the clients for their son's problem by stating that their parenting behavior does not facilitate his being healthy and independent. Whether or not this provider observation is accurate, it is MI-inconsistent, because the provider is taking sides and thus is likely to elicit defensiveness and discord.

Somewhat MI-Consistent: *"You and Margo have some differences of opinion in how to parent Benjamin, which seems natural. How should we work toward resolving those differences?"*

The provider statement is somewhat MI-consistent. It acknowledges the existing discrepancies between the parents' perspectives and normalizes the situation. The provider then asks an open question, which invites the clients to share their perspectives. However, the specific question asked focuses how to solve the problem, not exploring goals and values. Thus the provider has jumped to planning before evoking the clients' motivations for change.

MI-Consistent: *"You two are dedicated to Benjamin's health. At the same time you have different perspectives on how best to help Benjamin. I wonder if we could take some time to discuss your goals for Benjamin. What are the goals each of you have for him and his future? [Waits for clients to respond]. How might these goals relate to your perspective on what is best for him in relation to helping him manage his diabetes?"*

MI-Consistent: *"You two are dedicated to Benjamin's health. At the same time, you each have different opinions on how to best help him. Perhaps we can discuss some of your values as they relate to parenting. What are some of your values as a parent? [Waits for clients to respond]. How do these values relate to your approach to helping Benjamin manage his diabetes? How are these values similar and different from your partner's in relation to helping Benjamin?"*

This provider statement has several aspects that make it MI-consistent. The provider affirms that both parents are dedicated to the health of their son. Additionally, the provider highlights, in a non-judgmental way, the discrepancy between the parents. Next, the provider elicits from the clients their parenting values and how these values relate to their perspective on parenting the child.

Proposed Strategy 3: Decisional Balance

Given that one or both parents may initially be at a precontemplative stage in relation to the need to learn parenting skills or change their parenting practices, it might be valuable to examine the pros and cons of participating in parent training. If both parents are involved in the discussion, it is important to elicit pros and cons from both parents. One approach is to encourage the parents to collaboratively develop the list of pros and cons. Another approach is to ask each parent to identify their individual pros and cons and facilitate a discussion between the parents.

Example: MI-Consistent/Inconsistent Decisional Balance

The following examples will illustrate MI-consistent and MI-inconsistent decisional balance for parents.

Client Statement: *"Margo tends to micromanage everything Benjamin does. It seems like he needs more space to be himself and be a normal kid."*

MI-Inconsistent: *"You feel Benjamin needs more space to become a nor-mal kid. On the one hand, I agree that there are benefits to giving children space and letting them be 'normal'. On the other hand, I can see Margo's point that Benjamin may need structure from you to get his diabetes under control."*

The provider responds with a reflection that captures only part of the dis-crepancy that exists—the father's perspective. The provider then offers his or her own unsolicited opinion about the pros and cons of the father's per-spective rather than eliciting them from the clients. This may create the impression that the provider believes his or her opinion is more important than the clients and is likely to increase discord in the session.

Somewhat MI-Consistent: *"So the two of you have different perspectives on how to help Benjamin. Perhaps we can talk about some of the benefits of learning new ways you can help manage his behavior and some of the draw-backs of not learning new skills to help him."*

The provider begins with a reflection that highlights the different perspec-tives of the parents. Further, the provider seems to be incorporating a deci-sional balance by eliciting the pro-change side of the argument. However, the provider makes no attempt to explore the drawbacks of changing and benefits of not changing. Thus the provider has fallen into the taking sides trap. Additionally, within the context of two parents, the focus taken by the provider can be perceived as siding with one of the parents, which could elicit discord from the other parent.

MI-Consistent: *"Both of you are concerned about Benjamin and his healthy development. You have different perspectives on how to best help Benjamin. Perhaps we can talk through some of these differences by having each of you discuss the pros and cons of learning additional skills to help Benjamin improve his health. If it is okay with each of you, it might be helpful for us to discuss your perspective on the drawbacks of changing and not changing and the benefits of changing and not changing your behavior."*

The provider demonstrates an MI-consistent approach in several ways. The provider begins by affirming the parents' dedication to the health of their child. Further, the provider highlights that a discrepancy exists between the parents. The provider also reframes the discrepancy by sug-gesting both parents are trying to best help their son. The provider then facilitates the decisional balance by first asking about the clients stay-ing the way they currently are. Next, the provider asks the clients about potential change efforts. One important point is that the provider empha-sizes the need for both parents to discuss their perspective. This avoids a potential perception that the provider is siding with one or the other parent. Finally, the provider avoids advocating for one side or the other (i.e., changing or staying the same) which is an important feature of a decisional balance.

CLINICAL CHALLENGE 2: GROUPS

Description

There is an increasing need for health and behavioral health providers to reach larger groups of people, including at-risk populations (Kazdin & Blaze, 2011; Prochaska & Norcross, 2010). An increasingly popular method to reach wider populations is to use groups (Schneider Corey, Corey, & Corey, 2010). Using groups, whether to address mental health or medical issues, or facilitate self-help, allows providers to address common concerns among clients simultaneously, build off strengths and experiences of multiple clients, and facilitate mutual support (Forsyth, 2011). When thinking of groups, you may envision people sitting in a circle talking about their inner-most secrets, or a 12-step group where someone discusses his "rock bottom" and others discuss how they relate. Groups take on many different formats ranging from process-focused groups, which emphasize personal exploration, to treatment groups for specific problems (e.g., cognitive behavioral group for social anxiety), to educational groups such as a group for clients awaiting an organ transplant (Wagner & Ingersoll, 2013). Given the increasing importance of groups to address a wide array of behavior and health issues, providers are often in the position to facilitate a group. However, many may not have the necessary training or experience, especially to integrate MI into group work. Reflecting on our education and training as psychologists, we recognize that we encountered little to prepare us for group work.

Our goal here is to discuss how you might use MI to address clinical challenges encountered in group work. Given the diverse applicability of MI, there has been a proliferation of MI in group work. For instance, MI groups have developed for at-risk adolescent alcohol and drug use (D'Amico, Hunter, Miles, Ewing, & Osilla, 2013), promoting adherence to HIV medication (Holstad, DiIorio, Kelley, Resnicow, & Sharma, 2011), and reducing school truancy (Ena & Dafiniou, 2009), to name a few. However, the concept of stand-alone MI groups to facilitate behavioral change is relatively new. More often MI is integrated with other evidence-based change approaches like cognitive-behavioral therapy and the research support is limited (Wagner & Ingersoll, 2013). Because MI was developed with a focus on individual behavior change some aspects may be more difficult to adapt to groups. If you are interested in learning how to conduct MI-based groups, we encourage you to read *Motivational Interviewing in Groups* by Wagner and Ingersoll (2013) where this topic is addressed more fully.

Whether you have facilitated groups or not, you can likely appreciate that working with a group of individuals is vastly different than working with a single individual. As such, there are unique challenges encountered when working with groups. These challenges range from having to simultaneously focus on the needs and goals of multiple individuals, to more complex factors such as interpersonal issues between group members and members being at different stages of engagement in the group. Schneider Corey and colleagues (2010) outlined several challenges and problem behaviors that group leaders may face in facilitating a group. These challenges, which will be the focus of our discussion, include intrapersonal concerns and interpersonal difficulties in the group.

Intrapersonal Challenges

Individuals enter a group with their unique expectations, goals, and personal characteristics that will impact their overt and covert group behavior. Internally clients may have concern about their referral to the group, worry about group involvement, differing readiness to engage in a group and change, varying knowledge of the topic, and distinct apprehension about how they will relate to and be treated by other group members (Schneider et al., 2010). The task for the group leader related to these challenges is how to address clients' variability so that the group proceeds as a meaningful and valuable experience for all clients.

> Example: *Kayla is a nurse practitioner. As part of her work in a transplant clinic, she facilitates an education group for individuals newly diagnosed with liver disease. Because it is an educational group, she focuses on lecturing about liver disease and the transplant process. During a recent group, she noticed various responses from her clients in relation to the group. Tabitha focused on every word that Kayla said and took copious notes; however, she often seemed confused but never asked questions. Thomas did not seem to be paying attention. Jacob seemed to become increasingly anxious as she talked about the different topics. Stacy, a client who works as a pediatric nurse, acted as though she didn't need to be at the group and was bored by it. Kayla was worried as she didn't think the group members were interacting well with each other or learning the important information needed to help them manage their disease and treatment.*

Kayla's experience is often encountered when facilitating groups, especially educational groups. What her experience highlights is the various intrapersonal challenges that might influence the development and functioning of the group. As discussed throughout this book, one of the values of MI is fostering engagement among clients. Young (2013) demonstrated how the spirit and principles of MI, discussed in chapter 2, align well with developing group cohesion and goals. Further, Rollnick, Miller, and Butler (2008) discuss some strategies that might be helpful for making educational groups more engaging. As educators we recognize how easy it can be to fall into lecture mode and try to be cognizant of how to remain MI-consistent when educating and facilitating group interactions inside or outside the classroom. Here are some MI strategies that can be used to address some of the intrapersonal challenges in facilitating groups.

Proposed Strategy 1: Evocative Questions

Using evocative questions in group work can help a provider engage group members, avoid the expert trap, and establish a group environment focused on understanding the unique needs of each group member. Evocative questions are especially important for groups that have a specific focus, such as education or a structured treatment for a particular disorder (e.g., exposure group for obsessive compulsive disorder). Using evocative questions can help establish the norm of open discussion in the group.

Example: MI-Consistent/Inconsistent Evoking

The following examples will illustrate MI-consistent and MI-inconsistent evoking for groups.

MI-Inconsistent: *"Welcome to the living with liver disease group. How long have you had liver disease? Has anybody been to a group before? Who thinks this group will be helpful? Does anyone want to learn how improve their health?"*

These questions are MI-inconsistent because they are closed questions and are unlikely to facilitate clients opening up and engaging in discussion. Members of a group who are uncomfortable or uncertain about the group experience could easily respond with minimal answers. Some of these questions also could have a judgmental quality to them and could increase discord and withdrawal from clients, which is the opposite of what MI-consistent providers would want. Also, asking closed question after closed question could close off clients as the provider has succumbed to the question and answer trap.

Somewhat MI-Consistent: *"Thank you for coming to the living with liver disease group. What are the difficulties related to living with liver disease?"*

This statement is somewhat MI-consistent in that the provider provides an affirmation for the group and asks an open question. However, the provider falls into the premature focus trap by asking about the problems associated with living with liver disease. In a group setting, this premature focus could lead to discord and reduced involvement among the group.

MI-Consistent: *"Thank you for coming to the living with liver disease group. I'm sure some of you are unsure about this group—both what to expect and what is expected of you. That is natural. What are your expectations and concerns about this group?"*

This statement is MI-consistent for several reasons. First, the provider affirms the clients attending the group by thanking them for coming and normalizes that clients have expectations and concerns about the group. Rather than asking a closed question or jumping into education, the provider asks an open question to elicit expectations and concerns from the clients. In doing so the provider expressed her desire to learn about the clients, value for open communication, and hope that clients are engaged in the group.

Proposed Strategy 2: Discussing Pros and Cons of Group Work

Group members will likely be at various stages of readiness to engage in group work and to make the types of changes the group is intended to facilitate. Many have different expectations and concerns about the group, as well as diverse knowledge and experience with groups. Discussing the pros and cons of group involvement can help clarify for both the provider and the clients what the unique expectations, hopes, and concerns of a particular group of clients may be. When working with groups, providers will likely encounter shared and distinct pros and cons for each client. Thus, it is important for providers to ensure that each client has the opportunity to offer pros and cons, and this may require specifically asking a client or two to share.

Example: MI-Consistent/Inconsistent Discussing of Pros and Cons

The following examples will illustrate MI-consistent and MI-inconsistent discussion of the pros and cons of group work.

Client 1 Statement: *"I am not sure that this group will help. All I need is a transplant!"*

Client 2 Statement: *"I don't know—I guess we could learn some things that may help."*

MI-Inconsistent: *"It sounds like folks might have various perspectives about the value of this group. Let me take a little time now to tell you how this group can help each of you live better with your liver disease."*

The provider begins by highlighting the different perspectives expressed by group members using a reflection. However, rather than exploring the clients' perspectives on the pros and cons of the group, the provider begins to offer her own opinion about the pros of the group. She has fallen into the expert trap with this response by implying that her perspective is more valuable or valid. By focusing only on the pros, she also fell into the trap of taking sides, which is likely to elicit anti-group responses from the clients.

Somewhat MI-Consistent: *"You all are probably concerned about what will best help you with your liver disease. If it is okay with you, I'd like to provide some information on why the transplant team thinks these groups are important for all transplant candidates. Then I'd love to hear your perspectives at the end of the group."*

This statement is somewhat MI-consistent. The provider acknowledges that group members have ideas or concerns about how the group can be helpful, which expresses empathy. She also introduces the option to address any questions or concerns at the end of group and asks permission to share information, both of which somewhat enhance a sense of collaboration. However, by tabling the discussion of client concerns to the end of the session and setting the agenda for the session without any client input, the provider is assuming the expert role. This may enhance disengagement and discord among those who are uncertain about the group.

MI-Consistent: *"You all are probably concerned about what will best help you with your liver disease. Also, each of you likely have different thoughts on how this group may or may not help you. That makes sense given that you are unique individuals and want what is best for you specifically. Perhaps we can discuss each person's thoughts about the drawbacks and benefits of his or her own participation in the group. Tabitha, what are your thoughts about that?"*

This provider statement is MI-consistent for several reasons. The provider acknowledged that the clients are seeking what is best for them, thereby conveying a desire to collaborate with each group member. Next, the provider commented on the fact that each group member may have different opinions about the value of the group, normalizing these differences and emphasizing autonomy. Finally, the provider facilitates the discussion by asking about the pros and cons of participation in the group from each member, thus avoiding taking sides or "defending" the group, and communicates a desire for open discussion that includes dissenting opinions among all members.

Proposed Strategy 3: Elicit-Provide-Elicit

Most groups will likely require a provider to give information about a disease/disorder, specifics of an offense and legal issues, a treatment approach, group rules and norms, or any of a variety of other topics. The elicit-provide-elicit approach offers an MI-consistent and engaging way to share information with group members. Using elicit-provide-elicit, a provider can also gain valuable insight into what the group already knows or doesn't know about the topic through the initial eliciting. In contrast to how this strategy was discussed elsewhere in this book, in a group context a provider attends to all group members' responses and ensures that all members had an opportunity to respond before and after information is provided.

Example: MI-Consistent/Inconsistent Elicit-Provide-Elicit

The following examples will illustrate MI-consistent and MI-inconsistent elicit-provide-elicit in a group.

MI-Inconsistent: *"Let's begin today with talking about lifestyle changes in relation to liver disease. Many people think that all they need is medical treatment or a transplant to improve their health. However, there are many lifestyle changes you all can make that can help improve your liver disease. In fact, if you were to have a transplant there will be many behavior changes that will be required of you. We will talk about all of these today."*

This provider statement is MI-inconsistent and likely to elicit sustain talk—talk about not changing. The provider falls into the expert trap and essentially lectures the group. The provider does little eliciting to gain the clients' understanding about liver disease or different changes that need to be made. Similarly, there is no eliciting from the clients their reaction to the information the provider offered.

Somewhat MI-Consistent: *"There are a lot of different things that go into living with liver disease. Before we begin discussing these different things, I would like to learn what each of you already knows about managing liver disease. Who would like to discuss what they know about behavioral changes in relation to living with liver disease? [Waits for clients' responses]. Thank you for your information. The biggest changes that people can make are to stop drinking alcohol and take their medications. Does that make sense?"*

This statement is somewhat MI-consistent for several reasons. The provider communicates empathy, acknowledging there are many things that require change, and uses elicit-provide-elicit. However, the provider prematurely focuses on making behavioral changes versus remaining less focused to learn what group members already know, which could result in missed information. Additionally, the provider asks who would like to share, a closed question, versus explicitly stating she would like to hear what each member knows. After providing information, the provider asks a closed question that basically asks for agreement versus asking a question that is more likely to elicit client reactions to the information.

MI-Consistent: *"There are a lot of different things that go into living with liver disease. Before we begin discussing these different things, I would like to learn what each you already know about managing liver disease. If it works for you we can go around and each of you can share what you already know or have heard about living with liver disease, because my bet is that each of you have information you already know that you can discuss. [Waits for clients to answer]. It sounds like you all have a lot of valuable information already. If I might add, one thing we might discuss is the different lifestyle changes, such as stopping drinking and eating healthier, that can help you better manage your liver disease. What are your thoughts about that?"*

This statement is MI-consistent because the provider communicates empathy and that there is a lot of information about living with liver disease without talking about one specific aspect, thus avoiding the premature focus trap. Additionally, before providing any information she elicits what is known currently by the group and emphasizes her desire to hear from group members. This communicates that the provider believes that each member has important information about the topic and that she values hearing from each of them. After the client responses, the provider reflects and reinforces that the group knows a lot about the topic. She then announces that she would like to provide information, gives the information, and then elicits the group members' reactions to the information.

Proposed Strategy 4: Group Planning

Thus far we have discussed planning as an MI-consistent strategy for working with individuals; however, as discussed earlier, there are many differences in working with groups. One of those differences is that group members may have different goals that they want to achieve. These differences may stall the progress of the group or interfere with the accomplishment of more general goals. In chapter 3 we discussed MI-consistent planning. With some adaptations to account for multiple individuals, the planning process can be used to evoke from group members their individual reasons and goals for involvement in the group and then facilitate a discussion about developing group goals and outcomes.

Example: MI-Consistent/Inconsistent Group Planning

The following examples illustrate how a provider might use planning to help group members prepare to successfully participate in a group.

Client 1 Statement: *"I'm willing to try this group, but I'm not really sure about it."*

Client 2 Statement: *"Yeah, this seems like a hoop we need to jump through to get our transplant."*

Client 3 Statement: *"I don't know—maybe there are things we can learn to make our lives better."*

MI-Inconsistent: *"It sounds like some of you are uncertain about this group. You are probably more interested solely in a transplant. Part of the process for getting a transplant is to attend this group. Regular attendance is important even if you're not sure about it. In this group we will discuss many things including the transplant process, taking medications and lifestyle changes before and after the transplant. It is a lot of information but we will most likely cover something of interest to you."*

The provider starts with a reflection to acknowledge the different perspectives of the group members. However, her next few statements could be perceived as confrontational and could elicit discord from the group members who expressed concern about the group. Further, the provider is prescribing the plan for the group, neglecting to elicit any expectations or goals from group members. The provider also assumes (instead of evoking from clients) that the group will meet their goals in some way. Telling the client what to do and assuming her plan will meet the various clients' needs is not collaborative, and may diminish the clients' sense of autonomy or investment in the group.

Somewhat MI-Consistent: *"You all have different perspectives about this group. Before we move any further, perhaps we can take some time to discuss reasons for the group. [Waits for clients to respond]. There are a variety of reasons for attending this group. So what should our plan of action be?"*

This provider statement is somewhat MI-consistent. The provider begins with a reflection acknowledging that the group has different thoughts about the group and attempts to elicit reasons for the group from members. However, the provider does not explicitly elicit from each member of the group. Additionally, the provider attempts to elicit a plan but may miss important ideas from members with such a global question versus eliciting from each member.

MI-Consistent: *"I am hearing that you all have different perspectives about how the group may or may not meet your needs. This seems natural to me as each of you knows what things tend to work best for you. Before we move any further, perhaps we can take some time to discuss your individual reasons for coming to the group. [Waits for clients to respond]. There are certainly various important reasons for attending this group ranging from getting a transplant*

Table 7.1. GROUP PLANNING FORM

Group Plan—Example

The most important individual reasons why we want to participate in group are:

1. So I can live better with liver disease
2. So I can get a transplant
3. So I can learn more about my disease
4. So my wife stops nagging me

Our group goals are to:

1. Better understand liver disease
2. Learn about the transplant process
3. Better understand medication
4. Become more self-sufficient in our disease

For group to be successful we must:

1. Attend meetings regularly
2. Respect each other's opinions
3. Openly discuss our opinions and reactions in group
4. Participate in all group learning activities

Some things that could interfere with group success include:

1. Lack of participation of all members
2. Disrespect for differences of opinion
3. Disinterest in some aspects of group

We can help each other be successful by:

1. Providing encouragement
2. Providing reminders about group goals

What we will do if we are not "sticking with" group the way we had hoped:

1. Remind each other why we are attending group
2. Support each other
3. Remind each other of how the group has already helped

to learning about lifestyle changes that can help you live with liver disease. Now that we know why each of you is attending the group maybe we can talk a bit about our collective plan for getting the most out of this group?"

This provider utterance is MI-consistent. It begins with a reflection acknowledging and validating the different opinions of group members. Next, the provider elicits the various reasons for attending the group, reflecting and reinforcing the various reasons. Finally, the provider introduces the idea of developing a group plan to make the group valuable for each client. This approach is validating and collaborative, and the plan developed will likely be more salient to the group members. As with the other strategies for working with groups, the provider attends to each group member to ensure that he or she is involved. You could also use the form in Table 7.1 to guide group planning. Rather than giving the form to each individual member, you could use the questions as a guide and present them using a dry erase board, blackboard, or flip chart. You could also elicit volunteers from the group to assume scribe duty and write the answers for the group on the board or chart.

Interpersonal Difficulties

A group consists of multiple individuals, each with their own histories, personalities, idiosyncrasies, styles of communication, and pet peeves. Thus, interpersonal difficulties seem natural and to be expected—sort of like sustain talk and discord. One role of a group facilitator is to build interpersonal cohesion and manage these difficulties (Wagner & Ingersoll, 2013), and MI-consistent strategies may be particularly useful (Young, 2013). Schneider Corey and colleagues (2010) identified several "problem behaviors" that often occur in groups that are presented in Table 7.2. Some approaches to group facilitation suggest that you directly challenge these behaviors and encourage group members to do the same. The first task in MI-consistent responding to these behaviors is to view them from an MI perspective as naturally occurring discord. Reframing them from problem behaviors to discord can be a signal that something needs to change in focus or discussion or interaction approach of the group. You can use of some of the proposed MI strategies for interpersonal difficulties that follow to help manage some of these behaviors in group

Example: *John is a substance abuse treatment counselor who facilitates 12-member cognitive behavioral treatment groups at a community-based intensive outpatient substance abuse treatment program. In his current group, John has identified several clients that seem to be disrupting the group process. Steve is a very active participant, and John values his contributions and enthusiasm. However, Steve seems to monopolize a great deal of group time, leaving little time for other clients to share their thoughts and feelings. Additionally, Steve often makes comments or asks questions that are not*

Table 7.2. GROUP PROBLEM BEHAVIORS

Behavior	Description
Monopolizing	A group member taking up the majority of group time and talking about her or his concerns.
Off-topic discussions	A group member routinely diverting the discussion away from the topic of discussion.
Hostility	One group member responds in a passive or overtly aggressive fashion to another.
Acting superior	A group member may respond condescendingly or in a fashion that suggests he is better than the others.
Socializing	Group members engaging in side conversations or engaging the group in social discussions that are not group related.

Adapted from Schneider Corey et al., 2010.

consistent with the topic John is trying to cover. Shari seems generally disengaged from the group, and John has observed her rolling her eyes or making sarcastic comments under her breath as other group members ask or respond to questions. It has become apparent that Shari believes she is not as 'bad off' as the other group members and questions whether she can benefit from the group. Finally, Trisha, Bob, and Sarah frequently whisper and giggle among themselves, or pass notes to one another during group. John notes that those around them seem unsettled by their socializing during groups."

Proposed Strategy 5: Shifting Focus

Sometimes discord, such as that illustrated in this example, may be the result of the discussion topic. For some approaches to group therapy (e.g., process-oriented groups) challenging the discord is encouraged. However, that is MI-inconsistent. In MI, discord is an indicator of a need to change something. One strategy is to shift the focus away from what may be causing the discord. However, it is important to first acknowledge the group member's behavior and others' responses before shifting the focus to avoid communicating you are uncomfortable with what happened in the group and that group members can't openly express themselves. This approach can also be used if an individual is monopolizing group time to shift the focus of discussion away from the monopolizing member to others.

Example: MI-Consistent/Inconsistent Shifting Focus

The following examples illustrate how a provider might use shifting focus in an MI-consistent fashion to manage discord in a group.

Client Statement: *"I'm different than you all. I don't use bad drugs, I just drink alcohol."*

MI-Inconsistent: *"Let's not talk about whose drug use is better or worse. Let's discuss how our drug has affected our lives."*

This provider utterance is MI-inconsistent, because the provider dismisses the concern communicated by the client in relation to the group and adopts an expert role. The provider's response is also likely to raise more discord as it could be perceived as challenging. The response has the potential to make the client more passive rather than more active in the group.

Somewhat MI-Consistent: *"Thanks for sharing. In what ways has drug and alcohol use affected your lives?"*

This statement is somewhat MI-consistent as the provider acknowledges the client statement in a non-confrontational way and shifts focus. However, the provider avoids acknowledging the discord statement from the client, which may invalidate the client's concerns and communicate that dissenting opinions are not valued in the group. The result of this statement is that the client could disengage from the group and become less motivated to change.

MI-Consistent: *"You are concerned about the different types of substances used by the group members. We may be getting a bit ahead of ourselves in discussing the drugs used, and I wonder if we could talk about what each of you is hoping to gain from this group."*

The provider begins by using a reflection to acknowledging the client's concern but doesn't agree or disagree with it. The provider then shifts the focus of the discussion away from the differences in drugs used to a discussion about what each member wants from the group. This could also transition into a discussion about group rules and norms.

Proposed Strategy 6: Reflective Listening

Reflective listening is at the heart of MI and can be used at any time in an MI-consistent interaction. In groups, reflective listening can serve multiple purposes (Wagner & Ingersol, 2013). First, the group leader can use reflective listening to respond to interpersonal difficulties. By responding reflectively the provider models alternate ways group members can respond to others in the group. Second, the provider can facilitate group members responding to each other using reflective listening.

Example: MI-Consistent/Inconsistent Reflective Listening

The following examples illustrate how a provider might use reflecting to manage interpersonal difficulties in a group.

Client Statement: *"I'm different than you all. I don't use bad drugs, I just drink alcohol."*

MI-Inconsistent: *"This is a common misconception—alcohol is also a drug."*

This statement is not a reflection and is MI-inconsistent. The information the provider gives is accurate, but it is a direct confrontation of the client's statement. This could facilitate expressions of resentment or hostility from other group members who feel put down by the client's statement.

Somewhat MI-Consistent: *"You only use alcohol."*

This statement is a reflection and is somewhat MI-consistent. The provider validates the concern of the client and resists the righting reflex. However, this simple reflection is unlikely to move the conversation forward in a useful direction. Thus, although not wrong, with this response the provider is missing an opportunity to engage other group members, elicit more about the client's concerns and discord, or shift the focus to a topic that is more likely to facilitate change.

MI-Consistent: *"You're not convinced you belong in this group because you use only alcohol."*

This provider reflects the client's disagreement about their involvement in the group, which is MI-consistent. However, the provider does not indicate that he agrees or disagrees with the statement or directly confront the client's belief. He simply communicates that the provider is hearing what the client has communicated. Choosing to reflect this particular aspect of what the client has said is also likely to help shift the discussion to fruitful topics such as the different treatment needs and goals of each group member.

MI-Consistent: *"I hear what you are saying about your involvement in the group. At the same time I wonder what others in the group are hearing you say. Perhaps each of you can reflect back what you have heard. [Waits for each member to respond]. Thank you for your responses. Maybe you can reflect back to the group what you heard in their various responses."*

The provider's response is MI-consistent as he is attempting to facilitate a discussion using reflective listening. The provider acknowledges hearing the client. Next he prompts the other group members to reflect back what they hear in the client's statement. The provider affirms the members for their responses and invites the client to reflect back to the group what he has heard.

Proposed Strategy 7: Eliciting Group Member Strengths

There can be a tendency when clients in a group experience interpersonal difficulties with one or more other members to focus on others' negatives. Providers can attempt to minimize interpersonal difficulties by eliciting strengths and positive assets from group members who are having difficulties.

Example: MI-Consistent/Inconsistent Eliciting of Group Member Strengths

The following examples will illustrate MI-consistent and MI-inconsistent eliciting of group member strengths.

Client Statement: *"I'm different than you all. I don't use bad drugs, I just drink alcohol."*

Client 2 Response: *"Who are you to talk? Your situation is worse than each of us!"*

MI-Inconsistent: *"Okay, I'm going to jump in here as this is not appropriate group behavior according to our rules."*

This is statement is a common one in facilitating groups with the goal of reminding members how to participate in the group and to keep the discussion from escalating. However, the provider is assuming an expert role and is also judgmental by labeling the behavior as inappropriate. Although in some groups this might be a suitable response, especially to reinforce group rules and behavior, it is MI-inconsistent.

Somewhat MI-Consistent: *"You two seem to be heading in a direction that is concerning to me. If it's okay with you, let's step back for a moment and talk a bit about what strengths we see in each other."*

This provider statement is somewhat MI-consistent as it is not as confrontational as the first statement and the provider expresses his concern. However, the provider interrupts the discussion without asking permission. The provider only shares his perception of the situation and does not elicit the perceptions of other group members. Finally, the provider includes other group members in the discussion of positive qualities, making the situation solely about the two group members.

MI-Consistent: *"If it's all right with the group I would like to jump in for a minute. You two seem to be heading in a direction that is concerning to me and I wonder how others feel about it. [Waits for others to respond]. I wonder if we can step back for a moment and talk a bit about what strengths we see in each other and how that helps the group meet our goals."*

This provider statement is MI-consistent for several reasons. First, the provider asks permission to jump in to the discussion versus interrupting. The provider then shares his perception of the situation and asks for the perceptions of others in the group. Finally, the provider elicits from the group to comment on the strengths of each member and also how each member helps the group move forward.

CHAPTER SUMMARY

In this chapter we presented the clinical challenges of using MI with multiple individuals. Working with multiple individuals presents unique challenges for

Table 7.3. SUMMARY OF MOTIVATIONAL INTERVIEWING STRATEGIES FOR CLINICAL CHALLENGES RELATED TO MULTIPLE INDIVIDUALS

Clinical Challenge	Suggested MI Strategies
Parents: Differences between parents in relation to problem definition, motivation for change, and ideas for change	Giving information: Providing information in an engaging and objective fashion about the nature of the child's behavior and the relationship between parenting and child behavior change.
	Exploring goals/values: Elicit from parents their parenting goals, values, and goals for the child and contrast them with parenting behavior.
	Decisional balance: Facilitate decision making among parents by eliciting pros and cons about changing from both parents with the goal of developing shared motivation to change.
Intrapersonal challenges in groups: Individual factors and behaviors that may slow the development and progression of the group.	Evocative questions: Using questions aimed at genuinely understanding the client's concerns, motivations, and understanding about the group to engage each member in the group.
	Exploring pros/cons of group work: Engage participants in a discussion about the benefits and drawbacks of the group to address differences in readiness to change, motivations, and concerns about the group.
	Elicit-provide-elicit: Before providing information, elicit from all members what they already know about a topic and elicit reaction to the information from all members after providing it. This can be used to reconcile differences among group members.
	Group planning: Engaging the group in determining shared goals and methods to reach those goals within the group. It is important to develop some consensus among group members.
Interpersonal challenges in groups: Behaviors displayed by or between group members that affect the cohesion and functioning of the group.	Shifting focus: Acknowledging the discord in the group and shifting focus to a less discord-evoking topic.
	Reflective listening: Use of reflection to highlight the meaning in group members' comments either by commenting or eliciting reflections from group members.
	Eliciting strengths: Asking group members to comment on the positive attributes and strengths of other members with the goal to reduce discord.

using MI as different people may have different levels of motivation, reasons for changing or not, and perspectives of the concern/problem. Therefore, we emphasized throughout the chapter the importance of attending to these factors for all individuals involved in the session and demonstrated how you may achieve this with parents and groups using different MI strategies. While we did not specifically discuss MI groups, we invited you to envision how MI can be used to address intra- and interpersonal difficulties you may encounter when working with groups of people. In particular we encouraged you to be cognizant of applying MI strategies to the entire group versus one or two individuals. Many of the strategies we proposed can help you remain MI consistent while including multiple individuals and their perspectives. Table 7.3 summarizes the clinical challenges and suggested MI strategies.

8

Challenges in Learning to Use and Implement MI

As discussed in chapter 1, MI is not easy to learn. Most of the strategies and concepts presented in this book sound deceptively straightforward and intuitive. In fact, MI-consistent strategies are counterintuitive for many we have trained, especially in the situations in which they would be most useful (e.g., when clients are angry or upset, have limited motivation to change, or disagree with the provider). In this chapter we provide a number of tips that we have found useful in our own development as MI providers, applied in the MI trainings we have provided, and learned as MI researchers. Through these various experiences with MI we have learned valuable information from our trainees, clients, and participants that has solidified our appreciation for the nuances of learning MI. In many ways, our process has paralleled how Dr. William Miller developed his appreciation and understanding of MI (Adams & Madson, 2006). Thus, we offer these tips for your consideration as you begin to develop or strengthen your utilization of MI. As part of this discussion we also focus in greater detail on two challenges in learning to use MI: provider feelings of frustration and provider personal experiences that are similar to client experiences.

TIP 1: SET REALISTIC EXPECTATIONS

Many providers and students enter MI training with unrealistic expectations about the ease with which they will learn MI. This is probably based in part on the fact that many providers believe the practices they implement with clients are actually far more MI-consistent than they actually are (Miller, Yahne, Moyers, Martinez, & Pirritano, 2004). Whatever the source of the unrealistic expectations, they can result in disappointment and frustration during and following MI training.

Miller and Moyers (2006) observed that there eight separate tasks or stages involved in learning to successfully implement MI: (1) relinquishing the expert role and opening oneself to truly collaborating with clients; (2) developing skill in client-centered counseling, including accurate empathy; (3) recognizing and selectively reflecting change talk; (4) eliciting and increasing change talk; (5) managing discord; (6) engaging in MI-consistent change planning; (7) consolidating client commitment; and (8) integrating MI with other intervention styles. For some providers, particularly those with training in methods of psychological counseling or psychotherapy, the spirit of MI and the client-centered counseling aspects of MI may come relatively easy. In contrast, the more advanced and less familiar aspects of MI, such as recognizing and reinforcing change talk as well as eliciting and strengthening change talk, may come much less naturally. For providers from disciplines with training, practices, and philosophies that are less compatible with MI, all aspects of learning MI may present more of a challenge (Schumacher, Madson, & Nilsen, 2014). As noted in chapter 1, for many providers (including mental health providers), intensive workshop training followed by five sessions of coaching may be insufficient for expert competence or even beginning proficiency in MI to be obtained (Madson, Schumacher, Noble, & Bonnell, 2013; Miller et al., 2004; Moyers et al., 2008; Schumacher, Williams, Burke, Epler, & Simon, 2013; Smith et al., 2012). In fact, for many, learning proficient use of MI parallels the process (e.g., practice, observation and coaching) many providers undertook to learn how to practice in their disciplines.

We strongly recommend that providers and students set expectations that match the amount of MI training they will receive. Based on experience, if a provider is able to receive workshop training, plus up to 20 feedback-based coaching sessions, it seems highly likely that he or she will achieve expert competence in MI (Schumacher et al., 2013). If a provider, like many providers we train, does not have the time or resources to undertake that amount of training, he or she may still learn some valuable practices and principles of MI that can enhance work with clients. If a provider has not received any formal training in MI, but would still like to figure out how to apply at least some of the practices and principles of MI to his or her daily work, this book was written with that provider in mind. Although a novice provider is unlikely to be able to conduct a motivational interview after reading this book, he or she should be able to implement select strategies that may help better address common clinical challenges. However, remember the value and importance of the MI spirit that we emphasized throughout this book. Without adhering to the spirit of MI in implementing these strategies, they will likely be implemented in an MI-inconsistent fashion.

TIP 2: BE OPEN-MINDED

Many providers come to our MI training with very strong pre-existing beliefs about what types of strategies are best for a particular type of client (Schumacher et al., 2014). For example, many years ago, a fellow trainer shared the story of a provider who had said of MI, "this stuff probably works for some clients, but some clients just need to be confronted." As elaborated later in this chapter, it has been our experience that in fact the clients who are viewed as most appropriate for MI are often those who need it the least and vice versa. Other providers may draw seemingly premature conclusions about whether or not MI "works" on the basis of one or two attempts at using MI (often attempts that are not particularly MI-consistent). What we always encourage is that if a provider is considering adopting MI, he or she must keep an open mind. MI is not a panacea, that is, it will not be the solution for every client who is struggling with issues of motivation. But MI is also quite different from practice as usual (Miller & Rollnick, 2009), and is something that few providers (except those with extensive training in MI) just naturally implement in their day-to-day conversations with clients. We remember our early sessions attempting to implement MI. In the beginning we were uncertain about whether MI worked, because our implementation of the practices and principles was not yet expert. However, we also remember the first sessions when we really "got it" and clients seemed to almost miraculously move from just considering change (contemplation) or even not considering change at all (precontemplation) to fully committed to change and ready to act on a change plan (Prochaska & DiClemente, 1983). If providers are considering adopting MI (or select MI strategies), we encourage them to try it with their most challenging clients, the ones they are certain will only respond to confrontation. We also encourage them to try it repeatedly (not just once or twice) before drawing conclusions about whether or not it is a style that they would like to make part of their repertoires. We think it is important to remember the advice of Dr. William Miller—"learn the same way I did, from your clients" (Adams & Madson, 2006 p. 104).

TIP 3: GET OBJECTIVE FEEDBACK

As noted, individuals who are attempting to learn MI are generally not very good at gauging how MI-consistent their work is. Although in general, providers tend to overestimate how MI-consistent their performance is (Miller et al., 2004) we have also observed, especially among more self-critical trainees, an underestimation of how well they are performing. It is hard to imagine how a provider could improve their performance in implementing MI-consistent strategies, if he or she did not know how well they were currently implementing the strategies. Thus, getting objective feedback is generally recommended for anyone who is hoping to learn to implement MI (e.g., Miller et al., 2004). It has been our experience that providers perceive great benefits of receiving objective feedback and are very reluctant to submit work samples or allow observation of their practice so they can receive objective feedback. Interestingly, as we have conducted research to improve how we do MI training, one option we considered was not requiring work samples. We noted, as had many others, that providers were very reluctant to comply with requests to provide work samples for coaching (e.g., Schumacher, Madson, & Norquist, 2011; Schumacher et al., 2012). To test this assumption, we informally surveyed providers we had trained about the perceived value of getting feedback on work samples. Much to our surprise, even among groups of trainees who had shown great reluctance to submit work samples for feedback, responses were uniformly supportive of this practice.

MOTIVATIONAL INTERVIEWING TRAINER TIPS

Set realistic expectations
Be open-minded
Get objective feedback

TRAINING CHALLENGE 1: CLIENTS WHO FRUSTRATE YOU

Description

In MI training we deliver to providers who are already in practice (i.e., not students), those who attend the trainings will often describe de-identified examples of clients they see. The clients that providers discuss most frequently are those with whom they have a long-standing relationship. Sometimes they will discuss long-standing positive relationships with clients. These relationships are generally characterized by the client attending all appointments, following the provider's guidance, and speaking positively about their experience with the provider. In our experience, these cases are often discussed as examples of either (1) how the provider has already successfully used MI to motivate change in the past, or (2) a client for whom the provider believes MI would "work." Closer examination of the first case often reveals that the client was highly motivated for change at the outset of his or her interactions with the provider, and it was this intrinsic motivation that helped foster a long-standing positive relationship rather than MI. Remember, MI is not practice as usual and it is highly unlikely that a provider without training in MI is actually practicing MI (Miller & Rollnick, 2009). Closer examination of the second case often reveals that the client who is perceived as the "perfect MI client" actually does not need MI at all; he or she has sufficient intrinsic motivation to implement provider recommendations and/or develop and follow through on his or her own plan for change without MI.

More commonly, providers who attend our trainings will discuss clients with whom they (and sometimes the entire staff at a facility) have a long-standing negative relationship. From their perspective, the water that has passed under the bridge in these long-standing relationships is littered with missed appointments, requests for special treatment, non-compliance with recommendations, disruptive behavior, and so on. These clients are often presented as a challenge to the MI system—clients who cannot possibly benefit from MI and for whom a more confrontational, directive, and possibly even punitive approach is necessary. Although MI is not a panacea (Miller & Rollnick, 2009) and is not a guaranteed solution to every problem with every client, closer evaluation of these cases often reveals a pattern of provider-client interactions that may serve to entrench rather than reduce discord and sustain talk (Moyers, Miller & Hendrickson, 2005). From the client perspective, the water under the bridge in these long-standing negative relationships is often littered with lack of understanding, improper treatment (long wait times, insufficient time with a provider, rude staff), unsolicited advice, confrontation, and/or direct orders. Whatever the cause, long-standing negative client-provider relationships seem to be a source of significant frustration to providers. The following example illustrates a case in which a long-standing relationship may elicit frustration from a provider.

> Example: *Bob is diagnosed with a serious mental illness and has been a client at a community mental health center on and off for approximately 20 years. Over those 20 years the staff has seen Bob cycle through "good periods" when he takes his medications and attends other services such as counseling and vocational rehabilitation, and "bad periods" when he does not take his medication or follow other recommendations. During these "bad periods" Bob often ends up homeless or in jail. These bad periods are often very disheartening and frustrating to providers. It is also frustrating to providers that when Bob returns to the community mental health center for services after one of these "bad periods" he does not openly discuss what they perceive as the central cause of his recent misfortune—his lack of compliance with treatment. Instead he complains that his case manager is never available to drive him to doctor's appointments or to help him get his benefits check.*

Providers we train and work with also describe encounters with clients who seem to enter the client-provider relationship with a "chip on their shoulder." These clients may perceive that they have been mistreated (by the facility at which they are seeking service, their family, the criminal justice system, life circumstances, other providers, etc.), believe that the interventions offered are not appropriate or sufficient for their specific needs, or have other issues that lead to immediate or almost-immediate discord between client and provider. This can be very frustrating to providers who enter the relationship with optimism and a sincere desire to help. (The unique challenges presented by clients who have been forced to participate in an intervention are addressed further in chapter 4). I (JS) vividly recall an occasion when another provider's client came to the reception area of my office stating that he had a question about his medication and was told I was the person to ask. Being a psychologist (who doesn't prescribe), I wasn't sure how I could be helpful, but knew that the young man had misconceptions about my role in his treatment that needed to be clarified. As soon as we had found a confidential location to discuss his concerns, I was immediately accosted with very loudly voiced accusations that I had withheld medication from him. By using the spirit and strategies of MI, I was able to de-escalate and clarify the situation and, most importantly, avoid feeling frustrated or intimidated by this client. The following example illustrates a client with whom a provider may experience immediate frustration.

> Example: *After an hour in the waiting room, Rachel is called back to the exam area for her prenatal visit. After a nurse takes her vital signs and walks her to an exam room, she refuses to enter the room, stating, "You are just going to make me wait here again. I know I'm not a doctor, and I know this is a free clinic, but my time is valuable and I deserve some respect." After the nurse finally convinces Rachel to enter the exam room and have a seat on the exam table, Rachel proceeds to answer the nurse's questions about her health since the last visit with curt and hostile sounding replies.*

Proposed Strategy 1: Affirmation List

As described in chapter 2, during an MI session affirmations are used primarily to help clients see their strengths, resources, and previous successes from which a change effort may build. However, in our years of providing training to various audiences, we have come to identify another potential use for affirmations—to help providers see clients' strengths, resources, and previous successes, thereby reducing their frustration. In frustrating interactions with clients, whether the relationship is long-standing or brand new, we have observed that many providers seem to make what social psychologists have termed the "fundamental attribution error" (Ross, 1977). The fundamental attribution error describes the tendency of people to underestimate the impact of situational factors on others' behavior and to overestimate the impact of dispositional factors. We infer that many providers may make this error in thinking about the clients who frustrate them, because of what they tell us about those clients: "he just doesn't want to change," "you just can't talk to people like that," "she came in with a chip on her shoulder." It could also be inferred from what they fail to mention to us about the client or his or her situation: "she has had to wait at least an hour in the waiting room for every visit," "his medications cause terrible side effects," or "he has had 12 different case managers assigned to him over the last 20 years."

The foundational spirit of MI, as noted in chapter 2, requires not only evocation (of change talk), but also collaboration, acceptance, and compassion. Thus feelings of frustration and the negative thoughts about a client that likely accompany those feelings are impediments to MI practice. To help those we train, coach, and supervise overcome this common barrier to MI practice, we have found helpful to first ask them to list at least five (and ideally more) strengths or accomplishments that describe this client before discussing MI-consistent strategies that might be used. By focusing on the characteristics or accomplishments of a client that are worthy of affirming, provider perspectives of a client often shift and they are better able to be collaborative, accepting, and compassionate. In turn this spirit of collaboration, acceptance, and compassion better allows providers to see the role that situational factors (sometimes including the provider's own behavior!) may have played in eliciting non-adherence, complaints, or hostility from the client. With this fresh perspective, providers are often able to more effectively identify and apply other MI strategies to help clients move toward positive change.

Example: MI-Consistent/Inconsistent Affirmation List

The following examples will illustrate how to identify when you are frustrated with a client (like Bob or Rachel) and might benefit from developing an affirmation list, as well as how the list might look. You will notice that these examples differ from many of the other examples in this book as they do not represent sample dialogue between a provider and a client. Rather, they represent examples of what a provider might say to themselves or to another provider about a client.

MI-Inconsistent: *"Bob needs to take responsibility for his own mental health. He is in complete denial about his mental illness. He comes in here with such a strong sense of entitlement; he thinks case managers are like personal assistants."*

MI-Inconsistent: *"Rachel is a hostile person. She has no right to treat people that way and if she's not careful she's going to cross the line and get kicked out of this clinic. What does she expect from a free clinic, anyway?"*

This type of thinking about a client—a list of weaknesses, liabilities, and deficits—does not foster MI spirit and makes it very hard for a provider to apply other MI strategies that might promote change.

Somewhat MI-Consistent: *"We need to find someone to take Bob to pick up his benefits check."*

Somewhat MI Consistent: *"Rachel struggles with long wait times."*

The first example illustrates a provider thinking about a client in a way that shows compassion and a desire to help. However, it also suggests the provider is thinking of the client as a passive recipient of services who needs staff to "do" for him, rather than an autonomous person capable of collaborating in his own care. The second example illustrates a provider who is thinking about a client in a somewhat but not fully empathic and supportive fashion.

MI-Consistent: *"Bob has really shown perseverance. Despite the ups and downs of the past 20 years, he keeps coming back and trying to make changes in his life. He has also been very patient with us—I know these case management changes have been confusing and frustrating to him. He also knows a lot of what he needs to get back to health and stability, regular medical care, regular income, and so on."*

MI-Consistent: *"You've got to admire Rachel's dedication to her baby. She doesn't come from a social circle that really supports the importance of prenatal care, and the wait times people experience when they receive services here would try anyone's patience—and yet she keeps coming back."*

This type of thinking about a client or creating a list of strengths and accomplishments fosters MI spirit and makes it much easier for a provider to apply other MI strategies in a manner that will help promote positive change.

TRAINING CHALLENGE 2: CLIENTS LIKE YOU

Description

If you've lost 10 pounds, does that make you an expert on weight loss? What if you've lost 50 pounds? What about 100 pounds? If you used to have an alcohol use disorder and have been sober for 20 years, does that make you an expert on recovery? If you were a youth offender and turned your life around, does that make you an expert on offender rehabilitation? From an MI perspective, the answer would be: yes—sort of. it makes you an expert on how you successfully lost weight, stopped drinking, or turned your life around. And, if you are a weight loss counselor, an addiction counselor, or work in the juvenile justice system, there will undoubtedly be clients who will benefit from the wisdom of your personal experience. However, there will also undoubtedly be clients whose best strategy for weight loss, sobriety, or rehabilitation looks almost nothing like the strategy you successfully used to achieve those goals. In order to be MI-consistent in your approach to helping others, it is important to remember that in each interaction with a client there are two experts in the room: the client is an expert on his or her situation, values, preferences, etc. and the provider is an expert on how others (including possibly the provider himself) have successfully achieved changes in their lives (Miller & Rollnick, 2002).

Our experience in providing MI training is that many undergraduate students, graduate students, and professionals of all types are inclined to assume that the strategies that have worked for them will work for others. This is true in "real play" exercises in which participants in our trainings partner-up and take turns discussing changes they are considering and practicing MI skills. The changes discussed in these real play exercises are often typical, everyday changes that most people have tried to make; things like reorganizing a closet, starting an exercise program, or watching less television. It is quite common, especially during early practice exercises, for us to overhear comments such as, "Have you tried [strategy]? It worked for me!" Participants often find themselves drawing on their personal experience to advise their partner rather than sticking to the use of MI skills.

We also observe this tendency in role-play exercises, case discussions, and supervision sessions based on actual or role-played interactions with a client who is considering a bigger life change, such as abstaining from alcohol use after years of heavy drinking or better managing their blood sugar to get control of their diabetes. We have observed that providers who had successfully made the change being considered by their client often favored sharing the strategies that had worked for them rather than eliciting from the client the strategies that he or she believes might work best. Providers who had similar experiences also at times seemed to assume that the client's underlying motivations, hesitations, and so on were identical to the provider's. For example, during a case discussion, a provider presenting a client who repeatedly expressed the belief that substance abuse treatment was not the right place for him, because he was not as bad the other clients, might say, "I was just like him. I thought I was so different than everyone else. He just needs to get past that." Miller, Sorensen, Selzer, and Brigham (2006) note that there is evidence that substance abuse treatment providers who are in recovery may be less open to varied perspectives on substance abuse treatment, and the same may be true for providers in other areas who have overcome the same problems their clients are facing.

To combat what seems to be a fairly common tendency to assume that having had a similar personal experience gives us a unique understanding of the personal experience of our clients, we recommend using empathic listening strategies, particularly reflections and open questions. When beginning to implement MI, it may be most important to intentionally use these strategies when you are *most certain* that you understand the client's perspective. This will create opportunities to see firsthand that sometimes your assumptions are accurate and other times they are not. In cases where you lack certainty, checking your assumptions will likely come more naturally to you, and you probably won't have to be as intentional about it.

Proposed Strategy 1: Reflective Listening

In teaching the concept of reflective listening in MI, Miller and Rollnick (2013) often refer to Thomas Gordon's (1970) model of communication. In this model, communication involves three processes: encoding, hearing, and decoding. Encoding is the process whereby the speaker identifies what he or she wishes to express and chooses words through wish to express it. Hearing, as you might guess, is the process whereby the listener perceives the words uttered by the speaker. Decoding is the process by which the listener infers the speaker's meaning from the words he or she has heard. As Miller and Rollnick (2013) note, there are three places where communication can go awry: (1) the speaker may not clearly state what it was he or she hoped to express; (2) the listener may not clearly hear what the speaker said; or (3) the listener may mistake what the speaker meant by what he or she said.

QUICK REFERENCE

How Communication Can Go Wrong

Speaker doesn't say what he or she means.
Listener doesn't accurately hear what speaker said.
Listener misinterprets what speaker meant.

From an MI perspective, reflective listening is about confirming that what a listener thinks the speaker meant is what he or she actually meant. Thus reflective listening, when well done, can be very useful to help ensure that our assumptions about the ways in which our clients might be similar or different from us are accurate.

Table 8.1 is an example of how we presented this model of communication in a recent training session. As you review Table 8.1, imagine what would have happened if Mike had gone with his assumptions about what I (JS) meant, rather than using a reflection to check those assumptions. If he assumed I thought he was angry, he might have wondered what he had done that would have made me think he was angry. This in turn might have caused him to feel worried or irritated. If he assumed I heard his stomach growl, then he might have felt self-conscious and embarrassed. Worst of all, if he hadn't clarified what I meant, I might have missed the opportunity to try my first deep-fried tamale (if you're ever in the Mississippi Delta, I highly recommend it).

Example: MI-Consistent/Inconsistent Reflective Listening

The following examples will illustrate how to use reflective listening to ensure you aren't making assumptions about a client because he or she seems similar to you.

Client Statement: *"I admit I have problems, but I don't need substance abuse treatment. Everyone here is way worse than me."*

MI-Inconsistent: *"Do you think you are different than everyone else here?"*

Although this question seeks to clarify what the client meant, it is not a reflection and it is not MI-consistent. Closed questions such are often

Table 8.1. COMMUNICATION MODEL EXAMPLE

Encoding Error
Julie Thinks: "I wonder if Mike wants to grab lunch during the break."
Julie Says: "Are you angry?" (Instead of, "Are you hungry?")
Mike Reflects: "You think I'm angry with you."
Hearing Error
Julie Says: "Are you hungry?"
Mike Hears: "Are you angry?"
Mike Reflects: "You think I'm angry with you."
Decoding Error
Mike Hears: "Are you hungry?"
Mike Thinks: "Oh no, she must have heard my stomach growl."
Mike Reflects: "You heard my stomach growl."

perceived (and intended) as very confrontational, and thus are likely to result in defensive responding from the client (Miller & Rollnick, 2013).

Somewhat MI-Consistent: *"You don't need substance abuse treatment."*

This statement is somewhat MI-consistent. The simple reflection expresses empathy, but is likely to result in either a simple yes or no response or encourage sustain talk.

MI-Consistent: *"You think you are different than everyone else here."*

This statement is MI-consistent because it seeks to clarify what the client meant by his or her statement. The client is likely to respond by either correcting the provider if that is not what he or she meant or further exploring the ways in which he or she is different from and perhaps similar to the other clients in the treatment program.

Proposed Strategy 2: Open Questions

Open questions are another great way to test assumptions you may have about a client. When it comes to testing your preconceptions about a client, often the most important open question to ask is the one of which you feel certain of the answer. A classic example of this is in the Miller and Rollnick (1998) *Motivational Interviewing: Professional Training Series* videos. In one of the case examples in this series, John, who was referred from his employer subsequent to a positive drug screen, notes that if he had kids he might have to rethink his drug use. To this, Dr. William R. Miller responds, "And why would you do that?" Seems like an obvious, almost senseless question. Everyone knows that it isn't good for parents to use drugs, right? But drawing on the communication model, the MI provider is always aware that he or she might be surprised (perhaps very surprised) by the answer. John might have said, "Drugs cost money, and if I had kids I'd need to spend the money on the kids." Or he might have revealed, "I've had two prior arrests for drug possession, the next time I get caught, I'm going to prison for sure. You just can't do that to kids." Or he might have said, "My parents were heavy drug users and it really messed me up." Or he might have said any number of other things. By asking John an open question, Dr. Miller not only creates an opportunity for John to voice his own reasons for change (a central goal in MI), but also creates an opportunity to test any assumptions he might have about John's reasons for change based on his own experience as a parent or the experience of countless clients with whom he has worked over the years. Dr. Miller also avoids the potential discord that can result from erroneous assumptions. For example, if Dr. Miller had assumed that John's objection to parental drug use was a moral one (e.g., "everyone knows parents shouldn't use drugs") when in fact it was a practical one (e.g., "I think it is fine for parents to smoke marijuana, the problem is that it's illegal in this state, and I don't want my kids to suffer from the legal consequences."), John would likely have felt judged and discord would have emerged.

Example: MI-Consistent/Inconsistent Open Questions

The following examples will illustrate how to use open questions to ensure you aren't making assumptions about a client because he or she seems similar to you.

Client Statement: *"I admit I have problems, but I don't need substance abuse treatment. Everyone here is way worse than me."*

MI-Inconsistent: *"Do you think you are different than everyone else here?"*

This question is not an open question, it is a closed question. It is also MI-inconsistent because it is like to be perceived by the client (and possibly be intended by the provider) as a direct confrontation of the client's assertion that he doesn't need treatment. This is likely to increase discord in the interaction.

Somewhat MI-Consistent: *"In what ways are others worse than you?"*

This open question is somewhat MI-consistent in that it invites the client to elaborate. However, it invites the client to elaborate on why others are worse than the client. This is sustain talk and is unlikely to help the client move toward change on the problems he or she does have.

MI-Consistent: *"So you have problems, but you aren't sure this is the right place for you. Tell me a little more about the types of problems you have had."*

MI-Consistent: *"So you aren't certain this is the right place for you to solve your problems. What would be helpful to you?"*

These provider utterances are MI-consistent. Both begin with a reflection of the client's uncertainty about treatment. This is likely to reduce discord. Then the provider uses open questions to gather more information about the client's perspective. In the first example, the provider seeks to gain a better understanding of why the client perceives substance use as a problem. In the second example, the provider seeks to gain a better understanding of what type of treatment or assistance (if any) the client perceives he or she needs to overcome the problem. Although the questions will give the provider very different information, both are likely to help the provider gain a better understanding of this client's unique perspective.

SUMMARY

In this chapter we provide tips for learning and implementing MI-consistent practices in your daily work. We have found those who set realistic expectations, keep an open mind about the role of MI in their work, and get objective feedback about their use of MI have the most positive training outcomes and enjoyable training experience. We have also found two situations, summarized in Table 8.2, that impede implementation of MI for many providers. The first is clients with whom a provider feels frustrated. Intentionally focusing on the strengths, achievements, and positive qualities of these clients seems to help

Table 8.2. SUMMARY OF TRAINING CHALLENGES

Training Challenge	Suggested MI Strategies
Clients who frustrate you.	Affirmation lists: Developing lists of the positive qualities and strengths of clients to shift focus away from perceived deficits.
Clients who are like you.	Reflective listening: Use of reflection to better understand and appreciate the meaning of the client's comments and experience.
	Open questions: Using open questions aimed at genuinely understanding the client's concerns, motivations, and understanding.

providers adopt the spirit of MI in their interactions with them. The second impediment is a temptation to draw more heavily on the provider's personal wisdom and experience than the client's wisdom and experience when working with clients who are similar to the provider. Very intentional use of reflective listening and open questions may increase collaboration and support of autonomy in these situations. We believe that the practices and principles of MI are within everyone's grasp. With practice and appropriate training, you can achieve whatever level of expertise you believe is appropriate for your practice.

CONCLUSIONS

We hope you have enjoyed reading *Fundamentals of Motivational Interviewing: Tips and Strategies for Addressing Common Clinical Challenges.* We also hope that this book has provided food for thought on how the principles and practices of MI might be applied to a variety of ubiquitous, but nonetheless frustrating, clinical challenges. MI is a powerful communication style that can facilitate positive change in even the most seemingly hopeless situations. We have observed this phenomenon directly in clients we have treated and participants in our research studies. We have heard this feedback from providers we have trained and also experienced the benefits of MI firsthand. We both look forward to opportunities to participate in, as well as facilitate practice exercises, during the training we provide. That is because, depending on the particular exercise, participation provides opportunities for us to discuss a change we are considering in our own lives with a training participant who seeks to (1) empathically and collaboratively reflect or evoke our desire, ability, reasons, need, and commitment to change; and/or (2) affirm our strengths and past successes; and/or (3) help us develop a realistic and personalized plan for change. Those opportunities, in turn, provide a vehicle through which we develop or renew our motivation for changes in our own lives—from organizing a closet or file cabinet to healthy eating and regular exercise.

As noted in chapter 1, the body of research on MI is growing at an incredible pace (Lundahl & Burke, 2009). Moreover, this research indicates that almost invariably when MI is applied to clients experiencing a particular problem or challenge, it helps facilitate positive change—and in many cases with a smaller dose of an intervention (Burke, Arkowitz, & Menchola, 2003; Hettema, Steele, & Miller, 2005; Lundahl, Kunz, Brownell, Tollefson, & Burke, 2010; Rubak, Sandbaek, Lauritzen, & Christensen, 2005). However, it is also important to note, that for many problems and challenges to which MI is applied, the research support is still emerging. In those areas, we believe that MI is best applied as an adjunct to approaches with a longer track record and stronger evidence base rather than a stand-alone intervention. This book is designed to support this adjunctive use of MI. In the course of practice-as-usual, a provider may apply the relevant MI concepts, principles, and strategies described in this book as needed to help overcome hurdles introduced by less readiness to change, loss of momentum, psychiatric symptoms, and working with multiple individuals. To do this, however, we remind you of the importance of the MI spirit as a foundation for the integration of MI with practice as usual! In fact, our discussions of MI-consistent and MI-inconsistent applications of strategies often emphasized the importance of the MI spirit in guiding the application of a particular strategy. Based on our experience training others in MI we cannot over state this point.

In 1983, Dr. William R. Miller introduced an approach to helping clients achieve positive life changes that can best be described as revolutionary. This approach was elaborated by Dr. Miller and Dr. Steve Rollnick in 1991 with the publication of the first edition of the *Motivational Interviewing* text. Since that time, MI has been refined, studied, and practiced by countless others. We are excited to be a part of this ongoing revolution and invite you, our reader, to see for yourself how collaboration, evocation, acceptance, and compassion can help your clients overcome the most difficult challenges they face on the path to positive life changes. Whether this book is the beginning of your development as a MI-consistent provider or an addition to your MI library our hope is that we have contributed to your understanding of MI and its application to challenges faced in helping others change.

REFERENCES

Adams, J. B., & Madson, M. B. (2006). Reflection and outlook for the future of addictions treatment and training: An interview with William R. Miller. *Journal of Teaching in the Addictions, 5,* 95–109.

Ahmrein, P. C., Miller, W. R., Yahne, C. E., Palmer, M., & Fulcher, L. (2003). Client commitment language during motivational interviewing predicts drug use outcomes. *Journal of Consulting and Clinical Psychology, 71,* 862–878.

Ajzen, I., & Albarracín, D. (2007). Predicting and changing behavior: A reasoned action approach. In I. Ajzen, D. Albarracín, R. Hornik, I. Ajzen, D. Albarracín, & R. Hornik (Eds.), *Prediction and change of health behavior: Applying the reasoned action approach* (pp. 3–21). Mahwah, NJ: Lawrence Erlbaum Associates.

American Psychiatric Association. (2000). *Diagnostic and statistical manual of mental disorders* (4th ed., text rev.). Washington, DC: American Psychiatric Publishing.

American Psychiatric Association. (2013). *Diagnostic and statistical manual of mental disorders* (5th ed.). Arlington, VA: American Psychiatric Publishing.

Arkowitz, H., Westra, H. A., Miller, W. R., & Rollnick, S. (Eds.) (2008). *Motivational interviewing in the treatment of psychological problems.* New York: The Guilford Press.

Armstrong, M. J., Mottershead, T. A., Ronksley, P. E., Sigal, R. J., Campbell, T. S., & Hemmelgarn, B. R. (2011). Motivational interviewing to improve weight loss in overweight and/or obese patients: A systematic review and meta-analysis of randomized controlled trials. *Obesity Reviews, 12,* 709–723.

Atkinson, C., & Woods, K. (2003). Motivational interviewing strategies for disaffected secondary school students: A case example. *Educational Psychology in Practice, 19,* 49–64.

Bandura, A. (1977). Self-efficacy: Toward a unifying theory of behavioral change. *Psychological Review, 84,* 191–215.

Bandura, A. (2004). *Self-efficacy: The exercise of control.* New York, NY: Freeman.

Barwick, M. A., Bennett, L. M., Johnson, S. N., McGowan, J., & Moore, J. E. (2012). Training health and mental health professionals in motivational interviewing: A systematic review. *Children and Youth Services Review, 34,* 1786–1795.

Beck, A. T., & Steer, R. A. (1988). *Manual for the Beck hopelessness scale.* San Antonio, TX: Psychological Corp.

Bisono, A. M., Knapp Manuel, J., & Forcehimes, A. A. (2006). Promoting treatment adherence through motivational interviewing. In W. T. O'Donohue & E. R. Levensky

(Eds), *Promoting treatment adherence: A practical handbook for health care providers* (pp. 71–84). Thousand Oaks, CA: SAGE Publications.

Boardman, T., Catley, D., Grobe, J. E., Little, T. D., & Ahluwalia, J. S. (2006). Using motivational interviewing with smokers: Do therapist behaviors relate to engagement and therapeutic alliance? *Journal of Substance Abuse Treatment, 31,* 329–339. doi:10.1016/j.jsat.2006.05.006

Brehm, S., & Brehm, J. W. (1981). *Psychological reactance: A theory of freedom and control.* New York: Academic Press.

Brennan, L. M., Shelleby, E. C., Shaw, D. S., Gardner, F., Dishion, T. J., & Wilson, M. (2013). Indirect effects of the family check-up on school-age academic achievement through improvements in parenting in early childhood. *Journal of Educational Psychology, 105,* 762–773. doi:10.1037/a0032096

Burke, B. L. (2011). What can motivational interviewing do for you? *Cognitive and Behavioral Practice, 18,* 74–81.

Burke, B. L., Arkowtiz, J., & Menchola, M. (2003). The efficacy of motivational interviewing: A meta-analysis of controlled clinical trials. *Journal of Consulting and Clinical Psychology, 71,* 843–861.

Carcone, A., Naar-King, S., Brogan, K. E., Albrecht, T., Barton, E., Foster, T., & Marshall, S. (2013). Provider communication behaviors that predict motivation to change in black adolescents with obesity. *Journal of Developmental and Behavioral Pediatrics, 34,* 599–608.

Carey, K. B., Leontieva, L., Dimmock, J., Maisto, S. A., & Batki, S. L. (2007). Adapting motivational interventions for comorbid schizophrenia and alcohol use disorders. *Clinical Psychology, 14,* 39–57.

Catley, D., Harris, K. J., Mayo, M. S., Hall, S., Okuyemi, K. S., Boardman, T. et al. (2006). Adherence to principles of motivational interviewing and therapeutic outcomes. *Behavioural and Cognitive Psychotherapy, 34,* 43–56.

Clark, D. M. (1999). Anxiety disorders: Why they persist and how to treat them. *Behaviour Research and Therapy, 37,* S5–S27.

Coffey, S. F., Schumacher, J. A., Nosen, E., Littlefield, A. K., Henslee, A., Lappen, A., & Stasiewicz, P. R. (2013). Trauma-focused exposure therapy for chronic post-traumatic stress disorder in alcohol and drug dependent patients: A randomized clinical trial. Manuscript submitted for publication.

Cohen, L. J. (2010). Psychotic disorders. In Weiner, I. B., and Craighead, W. E. (Eds.), *The Corsini encyclopedia of psychology* (4th ed). (pp. 1394–1396). Hoboken, NJ: John Wiley & Sons.

Connors, G. J., DiClemente, C. C., Velasquez, M. M., & Donovan, D. M. (2013). *Substance abuse treatment and the stages of change: Selecting and planning interventions* (2nd ed). New York: Guilford Press.

Curtis, N. M., Ronan, K. R., & Borduin, C. M. (2004). Multisystemic treatment: A meta-analysis of outcome studies. *Journal of Family Psychology, 18,* 411–419.

D'Amico, E. J., Hunter, S. B., Miles, J. V., Ewing, B. A., & Osilla, K. (2013). A randomized controlled trial of a group motivational interviewing intervention for adolescents with a first time alcohol or drug offense. *Journal of Substance Abuse Treatment, 45,* 400–408. doi:10.1016/j.jsat.2013.06.005

Defife, J. A., Conklin, C. Z., Smith, J. M., & Poole, J. (2010). Brief Reports: Psychotherapy appointment no-shows: Rates and reasons. *Psychotherapy Theory, Research, Practice, and Training, 47,* 413–417.

DiClemente, C. C. (2003). *Addiction and change: How addictions develop and addicted people recover.* New York: Guilford Press.

DiClemente, C. C., & Velazquez, M. M. (2002). Motivational interviewing and the stages of change. In W. M. Miller, & S. Rolnick (Eds.), *Motivational intervewing: Preparing people for change* (2nd ed). New York, NY: Guilford.

Dimeff, L. A., Baer, J. S., Kivlahan, D. R., & Marlatt, G. A. (1999). *Brief alcohol screening and intervention for college students: A harm reduction approach.* New York, NY: The Guilford Press.

D'Onofrio, G., & Degutis, L. C. (2002). Preventive care in the emergency department: Screening and brief intervention for alcohol problems in the emergency department: A systematic review. *Academic Emergency Medicine, 9,* 627–638.

Doyle, A. C., & Pollack, M. H. (2003). Establishment of remission criteria for anxiety disorders. *Journal of Clinical Psychiatry, 64 (suppl 15),* 40–45.

Drymalski, W., & Campbell, T. (2009). A review of motivational interviewing to enhance adherence to antipsychotic medication in patients with schizophrenia: Evidence and recommendations. *Journal of Mental Health, 18,* 6–15.

D'Zurilla, T. J., & Goldfried, M. R. (1971). Problem solving and behavior modification. *Journal of Abnormal Psychology, 78,* 107–126.

D'Zurilla, T. J., & Nezu, A. M. (2007). *Problem-solving therapy: A positive approach to clinical intervention* (3rd ed.). New York, NY: Springer.

Enea, V., & Dafinoiu, I. (2009). Motivational/solution-focused intervention for reducing school truancy among adolescents. *Journal of Cognitive and Behavioral Psychotherapies, 9,* 185–198.

Ericsson, K. A., & Charness, N. (1994). Expert performance: Its structure and acquisition. *American Psychologist, 49,* 725–747.

Farbing, C. A., & Johnson, W. R. (2008). Motivational interviewing in the correctional system: An attempt to implement motivational interviewing in criminal justice. In H. Arkowitz, H. A., Westra, W. R. Miller, & S. Rollnick (Eds.), *Motivational interviewing in the treatment of psychological problems* (pp. 324–342). New York: Guilford Press.

Fenger, M., Mortensen, E. L., Poulsen, S., & Lau, M. (2011). No-shows, drop-outs and completers in psychotherapeutic treatment: Demographic and clinical predictors in a large sample of non-psychotic patients. *Nordic Journal of Psychiatry, 65,* 183–191.

Forsyth, D. R. (2011). The nature and significance of groups. In R. K. Conyne (Ed.), *The Oxford handbook of group counseling* (pp. 19–35). New York: Oxford University Press.

Frey, A. J., Cloud, R. N., Lee, J., Small, J. W., Seeley, J. R., Feil, E. G., et al. (2011). The promise of motivational interviewing in school mental health. *School Mental Health, 3,* 1–12.

Fromm, E. (1956). *The art of loving.* New York: Harper Perennial.

Gance-Cleveland, B. (2007). Motivational interviewing: Improving patient education. *Journal of Pediatric Health Care, 21,* 81–88. doi:10.1016/j.pedhc.2006.05.002

Gaughf, C. J., & Madson, M. B. (2008). The abstinence violation effect. In G. L. Fischer & N. A. Roqet (Eds.), *Encyclopedia of substance abuse prevention, treatment, and recovery*. Los Angeles, CA: Sage Publications.

Glynn, L. H., & Moyers, T. B. (2010). Chasing change talk: The clinician's role in evoking client language about change. *Journal of Substance Abuse Treatment, 39*, 65–70. doi:10.1016/j.jsat.2010.03.012

Gordon, T. (1970). *Parent effectiveness training: The proven program for raising responsible children*. New York: Harmony Books.

Graeber, D. A., Moyers, T. B., Griffith, G., Guajardo, E., & Tonigan, S. (2003). Addiction services: A pilot study comparing motivational interviewing and an educational intervention in patients with schizophrenia and alcohol use disorders. *Community Mental Health Journal, 39*, 189–202.

Heckman, C. J., Egleston, B. L., Hofmann, M. T. (2010). Efficacy of motivational interviewing for smoking cessation: A systematic review and meta-analysis. *Tobacco Control, 19*, 410–416.

Hettema, J. E., & Hendricks, P. S. (2011). Motivational interviewing for smoking cessation: A meta-analytic review. *Journal of Consulting and Clinical Psychology, 78*, 868–884.

Hettema, J., Steele, J., & Miller, W. R. (2005). Motivational interviewing. *Annual Review of Clinical Psychology, 1*, 91–111.

Hill, C. E., & O'Brien, K. M. (1999). *Helping skills: Facilitating exploration, insight, and action*. Washington, DC: American Psychological Association.

Hohman, M. (2012). *Motivational interviewing in social work practice*. New York: Guilford Press.

Hofmann, S. G., & Smits, J. A. (2008). Cognitive-behavioral therapy for adult anxiety disorders: A meta-analysis of randomized placebo-controlled trials. *Journal of Clinical Psychiatry, 69*, 621–632.

Holstad, M., DiIorio, C., Kelley, M. E., Resnicow, K., & Sharma, S. (2011). Group motivational interviewing to promote adherence to antiretroviral medications and risk reduction behaviors in HIV infected women. *AIDS and Behavior, 15*, 885–896. doi:10.1007/s10461-010-9865-y

Horvath, A. O. (2001). The alliance. *Psychotherapy, 38*, 365–372.

Houck, J. M., Moyers, T. B., & Tesche, C. D. (2013). Through a glass darkly: Some insights on change talk via magnetoencephalography. *Psychology of Addictive Behaviors, 27*, 489–500. doi:10.1037/a0029896

Ingersoll, K. S., Wagner, C. C., & Gharib, S. (2002). *Motivational groups for community substance abuse programs*. Richmond, VA: Mid-Atlantic Addiction Technology Transfer Center.

Interian, A., Lewis-Fernández, R., Gara, M. A., & Escobar, J. I. (2013). A randomized-controlled trial of an intervention to improve antidepressant adherence among Latinos with depression. *Depression and Anxiety, 30*, 688–696. doi:10.1002/da.22052

Ivey, A. E., & Bradford Ivey, M. (2003). *Intentional interviewing and counseling: Facilitating client development in a multicultural society*. Pacific Grove, CA: Brooks/Cole.

Janis, I. L., & Mann, L. (1977). *Decision making: A psychological analysis of conflict, choice and commitment*. New York: Free Press.

Jensen, C. D., Cushing, C. C., Aylward, B. S., Craig, J. T., Sorell, D. M., & Steele, R. G. (2011). Effectiveness of motivational interviewing interventions for adolescent substance use behavior change: A meta-analytic review. *Journal of Consulting and Clinical Psychology, 79*(4), 433–440.

Kazdin, A. E. (2005). Treatment outcomes, common factors, and continued neglect of mechanisms of change. *Clinical Psychology: Science and Practice, 12*, 184–188. doi:10.1093/clipsy/bpi023

Kazdin, A. E., & Blaze, S. L. (2011). Rebooting psychotherapy research and practice to reduce the burden of mental illness. *Perspectives on Psychological Science, 6*, 21–37.

Kessler, R. C., Chiu, W. T., Demler, O., & Walters, E. E. (2005). Prevalence, severity, and comorbidity of twelve-month DSM-IV disorders in the National Comorbidity Survey Replication (NCS-R). *Archives of General Psychiatry, 62*, 617–627.

Kessler, R. c., McGonagle, K. A., Zhao, S., Nelson, C. B., Hughes, M., Eshleman, S., Wittchen, H.-U., & Kendler, K. S. (1994). Lifetime and 12-month prevalence of DSM-III-R psychiatric disorders in the United States. *Journal of the American Medical Association Psychiatry, 51*, 8–19.

Lane, C. A., & Rollnick, S. (2009). Motivational interviewing. In S. A. Shumaker, J. K. Ockene, & K. A. Riekert (Eds.), *The handbook of health behavior change* (3rd ed.; pp. 151–167). New York, NY US: Springer Publishing Co.

Leffingwell, T. R., Neumann, C. A., Babitzke, A. C., Leedy, M. J., & Walters, S. T. (2007). Social psychology and motivational interviewing: A review of relevant principles and recommendations for research and practice. *Behavioural and Cognitive Psychotherapy, 35*, 31–45. doi:10.1017/S1352465806003067

Leukefeld, C., Carlton, E. L., Staton-Tindall, M., & Delaney, M. (2012). Six-month follow-up changes for TANF-eligible clients involved in Kentucky's targeted assessment program. *Journal of Social Service Research, 38*, 366–381. doi:10.1080/01488376.2011.651412

Levensky, E. R., & O'Donohue, W. T. (2006). Patient adherence and nonadherence to treatments: An overview for health care providers. In W. T. O'Donohue & E. R. Levensky (Eds), *Promoting treatment adherence: A practical handbook for health care providers* (pp. 3–14). Thousand Oaks, CA: SAGE Publications.

Lezak, M. D. (1995). *Neuropsychological assessment* (3rd ed.). New York: Oxford University Press.

Lundahl, B., & Burke, B. L. (2009). The effectiveness and applicability of motivational interviewing: A practice-friendly review of four meta-analyses. *Journal of Clinical Psychology: In Session, 65*, 1232–1245.

Lundahl, B. W., Kunz, C., Brownell, C., Tollefson, D., & Burke, B. L. (2010). A meta-analysis of motivational interviewing: Twenty-five years of empirical studies. *Research on Social Work Practice, 20*, 137–160.

Madson, M. B. Bonnell, M. A., McMurtry, S., & Noble, J. (2009). *HUB City Steps–motivational interviewing counselor manual.* Unpublished manual. University of Southern Mississippi.

Madson, M. B., Bullock-Yowell, E. E., Speed, A. C., & Hodges, S. A. (2008). Supervising substance abuse treatment: Specific issues and a motivational interviewing model. In A. K. Hess, K. D. Hess, & T. H. Hess. (Eds.), *Psychotherapy supervision: Theory research and practice* (2nd ed; pp 340–358). Hoboken, NJ: John Wiley and Sons.

Madson, M. B., & Campbell, T. C. (2006). Measures of fidelity in motivational enhancement: A systematic review of instrumentation. *Journal of Substance Abuse Treatment, 31*, 67–73.

Madson, M. B., Campbell, T. C., Barrett, D. E., Brondino, M. J., & Melchert, T. P. (2005). Development of the Motivational Interviewing Supervision and Training Scale. *Psychology of Addictive Behaviors, 19*, 303–310.

Madson, M. B., Landry, A. S., Molaison, E. F., Schumacher, J. A., & Yadrick, K. (in press). Training MI interventionists across disciplines: A descriptive project. *Motivational Interviewing: Theory, Research, Implementation and Practice.*

Madson, M. B., Lane, C., & Noble, J. J. (2012). Delivering quality motivational interviewing training: A survey of MI trainers. *Motivational Interviewing: Theory, Research, Implementation and Practice, 1*, 16–24.

Madson, M. B., Loignon, A. C., & Lane, C. (2009). Training in motivational interviewing: A systematic review. *Journal of Substance Abuse Treatment, 36*, 101–109.

Madson, M. B., Loignon, A., Shutze, R., & Necaise, H. (2009). Examining the fit between motivational interviewing and the counseling philosophy: An emphasis on prevention. *Prevention in Counseling Psychology: Theory, Research, Practice and Training, 3*, 20–32.

Madson, M. B., Mohn, R., Zuckoff, A., Schumacher, J. A., Kogan, J., Hutchison, S., Magee, E., & Stein, B. (2013). Measuring client perceptions of motivational interviewing: Factor analysis of the client evaluation of motivational interviewing scale. *Journal of Substance Abuse Treatment, 44*, 330–335.

Madson, M. B., Schumacher, J. A., & Bonnell, M. A. (2010). Motivational interviewing and alcohol. *Healthcare Counselling and Psychotherapy Journal, 10*, 13–17.

Madson, M. B., Schumacher, J. A., Noble, J. J., & Bonnell, M. A. (2013). Teaching motivational interviewing to undergraduates: Evaluation of three approaches. *Teaching of Psychology, 40*, 242–245.

Madson, M. B., Speed, A. C., Bullock Yowell, E., & Nicholson, B. C. (2011). A pilot study evaluating a motivational interviewing seminar on graduate student skill, self-efficacy and intention to use. *Rehabilitation Counselors and Educators Association Journal, 5*, 70–79.

Marlatt, G. A., & Witkiewitz, K. (2005). Relapse prevention for alcohol and drug problems. In G. A. Marlatt & D. M. Donovan (Eds.), *Relapse prevention: Maintenance strategies in the treatment of addictive behaviors* (2nd ed; pp. 1–44). New York: Guilford Press.

Martino, S., Ball, S. A., Gallon, S. L., Hall, D., Garcia, M., Ceperich, S., Farentinos, C., Hamilton, J., & Hausotter, W. (2006). *Motivational interviewing assessment: Supervisory tools for enhancing proficiency.* Salem, OR: Northwest Frontier Addiction Technology Transfer Center, Oregon Health and Science University.

Martino, S., Carroll, K., Kostas, D., Perkins, J., & Rounsaville, B. (2002). Dual diagnosis motivational interviewing: A modification of motivational interviewing for substance-abusing patients with psychotic disorders. *Journal of Substance Abuse Treatment, 23*, 297–308.

Martino, S. Ball, S. A., Nich, C., Frankforer, T. L., & Carroll, K. M. (2008). Community program therapist adherence and competence in motivational enhancement therapy. *Drug and Alcohol Dependence, 96*, 37–48. doi:10.1016/j.drugalcdep.2008.01.020

Mason, P., & Butler, C. C. (2010). *Health behavior change: A guide for practitioners.* New York: Elsevier.

Maughan, D. R., Christiansen, E., & Jenson, W. R. (2005). Behavioral parent training as a treatment for externalizing behaviors and disruptive behavior disorders: A meta-analysis. *School Psychology Review, 34,* 267–286.

McMurran, M. (2009). Motivational interviewing with offenders: A systematic review. *Criminological Psychology, 14,* 83–100.

Miller, W. R. (1983). Motivational interviewing with problem drinkers. *Behavioural Psychotherapy, 11,* 147–172.

Miller, W. R., Forcehimes, A. A., & Zweben, A. (2011). *Treating addiction: A guide for professionals.* New York, NY: Guilford Press.

Miller, W., & Mount, K. (2001). A small study of training in motivational interviewing: Does one workshop change provider and client behavior? *Behavioural and Cognitive Psychotherapy, 29,* 457–471.

Miller, W. R., & Moyers, T. B. (2006). Eight stages in learning motivational interviewing. *Journal of Teaching in the Addictions, 5,* 13–27. doi:10.1300/J188v05n01_02

Miller, W. R., & Rollnick, S. (1991). *Motivational interviewing: Preparing people to change addictive behavior.* New York: Guilford Press.

Miller, W. R., & Rollnick, S. (1998). Motivational interviewing: Professional training videotape series. The University of New Mexico Center on Alcoholism Substance Abuse, and Addictions (UNM/CASAA).

Miller, W. R., & Rollnick, S. (2002). *Motivational interviewing: Preparing people for change* (2nd ed.). New York: Guilford Press.

Miller, W. R., & Rollnick, S. (2009). Ten things motivational interviewing is not. *Behavioural and Cognitive Psychotherapy, 37,* 129–140.

Miller, W. R., & Rollnick, S. (2013). *Motivational interviewing: Helping people change* (3rd ed.). New York, NY: Guilford Press.

Miller, W. R., & Rose, G. S. (2009). Toward a theory of motivational interviewing. *American Psychologist, 64,* 527–537.

Miller, W. R., Sorensen, J. L., Selzer, J. A., & Brigham, G. S. (2006). Disseminating evidence-based practices in substance abuse treatment: A review with suggestions. *Journal of Substance Abuse Treatment, 31,* 25–39.

Miller, W. R., Yahne, C. E., Moyers, T. B., Martinez, J., & Pirritano, M. (2004). A randomized trial of methods to help clinicians learn motivational interviewing. *Journal of Consulting and Clinical Psychology, 72,* 1050–1062.

Miller, W. R., Zweben, A., DiClemente, C. C., Rychtarik, R. C. (1992). Motivational Enhancement Therapy Manual: A clinical research guide for therapists treating individuals with alcohol abuse and dependence. *Project MATCH Monograph Series, Vol. 2.* Rockville, Maryland: National Institute on Alcohol Abuse and Alcoholism.

Moos, R. H. (2007). Theory-based active ingredients of effective treatments for substance use disorders. *Drug and Alcohol Dependence, 88,* 109–121

Moyers, T. M. (2004). History and happenstance: How motivational interviewing got its start. *Journal of Cognitive Psychotherapy: An International Quarterly, 18,* 291–298.

Moyers, T., Manuel, J., Wilson, P., Hendrickson, S., Talcott, W., & Durand, P. (2008). A randomized trial investigating training in motivational interviewing for behavioral health providers. *Behavioral and Cognitive Psychotherapy*, *36*, 149–162.

Moyers, T. B., Martin, T., Manuel, J. K., Miller, W. R., & Ernst, D. (2010). *Revised Global Scales: Motivational Interviewing Treatment Integrity 3.1.1 (MITI 3.1.1)*. University of New Mexico, Center on Alcoholism, Substance Abuse and Addictions (CASAA): Albuquerque, NM. Retrieved on July 24, 2013 from http://casaa.unm.edu/download/MITI3_1.pdf.

Moyers, T. B., & Martin, T. (2006). Therapist influence on client language during motivational interviewing sessions: Support for a potential causal mechanism. *Journal of Substance Abuse Treatment*, *30*, 245–251.

Moyers, T. B., Miller, W. R., & Hendrickson, S. M. L. (2005). How does motivational interviewing work? Therapist interpersonal skill predicts client involvement within motivational interviewing sessions. *Journal of Consulting and Clinical Psychology*, *73*, 590–598.

Murphy, C. M., Linehan, E. L., Reyner, J. C., Musser, P. H., & Taft, C. T. (2012). Moderators of response to motivational interviewing for partner-violent men. *Journal of Family Violence*, *27*, 671–680. doi:10.1007/s10896–012–9460–2

Naar-King, S., Earnshaw, P., & Breckon, J. (2013). Toward a universal maintenance intervention: Integrating cognitive-behavioral treatment with motivational interviewing for maintenance of behavior change. *Journal of Cognitive Psychotherapy*, *27*, 126–137. doi:10.1891/0889–8391.27.2.126

Naar-King, S., & Suarez, M. (2011). *Motivational interviewing with adolescents and young adults*. New York: Guilford Press.

National Alliance for the Mentally Ill. (2013). *Mental illness: What you need to know*. Brochure retrieved Nov. 12, 2013 from http://www.nami.org/Content/Navigation Menu/Inform_Yourself/About_Mental_Illness/By_Illness/MentalIllnessBrochure.pdf.

Neighbors, C., Walker, D. D., Roffman, R. A., Mbilinyi, L. F., & Edleson, J. L. (2008). Self-determination theory and motivational interviewing: Complementary models to elicit voluntary engagement by partner-abusive men. *American Journal of Family Therapy*, *36*, 126–136. doi:10.1080/01926180701236142

Nelson, H. E. (2005). *Cognitive-behavioural therapy with delusions and hallucinations: A practice manual* (2nd ed.). Cheltenham, UK: Nelson Thornes Ltd.

Nicholson, B. C., Fox, R. A., & Johnson, S. D. (2005). Parenting young children with challenging behaviour. *Infant and Child Development*, *14*, 425–428. doi:10.1002/icd.403

Passmore, J. (2011). Motivational interviewing: Techniques reflective listening. *The Coaching Psychologist*, *7*, 50–53.

Peeters, F. P. M. L., & Bayer, H. (1999). 'No-show' for initial screening at community mental health centre: Rate, reasons, and further help-seeking. *Social Psychiatry and Psychiatric Epidemiology*, *34*, 323–327.

Pirlott, A. G., Kisbu-Sakarya, Y., DeFrancesco, C. A., Elliot, D. L., & MacKinnon, D. P. (2012). Mechanisms of motivational interviewing in health promotion: A Bayesian mediation analysis. *The International Journal of Behavioral Nutrition and Physical Activity*, *9*, 69–80. doi:10.1186/1479–5868–9-69

Prochaska, J. O., & DiClemente, C. C. (1983). Stages and processes of self-change of smoking: Toward an integrative model of change. *Journal of Consulting & Clinical Psychology*, *51*, 390–395.

Prochaska, J. O., & Norcross, J. C. (2010). *Systems of psychotherapy: A transtheoretical analysis* (7th ed). Belmont, CA: Thomson/Brooks Cole.

Rogers, C. R. (1959). The essence of psychotherapy: A client-centered view. *Annals of Psychotherapy, 1,* 51–57.

Rollnick, S., Miller, W. R., & Butler, C. C. (2008). *Motivational interviewing in health care: Helping patients change behavior.* New York: Guilford Press.

Rosengren, D. B. (2009). *Building motivational interviewing skills: A practitioner workbook.* New York: Guilford Press.

Ross, L. D. (1977). The intuitive psychologist and his shortcomings: Distortions in the attribution process. In L. Berkowitz (Ed.), *Advances in experimental social psychology* (Vol. 10, pp. 173–220). New York: Academic Press.

Rubak, S., Sandbaek, A., Lauritzen, T., & Christensen, B. (2005). Motivational interviewing: A systematic review and meta-analysis. *British Journal of General Practice, 55,* 305–312.

Rusch, N., & Corrigan, P. W. (2002). Motivational interviewing to improve insight and treatment adherence in schizophrenia. *Psychiatric Rehabilitation Journal, 26,* 23–32.

Ryan, R. M., & Deci, E. L. (2000). Self-determination theory and the facilitation of intrinsic motivation, social development, and well-being, *American Psychologist, 55,* 68–78.

Schneider Corey, M., Corey, G., & Corey, C. (2010). *Groups: Process and practice* (8th ed). Belmont, CA: Brooks/Cole.

Schumacher, J. A., Coffey, S. F., Stasiewicz, P. R., Murphy, C. M., Leonard, K. E., & Fals-Stewart, W. (2011). Development of a brief motivational enhancement intervention for intimate partner violence in alcohol treatment settings. *Journal of Aggression, Maltreatment, and Trauma, 20,* 103–127.

Schumacher, J. A., Coffey, S. F., Walitzer, K. S., Burke, R. S., Williams, D. C., Norquist, G., & Elkin, T. D. (2012). Guidance for new motivational interviewing trainers when training addiction professionals: Findings from a survey of experienced trainers. *Motivational Interviewing: Training, Research, Implementation, and Practice, 1,* 7–15.

Schumacher, J. A., Madson, M. B., & Nilsen, P. (2014). Barriers to learning motivational interviewing: A survey of trainers. *Journal of Addiction and Offender Counseling,* in press.

Schumacher, J. A., Madson, M. B., & Norquist, G. S. (2011). Using telehealth technology to enhance motivational interviewing training for rural substance abuse treatment providers: A services improvement project. *The Behavior Therapist, 34,* 64–70.

Schumacher, J. A., Williams, D. C., Burke, R. S., Epler, A. J., & Simon, P. (2013). *Competency-based supervision in motivational interviewing for psychology pre-doctoral interns and postdoctoral fellows.* Manuscript submitted for publication.

Seal, K. H., Abadijan, L., McCamish, N., Shi, Y., Tarasovsky, G., & Weingardt, K. (2012). A randomized controlled trial of telephone motivational interviewing to enhance mental health treatment engagement in Iraq and Afghanistan veterans. *Psychiatry and Primary Care, 34,* 450–459.

Seppala, E. (2013, June). The compassionate mind. *Observer, 26,* 20–25.

Seligman, L. W. (2008). *Fundamental skills for mental health professionals.* Upper Saddle River, NJ: Pearson Education.

Smith, J. D., Dishion, T. J., Shaw, D. S., & Wilson, M. N. (2013). Indirect effects of fidelity to the Family Check-Up on changes in parenting and early childhood problem behaviors. *Journal of Consulting and Clinical Psychology,* doi:10.1037/a0033950

Smith, J. L., Amrhein, P. C., Brooks, A. C., Carpenter, K. M., Levin, D., Schreiber, E. A., Travaglini, L. A., & Nunes, E. V. (2007). Providing live supervision via teleconferencing improves acquisition of motivational interviewing skills after workshop attendance. *American Journal of Drug and Alcohol Abuse, 33,* 163–168. doi:10.1080/00952990601091150

Smith, J. L., Carpenter, K. M., Amrhein, P. C., Brooks, A. C., Levin, D., Schreiber, E. A., Travaglini, L. A., Hu, M. C., & Nunes, E. V. (2012). Training substance abuse clinicians in motivational interviewing using live supervision via teleconferencing. *Journal of Consulting and Clinical Psychology, 80,* 450–464. doi: 10.1037/a0028176

Söderlund, L. L., Madson, M. B., Rubak, S., & Nilsen, P. (2011) A systematic review of motivational interviewing training for general healthcare practitioners. *Patient Education and Counseling, 84,* 16–26.

Stasiewicz, P. R., Herrman, D., Nochajski, T. H., & Dermen, K. (2006). Motivational interviewing: Engaging highly resistant clients in treatment. *Counselor: The Magazine for Addictions Professionals, 7,* 26–32.

Steinberg, M. L., Ziedonis, D. M., Krejci, J. A., & Brandon, T. H. (2004). Motivational interviewing with personalized feedback: A brief intervention for motivating smokers with schizophrenia to seek treatment for tobacco dependence. *Journal of Consulting and Clinical Psychology, 72,* 723–728.

Sterrett, E., Jones, D. J., Zalot, A., & Shook, S. (2010). A pilot study of a brief motivational intervention to enhance parental engagement: A brief report. *Journal of Child and Family Studies, 19,* 697–701.

Substance Abuse and Mental Health Services Administration. (1999). *Enhancing motivation for change in substance abuse treatment* (DHHS Publication No. SMA 99–3354). Rockville, MD: The CDM Group.

Thevos, A. K., Quick, R. E., & Yanduli, V. (2000). Motivational interviewing enhances the adoption of water disinfection practices in Zambia. *Health Promotion International, 15,* 207–214.

Thombs, D. L., & Osborn, C. J. (2013). *Introduction to addictive behaviors* (4th ed). New York: Guilford Press.

Van Minnen, A., Harned, M. S., Zoellner, L., & Mills, K. (2012). Examining potential contraindications for prolonged exposure therapy for PTSD. *European Journal of Psycho-Traumatology, 3,* 18805. Retrieved from http://dx.doi.org/10.3402/ejpt.v3i0.18805.

Vasilaki, E. I., Hosier, S. G., & Cox, W. M. (2006). The efficacy of motivational interviewing as a brief intervention for excessive drinking: A meta-analytic review. *Alcohol & Alcoholism, 41,* 328–335.

Wagner, C. C., & Ingersoll, K. S. (2013). *Motivational interviewing in groups.* New York: Guilford Press.

Walters, S., Clark, M. D., Gingerich, R., & Meltzer, M. (2007). A guide for probation and parole: Motivating offenders to change. U.S. Department of Justice, National

Institute of Corrections. NiC Accession Number 022253. Retrieved on December 23, 2013 from http://static.nicic.gov/Library/022253.pdf.

Walters, S. T., Matson, S. A., Baer, J. S., & Ziedonis, D. M. (2005). Effectiveness of workshop training for psychosocial addiction treatments: A systematic review. *Journal of Substance Abuse Treatment, 29*, 83–293.

Westra, H. A., & Aviram, A. (2013). Core skills in motivational interviewing. *Psychotherapy, 50*, 273–278. doi:10.1037/a0032409

Westra, H. A. (2012). *Motivational interviewing in the treatment of anxiety.* New York: Guilford Press.

World Health Organization. (2008). *The global burden of disease: 2004 update.* Retrieved Nov. 12, 2013 from http://www.who.int/healthinfo/global_burden_dis ease/GBD_report_2004 update_full.pdf

Young, T. L. (2013). Using motivational interviewing within the early stages of group development. *The Journal of Specialists in Group Work, 38*, 169–181.

Zeollner, J., Connell, C., Madson, M. B., Thomson, J. L., Landry, A. S., Molaison, E. F., Reed, V. B., & Yadrick, K. (2014). HUB City Steps: A 6-month lifestyle intervention improves blood pressure and psychosocial constructs among a primarily African American community. *Journal of the Academy of Nutrition and Dietetics, 114*, 603–612.

Zoellner, J. M., Connell, C. C., Madson, M. B., Wang, B, Reed, V. W., Molaison, E. F., & Yadrick, K. (2011). H.U.B City Steps: Methods and early findings from a community-based participatory research effectiveness trial to reduce blood pressure among African Americans. *International Journal of Behavioral Nutrition and Physical Activity, 8*, 59–71. doi: 10.1186/1479–5868–8–59

Zweben, A., & Zuckoff, A. (2002). Motivational interviewing and treatment adherence. In W. R. Miller & S. Rollnick (Eds.), *Motivational interviewing: Preparing people for change* (2nd ed; pp. 299–319). New York: Guilford Press.

ABOUT THE AUTHORS

Julie A. Schumacher, PhD, is an Associate Professor and Vice Chair for Professional Education and Faculty Development in the Department of Psychiatry at the University of Mississippi Medical Center and Director of the Mississippi Psychology Training Consortium. She is actively involved in motivational interviewing practice, training, supervision, dissemination, and research and has received multiple NIH grants for her work in this area.

Michael B. Madson, PhD, is an Associate Professor in the Department of Psychology at the University of Southern Mississippi. He is actively involved in training, supervising, and researching motivational interviewing as part of health and harm reduction interventions. His work has been funded by multiple agencies, including the NIH and the American Psychological Foundation.

Page numbers followed by "f" and "t" indicate figures and tables.